Nonviolent Resistance in Trauma-Focused Practice

This book presents Nonviolent Resistance (NVR) for trauma-focused care, adopting a systemic and trauma-orientated approach to aggressive and self-destructive behaviours in young people. Based on systemic therapy methods and principles in socio-political NVR, NVR targets aggressive and self-destructive child behaviours in a relational way to help parents develop self-efficacy in responding to the problematic behaviour and grow a supportive community around the family. In this book, Peter Jakob integrates the original NVR model with aspects of trauma and attachment theory, solution-focused therapy and narrative therapy, in order to expand the efficacy of NVR in trauma-focused work. Grounded in Jakob's extensive clinical experience and research, the book will help the reader navigate the complexity of working across various systems in family therapy and counselling, particularly within challenging contexts such as multi-stressed families, adoptive families, foster- and residential care. Method descriptions and illustrative case examples are featured throughout the chapters to ultimately help readers contribute to their clients' (re)discovery of their internal and interpersonal resources and ultimately promote healing from trauma for everyone involved. This text is an essential resource for a wide variety of mental health professionals, social workers and family workers, as well as caregivers and managers in residential care.

Dr Peter Jakob is a Consultant Clinical Psychologist, and Systemic Therapist in private practice, Partner in "Connective Strength" and Co-Director of the Canadian Center for NVR Therapy and Practice. He is a renowned international speaker, and has trained many professionals in using the approach, leading to its integration in the work of many local authority children's services and child and adolescent mental health services in the UK.

"Beyond offering a resourceful, creative, and effective approach for dealing with trauma, Peter Jakob's Nonviolent Resistance in Trauma-focused Practice presents a humanizing alternative to pathologizing and manualized approaches. His emphasis on possibilities, exceptional moments where carers and children have somehow avoided enacting their typical problematic patterns, and the creation of a caring community illustrate the power of NVR as practiced from a collaborative, relational stance. Complete with case examples and illustrations of method, Jakob gives his readers a rich compendium of treatment resources that emphasize a socially just approach to trauma."

Sheila McNamee, *PhD, Professor Emerita, University of New Hampshire, Co-Founder and VP, Taos Institute*

"Peter Jakob is a bricoleur of ideas. With utmost and steadfast care he addresses difficult and distressing situations families and communities face in ways that reveal relational pathways out of despair into hope and justice. He draws together ideas from NVR, narrative therapy, social constructionism, philosophy, and systems theory to imaginatively respond to complex circumstances without over-simplification. Peter's voice and experience come through in the evocative examples and his storehouse of questions. Anybody who cares for families in any capacity must read this book."

Sally St. George and Dan Wulff, *Professors Emerti, Faculty of Social Work, University of Calgary*

"Peter Jakob deserves commendation for skillfully integrating three prominent therapeutic approaches: narrative therapy, solution-focused therapy, and nonviolent resistance. Through a diverse array of case studies, he adeptly navigates the reader through the process of cultivating profound empathy necessary for effectively engaging with the most challenging clients and families encountered in professional practice. This book is not one to be hastily consumed over a weekend; rather, its meticulous structure allows for thorough examination of each chapter at one's own pace and in a preferred sequence."

Ben Furman, *psychiatrist and solution-focused psychotherapist, Finland.*

"Nonviolent resistance in trauma-focused practice is that rare book in which theory and practice do not merely inform each other but are presented, understood, and practiced as a unity. Jakob takes us into the world of troubled families mired in, sometimes violent, abuse, who have come to his therapy practice. In telling the family stories and their therapy stories, he shows us a uniquely respectful, humane, and hopeful conversational process. What comes through clearly in the dozens of case studies is how NVR transforms "resistance" into a humanely positive creation of new forms of relating to self and other."

Lois Holzman, *PhD, Co-founder and Director, East Side Institute, NY USA*

"We have an ethical responsibility for the way we speak about our clients. Deconstructing pathologizing language, Peter Jakob engages with the utmost respect for the traumatizing experiences of his clients in dialogical conversations that create space and give back the clients their own voice. He doesn't locate the problem in the person, not reifying it as a fixed identity. He combines the eco-systemic approach, engaging the larger system around the family, with NVR perspectives, caring and appreciative dialogues and compassionate and appreciative witnessing."

Jan Olthof, *Psychotherapist, Author of The Handbook of Narrative psychotherapy, Trainer and supervisor in Family Therapy*

Nonviolent Resistance in Trauma-Focused Practice

A Systemic Approach to Therapy and Social Care

Peter Jakob

Routledge
Taylor & Francis Group

LONDON AND NEW YORK

Designed cover image: ©Shutterstock Images

First published 2025
by Routledge
4 Park Square, Milton Park, Abingdon, Oxon OX14 4RN

and by Routledge
605 Third Avenue, New York, NY 10158

Routledge is an imprint of the Taylor & Francis Group, an informa business

First German edition published Dem Trauma Widerstand
leisten: Neue Autoritat als familientherapeutischer und
traumapadagogischer Ansatz © 2022 Peter Jakob p/a
Vandenhoeck & Ruprecht GmbH & Co KG

Originally published by Vandenhoeck & Ruprecht GmbH & Co KG

British Library Cataloguing-in-Publication Data
A catalogue record for this book is available from the British Library

ISBN: 9781032717128 (hbk)
ISBN: 9781032697390 (pbk)
ISBN: 9781032717111 (ebk)

DOI: 10.4324/9781032717111

Typeset in Times New Roman
by codeMantra

Contents

Foreword by Haim Omer

Since its beginnings about 25 years ago, the implementations of NVR have been extended over and beyond the original target population of children with disruptive, violent, anti-social and high-risk behaviours. I think the two most important extensions were in helping parents and children with anxiety disorders (Lebovitz and Omer, 2013) and massive traumatic experiences. Peter Jakob almost single-handedly developed this major adaptation of NVR to multi-stressed families, showing a cross-generational pattern of distress that often includes domestic violence, rape, sexual abuse, child physical abuse and severe neglect.

Jakob's three major adaptations of NVR to those cases are (a) providing a safe frame for creating a support network for those families, (b) emphasising elements of NVR that make it function as trauma therapy and (c) developing steps to reinstate the caring dialogue that has often been constrained in these families.

Growing a support network is a core element of the NVR intervention. However, for families exposed to many different, often traumatic stress factors, it may be especially difficult to develop a support network, because parents often feel criticised, delegitimised or endangered by people in their surroundings. It is imperative to help the parents to build a safe support network that would protect them rather than exposing them to critical, blaming or coercive interactions. Jakob posits that the first stage in working with the parents and children in these families, or in foster families, adoptive families or residential homes for young people, lies in creating a safe network by helping the parents and other caregivers to differentiate between the positions people take. They are asked to consider these persons individually, focusing on their own feelings and body sensations while they imagine talking to them about their difficulties or asking them to be present in certain situations, such as the NVR sit-in. In this way, the parents can learn to trust their own perception and determine whether the other person acts in a way that is emotionally safe and potentially supportive, well-intentioned but critical and prescriptive, or coercive and dangerous. The first category will constitute the core of the parents' support system. People in the second category are invited to a session in which they are helped to empathise with the parents' condition and learn about their plans to change the situation. This experience often results in a change of attitude. Some of them become active supporters, while others diminish their critical stance. Regarding the members of the third category, the parents are helped to resist their coercive and destructive acts and keep them at bay with the techniques of NVR. The book illustrates in inspiring ways, how helping those parents to resist the attacks by others from within or outside the family (including those by their own children) in effective but rigorously non-violent ways, systematically increases their self-worth, courage and ability to anchor themselves and serve as an anchor for their child. I find how Jakob helps us understand and modify the attitudes of colleagues in the helping professions, who sometimes relate to the parents from a critical-prescriptive perspective, of particular value.

The second adaptation developed by Jakob is to utilise some central elements of NVR as a form of trauma therapy in their own right. Traumatised parents or other caregivers often have a hard time regulating themselves emotionally when faced with their child's difficult behaviours. Being faced with provocations often reawakens traumatic memories of previous events in which they completely lose their self-control. NVR helps them to cope with this challenge. One example is helping the parent to focus on a trusted supporter's embodied presence as an aid in self-regulation in the face of the child's threatening and aggressive behaviour when they are taking positive action. The result is that most parents become able to successfully perform positive action such as the sit-in, which serves as a corrective emotional experience to themselves and their child. Discussing the experience, before and after the event, and adding layers of meaning to such action is an important element of NVR as trauma therapy. This adaptation of NVR includes some of the effective elements of acknowledged forms of trauma therapy, such as cognitive and emotional preparation, controlled exposure, the creation of a safe context of experimentation and rehearsal of sensory-motor cues to enable self-regulation (Monson and Shnaider, 2014).

The third adaptation regards the need to renew the caring dialogue, in which the parents respond to needs articulated by their child, and which has been impeded by the parents' avoidance or the child's rejection of the parents' caring messages. Learning how to withstand the expected rejection in therapy while maintaining their caring stance, parents can once again engage in this dialogue. Jakob presents many cases in which specific, targeted gestures of reconciliation, which address a child's hitherto insufficiently met needs, bring parent and child closer.

This listing of the three chief additions that Jakob has brought to NVR is however far from doing justice to the book's richness. I have always viewed NVR as a method to be integrated with a therapist's, counsellor's or teacher's experience, knowledge and abilities. This book is a valuable lesson in such integration. I found it highly rewarding to see how Jakob utilises the insights of narrative and solution-focused therapy, the utilisation techniques of Milton Erickson and the understandings of Wilson's child-focused therapy to enrich the therapeutic palette of NVR. Particularly satisfying for me were the special, highly original uses of the support group that make it into an invaluable tool of NVR as trauma therapy.

The detailed and systematic presentations of principles and tools render this book almost into a treatment manual. One can definitely use the book to learn, implement and supervise parent-training in NVR with multi-stressed families, adoptive and foster families and caregivers in residential children's homes. And if, among the readers, someone should have the research interest and courage to build upon this quasi-manual for the development of an empirical study, the benefits would be multiplied.

We're sometimes asked whether NVR is a 'trauma-informed therapy'. This book shows that it may be a lot more than that. Resisting Trauma may prove to be not only a major contribution to NVR, but also a milestone in our ability to understand and treat complex trauma in individuals and families.

Reference

Monson, C. M., & Shnaider, P. (2014). *Treating PTSD with cognitive-behavioral therapies: Interventions that work*. Washington, DC, American Psychological Association.

Why this book matters – Foreword by Jim Wilson

Peter Jakob's approach to the treatment of Trauma by Nonviolent Resistance embraces a width of vision that is grounded in an eco-systemic perspective and embedded in his appreciative, courageous and dignified orientation to all those he endeavours to help.

Trauma theory and the experience of traumatic events are given particular attention, are fully developed and made accessible through Peter Jakob's many vivid examples of effective methods and techniques that populate the chapters of this book.

He illustrates an approach to trauma that is concerned with creative possibilities rather than fixed pathologies and with resourceful rather than deficit descriptions of people. He locates his practice as a social, relational and systemic process, without losing sight of an individual's experience. In this volume, Peter Jakob shows his acute sensitivity to working collaboratively with parents/carers who have experienced earlier trauma in life and are presently faced with violence from a child in their family or care. To begin to matter emotionally (again) to one another is to experience intimacy where safety and a sense of belonging are restored. This is an important dimension that Peter Jakob develops in this expansive exploration of the possibilities within NVR.

Appreciative praxis matters

Peter Jakob guides the reader within a collaborative, appreciative and relational orientation to extend NVR practices with coaches, counsellors, parents and carers. I could also see how many elements of the author's approach to therapy can have direct relevance in related fields of therapeutic and social practice, including family therapy.

Peter Jakob's creativity is shown in the plentiful accounts he offers from practice, where he shares tips, suggestions, examples of useful questions, practice-based methods and a wide knowledge base that help counsellors and others to be clear about what methods can help in meeting with parents and carers where traumatic events and processes still affect their ways of responding to violence from their child. The detailed case vignettes reveal a wide repertoire of methods and techniques, including Peter's engaging with a family member's 'script' that has been shaped by traumatic experiences, while gently exploring exceptions and the pursuance of more creative, less-confining 'scripts'. He provides examples of various uses of role play, hypothetical future conversations and examples of creative therapeutic rituals. In his practice, he also employs mindfulness and attends to embodied responses in his meetings with others. These extensive skills show an attitude of inclusivity that frees practice from the confines of any one 'school of thought'. All of his practice is seen within the wide-angle systemic lens of the client's social milieu, their family, support group and resource network.

Instead of dedicating himself to following grand theories to explain the phenomenon of violence and trauma, Jakob eschews this view and draws instead on ideas that have direct practical use. In this way, his approach is rich and resource-based, utilising knowledge from trauma theory, narrative practices, solution-focused practices, attachment theory and the aforementioned eco-systemic framework.

Hope and vision also matter

In Peter Jakob's approach, traumatic experience is not a life sentence; rather, new life is developed in the exploration and application of co-creative NVR practice. He describes an orientation to practice that is imbued with both expertise and humility, determination to expand possibilities for creative opportunities, the avoidance of pathologising thinking or language, optimism without naivete and a lively imagination to stimulate creativity.

Peter manages to create a vision of future possibilities while at the same time enduring the here and now challenges and apparent hopelessness that confront all where violence and trauma are being (re)experienced. This is a central theme running through the book. He seems to say to the reader, "Stay with it, even when there are setbacks and the outcome looks bleak, because there are possibilities just around the corner".

Helping parents and carers to become child focused during, and especially after, the cessation of violence, enables both child and parent to begin (again) to matter to one another. When a mother looks into the eyes of her child and sees that she matters, the mother can also begin to feel that she matters to herself. Mattering to one another is the counterpoint to the 'adversary' of violence that haunts relationships.

The hope that pervades Jakob's writing reminds me of Vaclav Havel's statement that "Hope is not the conviction that something will turn out well but the certainty that something makes sense regardless of how it turns out" (Havel, 1991 in Wilson 2017, p. 181). To open the pages of this book is to enter into a study of trauma, violence and the creativity involved in helping children, parents and all involved to find alternative ways of relating beyond violence and beyond the entrapment of traumatic life experiences.

Practice needs a vision of alternatives that moves beyond seemingly intractable difficulties. Jakob's vision of practice in this volume provides an abundance of alternatives. Imagination and courage are hallmarks of his practice, and he demonstrates in the chapters ahead how one's practice can be enriched by taking ideas and methods and applying them in one's own way in NVR. In reading this book, I am inspired to take fresh steps and find the courage to explore new ideas and methods in my practice. I hope you may also find similar satisfaction in your reading of Peter Jakob's approach.

References

Havel, V. (1991). *Disturbing the peace*. New York: Vintage.

Wilson, J. (2017). *Creativity in times of constraint; A practitioner's companion in mental health and social care*. London: Routledge.

How to read this book

Nonviolent Resistance therapy, in its original conceptualisation, is an evidence-based approach to helping caregivers deal with harmful or self-destructive behaviour in children or young people who do not engage or do not engage constructively in therapy to ameliorate these difficulties. The adult is the client; adult and child are benefactors of the systemic change that is brought about. If you are entirely new to NVR, you may wish to read literature which introduces the core approach, such as Omer's 'Non-violent Resistance' (2021c), or attend an introductory seminar to familiarise yourself with the basic tenets of NVR, and the methods it offers to caregivers. However, this book is structured in such a way that mental health clinicians or social care practitioners of all kinds of orientation, training and background can, it is hoped, take ideas and inspiration for their own practice from its pages.

Nonviolent Resistance in Trauma-focused Practice leads the reader into an adaptation of Nonviolent Resistance therapy, for working with people who have experienced severe disadvantage and oppression. In doing so, it integrates within a social justice framework many aspects of different systemic therapy traditions, as well as research in social interaction, trauma, attachment and neuroscience. The book is subdivided into three parts, which represent three planes or fields of the systemic processes which restrict or enable recovery from trauma; these begin with the larger system around the family, move on to the parent in interaction with this larger system and the child, and finally to the child themselves. Each part builds upon the previous ones, and it can therefore help to develop a fuller understanding of its ideas and methods if you read the book from start to finish, rather than taking individual chapters out of context.

There are numerous method sections in this book. I would recommend experimenting with these methods with colleagues first, before bringing them into your work with clients. Experimenting with the methods will help to develop a felt sense of their transformative qualities and enable you to develop fluency in their application. None of these method sections are stand-alone protocols for practising therapy in a manualised manner, but instead should be understood to help facilitate movement within a therapeutic system that is geared towards change. In using these methods, the practitioner or therapist must be authentic and congruent, *real*, if they are to be helpful to the client.

DOI: 10.4324/9781032717111-1

The many case examples aim to bring the ideas in this book to life. They are vignettes, the purpose of which is to illustrate certain theoretical or practical aspects of working with NVR in regard to trauma, but not exhaustive case studies. To fully protect the identity of clients, I have routinely changed many demographic details in these case examples, and have often used composite case methodology, whereby elements of two or more cases are brought together in a description of the therapeutic processes, but in a manner that is true to life.

A word about 'needs'. This book frequently refers to 'insufficiently met need', 'need signalling', 'child needs', 'parental need', etc. The word need is not used here to indicate that something is pathological in the person. Children have needs which are addressed in life, more or less sufficiently, by parents and other caregivers as a matter of course; parents have needs, and so forth. The interest in this book lies in how such needs can be addressed in interaction, and what transforming and ultimately healing interpersonal processes can be pivotal for this in work with NVR.

Introduction

Trauma-focused nonviolent resistance

In the two and a half decades since its inception (Omer, 2001), therapeutic work with parents based on nonviolent resistance, or short 'NVR', has found its way into the canon of systemic approaches in the UK and many Western European countries. NVR is beginning to become known among mental health and social care professionals in North America and places such as Australia, as well. Its respectful and humane starting point – resisting harm without doing harm – has generated many answers to hitherto unsolvable problems that left parents, other caregivers, teachers, mental health professionals and the communities around them feeling helpless, and often despondent. One of its strengths lies in the principle of one-sided action, a core tenet of the approach: the NVR practitioner – a therapist, counsellor, family support worker or parent coach – will help the adults who are responsible for the care of a young person who is showing harmful or self-destructive behaviour to take action in new ways, even if the younger person does not cooperate with them. These ways of taking action are built on raising presence rather than attempting to exert control. Parents do not need to rely on their child's cooperation, which will so rarely be forthcoming; yet, they will be able to act in a way that does no harm.

NVR is a trans-diagnostic approach. It was not developed as a 'treatment' for any kind of specific, diagnosable 'condition'. Instead, it occupies itself with the transformation of communication systems which have grown around habitual behaviours that are harmful to others and self. NVR does not ask *Why? What is the underlying causation?*; it asks: *How do we change the ecology of the problem and make it difficult for it to persist?* In this way, NVR can begin to address the very essence of destructiveness in interpersonal relationships, and we continue to learn more in the course of its practice. It is therefore not a manualised approach set in stone, but an ongoing effort in discovering the principles of nonviolence. While NVR seeks to transform communication processes around destructive- and self-destructive behaviours, it is consistently changing and re-inventing itself. The trauma-focused approach to NVR, which this book is about, is such an effort.

Nonetheless, practitioners in the field are frequently asked questions which frame NVR as a kind of 'treatment', which should have its indications and counter-indications based on an individual client's diagnosis or psychological formulation: *Can you do NVR with autism? Can you do NVR with eating disorders?* or *Can*

DOI: 10.4324/9781032717111-2

you do NVR where there has been trauma? It is this last question which forms the starting point for this book. However, the reader will discover that this question has been turned on its head, and we will go on to examine: *How can NVR help to overcome many effects of trauma in parents, caregivers, children and young people, and the wider systems around them?* We will explore the therapeutic properties of the approach for ameliorating or overcoming psychological difficulties which are associated with traumatic stress. We will examine the kinds of relational rupture and alienation that can grow between parents and other adults, and between parents and their children in the wake of traumatic experiences – and develop perspectives on how interpersonal reconnection may be promoted within the methodology of NVR. Finally, we will look at how healing takes place within a communication system that is in the process of transforming itself.

Nonviolent resistance as an approach to traumatic stress

The kids are really aggressive, but you can't work with NVR, it's not indicated – the mother is much too traumatised!

This is how a child psychiatrist introduces a family he would like to refer to me as a known 'expert in child aggression'. Without a doubt, this first sentence expresses his very best intentions.

But at the same time, a raft of unquestioned assumptions about trauma, the mother, the family, NVR as an approach, our professional relationship and myself as a therapist are embedded in this sentence. How do these kinds of invisible assumptions, which are not obvious to the speaker nor, at first, to the listener, affect me? Helplessness and professional self-doubt immediately show their ugly faces: *Will I be able to meet the challenges of this 'complex' case*? A familiar kind of annoyance makes me feel uncomfortable; yet, the emerging tension is difficult to address, as the psychiatrist and I are also personal friends. As a result, the conversation turns out to be rather taciturn. I know my own reaction well; it usually abates very soon.

However, this brief exchange says a lot about how our professional language, and the way we speak about 'trauma', can profoundly influence, if not shape our emotions, our cognition, behaviour, body sensation and interaction. First, I would like to point to the way a so-called 'regressive narrative' has been introduced: a manner of storytelling that describes this family in a static way; an entirely problem-focused narrative that tells 'how things *are*', that purports to tell facts, a snapshot depicting pathology, which then defines the person of the parent. The psychiatrist's account leads into a narrative of a kind that leaves little conversational space for appreciating and developing understandings of constructive change; it has an immediate discouraging effect on the therapist – on me. If such a regressive narrative of a family that has experienced trauma became the meta-narrative within which we construct therapeutic reality, we would do well to ask some pertinent questions:

- *How would the therapist relate to a child's parents, if they unquestioningly adopted the view that is implied by the referrer's first sentence?*

- *What questions does the family practitioner ask? And, as importantly, what questions do they not ask?*
- *What does the body language of a residential carer or foster carer tell the parents about their belief in the possibility of reconnection between a young person and their parent, or even their rehabilitation into their parent's care? What does their body language tell their colleagues about the assumed prospects of such a rehabilitation for the future?*
- *How does all this affect the parents' ability to imagine positive changes in their relationship with the child, in their own and in the child's behaviour, in their relationship with one another?*
- *How does it, in turn, affect the practitioner's ability to generate hope for change within themselves, develop a sense of professional agency and an expectation of self-efficacy in working with parent or parents and child?*
- *How does the regressive narrative of a family with a '**much too traumatised mother**' influence the images that carers, teachers, social workers and other professionals will develop of the parent, and how will those images, by virtue of the professionals' interaction with the parent and the young person respectively, influence the future relationship between mother and child?*
- *What does such a story mean for the young person's future?*

As professionals, we have an ethical responsibility to reflect on the possible implications of how we speak about clients and how we communicate with others about them. This is especially salient when it comes to clients who are facing multiple challenges. Given the power we carry as professionals, our preconceptions can have enormous implications for their lives. A first step can be to bring the invisible, unquestioned assumptions about the 'traumatised mother' to light, and then to augment the narrative by enriching it with an 'alternative history' – one that tells of possibilities for change, describes parental responses that were different to her normal reactions and attributes meaning to them, an account that highlights intrapsychic and interpersonal strengths, resources and resilience.

Where a pathologising narrative has become a veil that conceals discouraging paradigmatic assumptions about parents and children, which nonetheless percolate up into our implicit and explicit understandings of them, we can deconstruct it and create space for alternative descriptions. Examining the psychiatrist's sentence, we recognise that he does not use the word 'trauma' as a reference to a broad range of phenomena in the life of the mother, which are in some way associated with the many injuries she will have suffered, the very specific consequences of these injuries in the here and now, how she responds in different ways to the kind of aggressive behaviour her child often demonstrates, how she faces the challenges of dangerous and aggressive adults around the family, or how she manages to live on and sometimes act constructively in spite of all these difficulties. Instead, the concept of trauma has become set in stone, reified in a way that in philosophy is described as a 'thing in itself',[1] an object whose existence is considered to be a fixed entity, regardless of the perspective of the observer. 'Trauma' is thus declared to be a characteristic or personality trait of the mother, who now '*is* like this' and therefore '*cannot*'. It is an attribution of a trait that is made without the mother having power to accept or reject it, or to choose from a host of attributions.

However, if we use the word 'trauma' in a manner that does not incorporate a fixed and often reductive meaning, our position towards the mother and thus towards her child changes immediately. We are no longer 'experts' who *know* all about *her trauma*, and hence about her, but become interested participants in a relationship with her as a person, whose responses can show a measure of fluidity, who has embarked on a process of change. Curiosity and a benevolent search for understanding can take the place of the previous, ascriptive view of the mother, whose life experience in relation to abuse is broader than a mere description of injury she may have suffered. This allows new questions to emerge:

- *Exactly what injuries have been and, importantly, continue to be inflicted upon her?*
- *How has she defended herself and resisted violence and injustice?*[2]
- *What does this say about her potential ability to protect herself and her children, and to maintain the integrity of her nuclear family?*
- *How has she endeavoured to protect her child from harm in the past, even if this was often not obvious, recognised or appreciated by professionals and non-professionals around the family?*
- *What tell-tale signs of healing from the consequences of trauma can we recognise in her, in her child, in the relationship between her and her child?*
- *How is she beginning to use NVR methods to eradicate more and more the traces of abuse in her own life, and in the life of her child?*
- *How does she see herself changing in the course of this process?*
- *How will the process of 'resisting harm, together, in a caring way'* (Dulberger, 2021) *affect her and her child's process of healing from the injuries they have suffered?*

Such questions are reminiscent of the repertoires of Solution-focused and Narrative Therapy. These ways of working and understanding the therapeutic process are woven into the trauma-focused approach to NVR that is the subject of this book. We will now take our first steps towards an understanding of how working with NVR can help ameliorate the pernicious effects of trauma on the person of the parent and the child.

Deconstructing the psychiatric concept of trauma can become a vaulting pole for us to leap over some of the obstacles that would otherwise impede the healing process of parents and children who have experienced mistreatment in close relationships. Parents themselves can relate *their own perspectives* on the injuries they have suffered, how they have survived and resisted, where they succeed in remaining self-determined, how they are able to act constructively in spite of the abuse they have been subjected to, what pathways to healing they can identify for themselves and their children, and how they envision a better future. This is not to say that change is always easy; the injuries to parents and children, which include harrowing experiences such as partner violence and coercive control, emotional abuse, sexual violence and child abuse, run very deep. Nonetheless, parents – and by extension their children – can make giant leaps in their recovery by deconstructing reified concepts of 'trauma'.

Such leaps need to be made skilfully. They require discipline, practice, perseverance, encouragement, a suitable methodology and a solid social support network. The support of a proactive, caring community around a family, foster family or residential home is an essential ingredient for fomenting a social system that can enable a healing process.[3] Facilitating all this is the task of the trauma-focused NVR practitioner. There can be no expectation on the part of this practitioner of what prerequisites clients who face multiple challenges should bring to the process, in order to qualify for the intervention. Young people's controlling, aggressive, degrading or rejecting behaviours open up old wounds in their parents, their siblings – and in themselves, and threaten to inflict new wounds on caregivers and others around the child. Where this is the case, this book aims to help professionals involved in family support or therapy, foster care or residential care to find new ways of navigating what may have hitherto felt like impossibly complex situations.

The example of the referring psychiatrist illustrates an important principle: if parents and children who act in harmful or self-destructive ways are to recover from trauma, they require an emotionally safe social environment, in which an unshakeable belief in everyone's ability to change pervades and is powerfully communicated in explicit and implicit ways. This is a social environment, in which there is an appreciation of parents' and other caregivers' self-efficacy, and an appreciation of the child's propensity for personal growth.

But how can the NVR practitioner facilitate the growth of such a social environment which helps the family, foster- or children's home become a nurturing ground for overcoming the deleterious effects of serious trauma? That is the theme of *Part I* of this book. We no longer ask, *Can you use NVR where parents or children have experienced severe trauma?* The question has become: *How does systemic work with NVR contribute to overcoming their trauma?*

NVR as a therapeutic agent for trauma?

NVR as a therapeutic approach takes its inspiration from traditions of socio-political nonviolent resistance by liberation movements such as the Indian struggle for independence from Britain or the American Civil Rights Movement, or, more latterly, the Velvet Revolution, or Black Lives Matter. Unlike other forms of political revolt which aim to disempower or even annihilate an enemy, nonviolent resistance does not have enemies, does not consider other people or groups of people as entities that should be harmed so they lose their power over the resistors. Its target is always violence, controlling behaviour, the oppression, and degradation of people per se. Its aims are to re-balance power and, insofar as this is possible, the conversion of the opponent (Weber, 2001). Resistance is directed at attitudes, dominant discourses, structural violence and institutional discrimination that legitimise mistreatment. Nonviolent resistance thus avoids any perpetrator-victim dichotomy; all are victims of discourses and structures that legitimise violence, even those who instigate it.

Leaders of socio-political nonviolent resistance such as Mahatma Gandhi, Martin Luther King and Rosa Parks externalised the problem. They did not locate it in the person or people who acted in violent ways, but saw it as existing outside of the person who oppresses – in the language of NVR, the person showing controlling behaviour – and existing outside the person who is oppressed – in the language of NVR, the person who is affected by controlling behaviour. This did not mean they failed to acknowledge harmful attitudes, but they separated attitude from person, and from the possibility of how the person may see the world in the future.[4]

The notion of nonviolent resistance opens new horizons for change in families and communities: Were we to resist the child's *attitudes* that make violence possible, not the child themselves, and in the process of resisting became more able to appreciate, embrace and support the *person* of the child, we would simultaneously act in both our own and in our child's interest.

Parents' de-escalation can counteract their own potential for aggression. At the same time, carefully planned and executed action, instead of spontaneous, immediate *re*-action, will help overcome their own tolerance of controlling behaviour and their submission to it. In the experiential and self-reflective process that accompanies this, parents can learn much about themselves and others, develop their personal agency, and a greater sense of self-efficacy.

People who oppress, and people who are oppressed, *change as a person* in the process of resisting in nonviolent ways. Gene Sharp (2012), who has carried out extensive research into nonviolent political action and acted as a consultant to various civil resistance movements such as Ukraine's 'Orange Revolution' of 2004/2005, has investigated the 'conversion of the opponent'. He posits that personal insight into the injustice of their own position, which can come about as a result of the nonviolent action of others, will eventually lead to changes in the attitudes of a significant number of people who had previously participated in oppression and discrimination, and will eventually result in changes to their behaviour.

We can now raise the question: *How* does resisting in itself change the person of the resistor?

Rosa Parks, the initiator of the Montgomery bus boycott, which lasted almost a full year from December 1955 through to December 1956, expressed her experience that, with the determination to act, and the knowledge of what needs to be done, fear diminishes (Reed and Parks, 1995). While Omer, like Gandhi himself, often speaks of courage (Omer, 2021a, 2021b), it is important to stress that a courageous attitude in the parent should not be seen as a prerequisite for working with NVR or as an essential virtue. Instead, we can consider 'courage', in a systemic sense, to be a manifestation of an 'interpersonal mind', not just growing out of an individual disposition alone: a growing network of supporters who continually convey the message: '*You are not alone. We are with you. What can we do?*' en-*courages* parents. Embedded in this network, their ability to face rather than fearfully avoid difficult challenges relating to their child increases, as their competence and experience of self-efficacy, and the interpersonal nurture of such self-efficacy, grow.

The previously enslaved abolitionist Frederick Douglass (1845/2003) once put up a fistfight to deter an enslaver from whipping him. In his autobiography, he described this as a psychologically transformative experience, despite the mortal danger he put himself in:

> It rekindled the few expiring embers of freedom and revived within me a sense of my own manhood. It recalled the departed self-confidence and inspired me again with a determination to be free. ...My long-crushed spirit rose, cowardice departed, bold defiance took its place; and I now resolved that, however long I might remain a slave in form, the day had passed forever when I could be a slave in fact.
>
> (p. 69)

I do not wish to compare a parent's experience of child to parent violence and abuse with Douglass' experience of enslavement. However, our concern is in working with parents whose vulnerabilities have been exploited, often since their own childhood, and who will have suffered abuse throughout most of their lives, subjugated to the dominance of others who have held sway over them. Their exposure to child behaviours, which to them become associated with such a long string of abuse, will be merely the latest chapter in a life history of agony that has been brought about by their unfreedom. Therefore, I see much merit in examining the psychological transformation that Douglass describes as coming about in the process of resistance.[5] In his memoir, he also draws attention to the role that other enslaved people played in his resistance against the slave master's brutality and which supported his psychological process of change. This may give us some indication of the psychological transformation that can come about in a parent or caregiver who shows resistance to controlling behaviour.

Of course, they are at the same time also responding to a person who is their child, a young person they love, a person who is in need of their loving commitment, for whom they bear the responsibility of care. We will examine some of the complexities inherent in this similar, yet different relationship in *Part III* of this book.

Strikingly, Douglass equates his inner experience with his existential reality – he *is* no longer *a slave* due to his psychological transformation, while materially, he remains in bondage. Douglass describes here the manner, in which his resistance dissolved the internalisation of his oppression, how he overcame his fear, and how he developed courage, determination and self-confidence by virtue of resistance itself – in spite of the external circumstances of his situation. The phrase, *my long crushed spirit rose* suggests that Douglass experienced the change that came with his resistance as healing. That his own actions *revived within (him) a sense of (his) own manhood* speaks to the perceived restoration of his self-determination and human dignity.

Rosa Parks' and Frederick Douglass' experiences can give us an idea of the possibilities that are inherent NVR: resisting can become a therapeutic agent for core features of traumatic injury such as fear, anxiety, a profound sense of helplessness and internalised negative self-attributions. This can be the case for parents who have experienced abuse in the course of much of their lives, or for parents who have adopted their children, or for carers suffering from secondary trauma. Trauma-focused work in NVR can, in my therapeutic experience, prove successful in ameliorating the kinds of psychological injury they have sustained. Their resistance to behaviours which, if tolerated, would re-traumatise, can contribute to the improvement of the parents' sense of self-worth and self-assurance, and help reduce specific symptoms of traumatic stress, understood as common shock, which manifest themselves in so-called 'disorders' or 'conditions' such as 'PTSD', 'EUPD[6]', 'clinical depression' or 'burnout'.

We can see NVR as a therapeutic agent which can help parents, who have been burdened by so-called 'historic trauma', begin to recover from the arc of abuse injury over time. However, specific adaptations of the NVR methodology are needed to facilitate this process. Such adaptations are described in *Part II*.

Post-traumatic stress disorder or 'common shock'?

Thirty-eight per cent of cases referred for NVR to CAMHS[7] in Birmingham, England, over a one-year period were so-called 'multi-stressed families' (Freeman et al., 2013). These are families, in which people have experienced domestic violence and abuse, emotionally controlling behaviour, sexual violence and child physical or sexual abuse, often in association with one another, for many years, sometimes over generations. Families with such high rates of adverse childhood experiences in parent and child are at greater risk of problematic drug or alcohol use, which begins as a form of self-medication. Misogyny, social and economic disadvantage, discrimination against members of ethnic minorities and racism, ableism and discrimination against members of LGBTQ+ communities further exacerbate the pressure on individual family members and their interaction with one another. We can, in therapy, track how such factors directly influence the psychological states of family members and their interaction with one another, by paying attention to them and giving them space in therapeutic conversation. As van der Kolk (2014) points out, trauma is an everyday occurrence in the social sphere: 20% of all Americans have experienced some kind of sexual abuse as a child; 25% were hit by their parents with enough severity to leave traces on their bodies; intimate partner violence is perpetrated in 1/3 of all couple relationships; one-fourth of all respondents grew up with relatives who had serious alcohol problems, and every eighth person has witnessed their mother being hit or beaten. Most of the violence is directed at women and children.

The classical diagnosis of post-traumatic stress disorder is based on a specific symptomatology, which is understood to arise from experiences that have been existentially threatening and have caused a profound sense of helplessness in the individual, whose innate threat responses could not perceivably protect the individual from harm in the moment. However, this understanding of trauma, based on the diagnostic category of PTSD, cannot extend to describe the variety of severe emotional injuries that occur in close interpersonal relationships.

A particular kind of injury, which occurs in the wake of controlling child behaviour, emerges when parents become helplessly exposed to communication that casts them as being irrelevant to their child. Such prolonged communication can result in internal fragmentation in the parent, and the fragmentation of their social relationships with people from outside of the nuclear family. In this book, I am using the concept of parental 'erasure' (Dulberger, Fried and Jakob, 2016; Beckers, Jakob and Schreiter, 2022), which can explain social avoidance by parents, when they are in states of consciousness that concur with this kind of communication and its subsequent internal psychological fragmentation. These states of consciousness are, in our experience, accompanied by a severe reduction of parental presence in the life of the child.

The historic psychological/psychiatric concept of trauma can be questioned – not only in regard to the scope of its applicability, but also in regard to its individualisation of suffering. This individualisation is based on a medical understanding, according to which traumatic experience becomes inherent in the human being, as a kind of personality trait. Lannamann and McNamee (2020) write: *"…we simply note that, in defining the person, psychology in the modern era adopted a stance of possessive individualism…"*. Quoting MacPherson (1962, p. 3), they elaborate

… where persons were understood as 'a conception of the individual as essentially the proprietor of his own person or capacities, owing nothing to society for them'. "Understood as a self-contained individual … the person becomes the repository of various internal, skin-bound attributes and mental conditions, including 'traumatic neurosis'".

(pp. 332–333)

Such individualisation of 'trauma' enables the emergence of victim narratives that are told by professionals *about* the person. The person who has been affected both by abuse, and by the stories told about them, has no say in how they are described by those who are in more powerful positions – they have, both literally and figuratively speaking, 'no voice'. There are certain parallels between the psychological and diagnostic narratives that are formed by socially authorised professionals, and narratives that are formed by people who have acted with abuse, e.g. by perpetrating domestic violence: *"Both kinds of storylines focus primarily on attributions of personal defect, are authored by other individuals who are in a hierarchically higher or more powerful position, and offer little or no narrative space for clients' positive traits or resources"* (Jakob, 2021, p. 11; translated by the author).

We need a way of conceptualising trauma that enables us (1) to locate it in its various social contexts, and (2) allows us to develop narratives together with parents, children and young people, which have space for storylines depicting individual and interpersonal sources of strength, resilience, of personal and of systemic growth.

Where in this book the word 'trauma' is used, it is understood with Weingarten (2003), as 'common shock'. Weingarten assumes that violence, in a broad sense, is a direct or indirect everyday experience. Often, but not always, this is perceived as existentially threatening; however, it always represents some kind of assault on our own integrity, or on the integrity of others. We become witness to, or suffer, physical or psychological injury. Such violence is an affront to our own human dignity and that of others.

The process of healing from traumatic injury takes place on both the individual *and* the social level. Weingarten sees the restoration of human dignity as a starting point for such a healing process. This can be initiated by creating conversational space for the person to share *their own* account of common shock from abuse and victimisation, and enabling others to become compassionate witnesses to their distress and suffering. In her model, certain personal capacities enable competent, compassionate witnessing. These are awareness of the other, providing physical and emotional safety, empathy, righteous shame[8] and compassion. In work with NVR, the practitioner can facilitate the competence that will enable others around the family to become such compassionate witnesses; in this way, they can contribute to the restoration of an abused parent's dignity. In my experience, it is this very restoration of human dignity that often enables a client to feel justified in resisting, whether it is their child's harmful behaviour or the harm that is being caused by another individual or people in the nuclear family's social environment. In other words, the re-humanisation of the parent, which takes place in an NVR social support network, that provides compassionate witnessing, is what enables them to feel entitled to step out of the victim position and take positive action. This will be discussed in *Part I*.

A further form of witnessing can be generated in co-authorship between practitioner and client and contributes to the emergence of an alternative, non-pathologising, non-victim-blaming narrative of the parent self. I refer to this as *appreciative witnessing* and consider it, alongside compassionate witnessing, to be an indispensable ingredient in the recovery from trauma, whether it occurs spontaneously within the support network, or is facilitated in a targeted way by the practitioner. New, helpful narratives of resistance in NVR can grow, when parents or other caregivers resist abuse, be it violence shown by the child or dangerously controlling behaviour in the family's social environment, and do so with the support of others. These narratives can emerge, when the practitioner creates conversational space for the parents' own efficacy in meetings with supporters, and for the kind of *interpersonal efficacy* that manifests, when parents and their supporters act in unison with one another. When the practitioner facilitates the expression of appreciation in the supporters, resistance narratives gain credibility. Their credibility increases further, the more they are associated with memories of direct positive action, as in the following example:

Brianna reports proudly, and at the same time thoughtfully:
We made the announcement to Erik that we won't accept his violent behaviour any longer. It was different from usual. I didn't shout or tell him off, but I didn't

let myself get discouraged either. I stayed serious and I persisted. I respected myself, but I also respected him. I don't think I could have done it without Jill. She was proud of me, too.

Here, a parent gives an account of her own personal agency, of the interpersonal efficacy demonstrated by her and her supporter, and of the witnessing of her agency by her supporter. Her account of dignified self-assertion contrasts with her earlier responses, such as angry shouting or withdrawing when she felt discouraged. There is a sense of showing *herself* respect, while at the same time remaining respectful towards her son – seeing herself, and being seen by a supporter and witness, as responding in a way that is commensurate with her values. She has acted as the parent she wants to be.

By experiencing their own self-efficacy when they actively resist abusive or harmful child behaviour, but also when they stand against untoward pressures from within the larger system around the family, parents eventually become more able to address insufficiently met psychological needs of their child. When this takes place, parents become empowered as compassionate witnesses of their own child's traumatic experience. They can, in turn, help the child find *their* own human dignity restored. This can help re-build the parent's sense that their care for the child *matters*.

The concept of 'mattering' (Marshall and Lambert, 2006) describes a person's sense of being significant and relevant to others. It is an understanding of self as an important agent in another person's life. One's own well-being depends on such an understanding. I consider it a key psychological need for parents to feel they have a significant role in their child's life – a sense of mattering without which their emotional well-being would be in jeopardy (see Beckers, Jakob and Schreiter, 2022), and which forms part of their identity. Some ways in which we can help them restore their sense of parental mattering – even against the backdrop of past psychological injury, re-traumatisation by their child's harmful behaviour and dismissive and rejecting communication which has led to the experience of erasure – will be discussed in *Part II* of this book.

From alienation to dialogue

Herman (2015) illustrates how social alienation follows in the wake of interpersonal abuse. She also addresses the perceived existential loss of meaning that accompanies such alienation.

Parents often associate acts of violence or other kinds of controlling[9] or self-harming behaviour by their child with earlier abuse they themselves have been subjected to, in their own childhood, and in casual or intimate partner relationships with other adults, generally men; they often end up experiencing the young person's behaviour as a continuation of such earlier abuse. This may be experienced only implicitly, while at other times, parents will articulate their experienced continuity between earlier abuse, and current child to parent abuse, in a cogent manner. They sometimes refer to the child's behaviour as 'domestic violence', and often feel guilty for drawing this comparison. Such an arc of abuse tends to leave the parent feeling in some way substantially different from other human beings; it can create a sense of existential isolation and leave a residue of shame. They may show avoidance of others within or around the family, whether physically avoiding them, or avoiding physical or emotional intimacy. As a result, further painful interpersonal alienation ensues.

In work with families in which there has been child to parent abuse, a profound sense of isolation felt by both parents and children can often be identified, where either the young person, the parent or both have experienced or witnessed abuse. The lack of a sense of belonging and the absence of felt mutuality among family members often manifests itself in relationships in which aggressive escalation, depreciative and denigrating communication, rejection and interpersonal avoidance occur on a daily basis. The ensuing alienation between parent and child often stands in the way of recognising child need. Insufficiently met psychological needs of children who have experienced early life abuse, and which may be obscured by their controlling behaviour – fall, in my experience, into five key areas:

1 the need for protection, physical and emotional safety,
2 the need for autonomy and self-determination that are commensurate with the child's developmental stage,
3 the need for belonging,
4 the need for a coherent and sufficiently positive attachment narrative (Dallos and Vetere, 2021), i.e. a narrative of family and self in relation to this family, the recollection of which enables the child to feel connected, cared for and experience sufficient emotional comfort and well-being (Jakob, 2019) and, finally,
5 the need for justice.

Jim Wilson (2018) has introduced child-focused practice into systemic therapy. He postulates, from a dialogical perspective, that the adult becomes more able to hear the 'voice of distress' in the young person when they position themselves with a focus on the child. However, for a number of reasons, caregivers may find it difficult to inhabit a child-focused position: they may become victimised by emotional or physical abuse, feel 'erased' due to dismissive and derogatory communication and end up believing they have no significant role to play in the child's life, may be constantly reminded of their own childhood abuse or intimate partner violence, or feel dehumanised, objectified and criticised by professionals or by members of the community or the larger family. Attention and attunement to the child become difficult, when one feels threatened by this very child, or is affected by the repercussions of the child's behaviour in the wider social environment. Psychologically and physically being in a victim position dictates survival reactivity and may interfere with their own or professionals' normative expectations of parenting, and the wish to be able to care and experience mutuality with the child.

This becomes further aggravated, when children or young people do not articulate their needs clearly and act in ways that feel dismissive or devaluing of the parents' care attempts. For example, parents who have adopted children, who, in turn, were abused, neglected and often witnessed domestic violence prior to their placements, often complain that their children resist intimacy and comfort, or are overly clingy or show affection indiscriminately (Selwyn, Wijedasa and Meakings, 2014).

Many adolescents, who show highly aggressive or self-destructive behaviour, will refuse to attend formalised therapy, or if they do, they will be unlikely to use the therapeutic input to give up harmful behaviour. Parents need to escape from a victim position if they are to feel they have agency in caregiving. Therefore, the persistent resistance of caregivers to the child's problematic behaviour and, their persistent resistance to dominance by other adults, gains central importance for the well-being of everyone in the family, including the child which is showing harmful behaviour.

Parents' resistance serves to protect themselves, and siblings of the child who is acting in harmful ways, from the ill effects of abuse; it enables them to not only physically, but also psychologically move out of a victim position. When caregivers increasingly show strength by acting in a determined yet non-injurious way in the face of dangerous or harmful behaviour, they can become an 'anchor' which enables greater attachment security for the child (Omer et al., 2013). By embodying, in a non-threatening way, a boundary that protects the child from their own destructive impulses, they help the child feel safer. This becomes particularly important for children who have experienced 'boundary setting' as threatening and abusive. Moreover, when they themselves are no longer mired in survival reactivity, parents also become psychologically more able to position themselves in ways that help them focus their attention on the wider psychological needs of the child. While Omer posits that acting as a deterrent from harmful or self-destructive behaviour can make children and adolescents feel less anxious and more secure, thereby emotionally 'anchoring' the child in the stormy sea of their own impulses, children with traumatic experience need to experience this deterrence from caregivers who have become empowered to go the extra mile and can reassure the young person they are neither hostile, nor negligent or scared of them. In this book, I will investigate this *anchoring function of attachment* in terms of its relevance for children who are recovering from serious trauma and attachment difficulties – young people, for whom the *non-threatening* nature of the parental boundary, in the widest sense, is of the utmost importance.

While the parental anchoring function creates the preconditions for a growing sense of security in the child, a new dimension of attachment between the adult and the child, one or both of whom have experienced trauma, becomes possible. Beyond the anchoring function, I add a further parenting aspect, that of the *focus on the child*, and describe how it is particularly relevant for children and young people with high levels of prior adverse experience.

While in general, self-efficacy increases with parenting experience, persistent behavioural difficulties in the child tend to diminish the parents' appreciation of their own parenting abilities (Maniadaki, Sonuga-Burke and Kakouros, 2005). By counteracting what is often experienced as an onslaught on the parents' positive self-identity as a caregiver, peaceful resistance can help them regain their sense of agency and self-efficacy expectation. This tends to generate the hope in the parents that they and their child may eventually find an avenue to engage with one another in a *caring dialogue* – one which enables child needs to be addressed and the parent to feel validated by the child's articulation of their need and acceptance of the adult's care. It is within this caring dialogue that the child's recovery from the ill effects of traumatic injury is supported. This process of reconnection between parent and child is a central theme in Part III.

From the outside in: Moving through different levels of the system

NVR practitioners can work competently in the different social fields which are of relevance for bringing about change.[10] Figure 0.1 illustrates such key social fields.

Instead of attending to the parent-child dyad alone, the trauma-informed NVR practitioner should be in a position to consider all social fields that may be relevant for the recovery of each and all family members from traumatic injury, regardless of the structure of their organisation or their original remit. In other words, the intervention must follow the needs of the child and family, and those who are supporting them, not the other way around. In order to find their way around this complex and confusing eco-systemic landscape, the practitioner may want to distinguish three system levels:

- the *larger system*, in which all those people communicate, who are directly or indirectly involved with the child or young person or with the nuclear family in regard to problematic behaviour, and/or are affected by such behaviour,[11]
- the *parents* or other *caregivers*,
- the *child.*[12]

We will initially focus on ways in which the NVR practitioner can facilitate emotionally safe and supportive interaction between participants of the larger system and the nuclear family or the residential or foster home. The next step will address how practising nonviolent resistance to harmful or self-destructive child behaviour can affect the parents' recovery from trauma in a positive way. Finally, we will explore how connective resistance facilitates change within the young person themselves, representing the innermost system level.

Change within the larger system, and between the larger system and the family, can help 'anchor' parents and/or other caregivers, providing greater security and enabling strength to emerge in the parent. This, in turn, can enable the parents to become an 'anchor' for the child, providing them with a more secure base from which they can begin their process of healing from the many injuries they have sustained in their young lives (Figure 0.2).

Moving from the outside in is of course an ideal-typical imagination of the therapeutic process. Real life is messy, especially when trauma plays into it, making

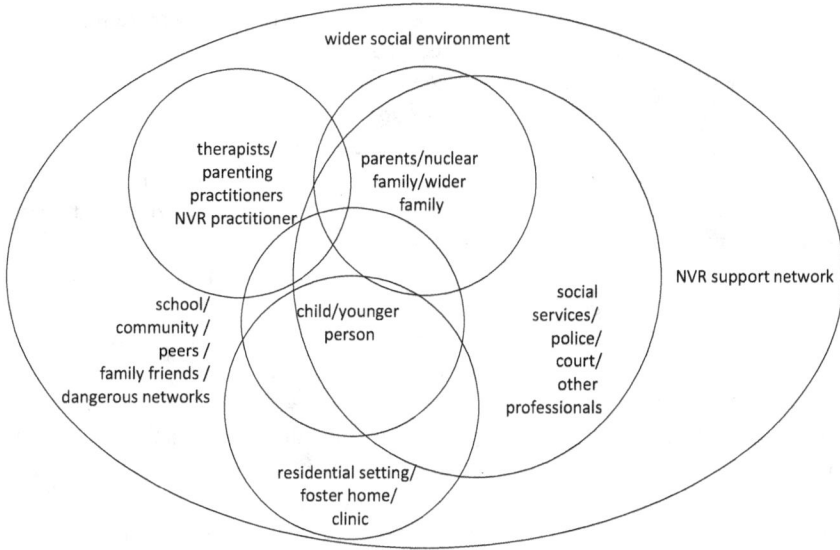

Figure 0.1 Key social fields.

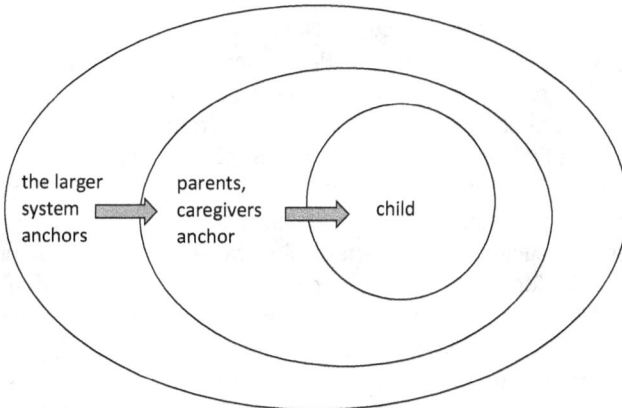

Figure 0.2 System levels.

it very difficult to adhere to a planned, linear progression. The NVR practitioner will therefore aim to move fluidly back and forth between these system levels in responding competently to clients' therapeutic needs.

But even moving fluidly between system levels poses significant challenges to the practitioner. Working with trauma-related difficulties often feels like sailing stormy seas in a tiny boat. Setbacks are very common in systems where people have experienced traumatic injury. They can occur very suddenly, are hard to predict and may be particularly severe. They can have a powerful emotional impact on the practitioner and lead to increased professional uncertainty or a resort to unsafe professional 'certainty'. Professionals within the larger system around the family, such as social workers, teachers or staff members in residential children's homes often experience high levels of stress and anxiety in responding to children and families where there has been trauma, due to the many ways in which their psychological injuries may give rise to dangerous or harmful behaviours, influencing their attitudes and responses towards their clients.

In social environments with high levels of controlling behaviour, escalation or new problems can emerge suddenly. 'Sub-systems' may move in completely different directions to the therapist/parent dyad. Finally, the often extreme pain and suffering of parents and children who have experienced traumatic injury can give rise to an entire host of difficult emotional responses within the practitioner, which need to be 'processed' if they are to have therapeutic agency and engage with clients and others in the family's social environment in helpful ways. The same maxim we posit for parents and caregivers applies to the NVR practitioner: "*You can't do it alone!*" Just as the parental anchoring function is essential for the sense of security in children with traumatic experiences, just as parents who have been abused need anchoring within an emotionally safe support network, we as practitioners in this field also need a well-functioning team that can support us effectively in our work with people who have experienced severe traumatic injury. Competent clinical supervision and peer supervision with colleagues who are conversant with and experienced in working with NVR, competent in responding to relational trauma, and who are able to inhabit positions which are marked by curiosity and non-judgemental attitudes, rather than critical and prescriptive responsiveness, are essential for work that is both efficacious and protective of the practitioner's emotional well-being. High ratios of clinical supervision to direct client contact hours are necessary, and peer supervision should take place in addition. Employers must responsibly create such support structures for practitioners, and also provide sufficient opportunity for relevant continuing professional development, if they are to ensure competent work and fulfil their duty of care to their staff and support their emotional well-being, professional confidence and workplace competence.

As a first step towards working with NVR that is both systemic *and* trauma-informed, the practitioner is well advised to establish that they can ensure not only their self-care, but also other-care, by availing themselves of a similar kind of anchoring to that which their clients require. Increasing professional competence and emotional well-being are not only individual personal traits – they are nurtured systemically and grow within the professional's own support network. I consider there to be an ethical systemic requirement to enable practitioners to develop and maintain the competencies which are essential for qualified and successful work with families and persons within the families' social environs. Such competencies are not professional and methodological knowledge alone; therapeutic work or parent coaching in NVR cannot just follow simple protocols, but instead must engage the 'whole person' of the practitioner.

The many method sections in this book aim to illustrate some new possibilities for the practitioner who is navigating a difficult terrain, but are not intended as a prescriptive, heavily manualised guide to working in this area. The professional who works within the many social fields the family moves in, who engages as a whole person, who is anchored by the emotionally safe support structures of their own organisation, must be able to maintain the flexibility that is required to respond adequately to the challenging situations they will face. Not only do they have the right to receive the kind of support they need, but it is also a professional necessity. Working in social systems that have been influenced by often extreme violence and abuse, with people who have experienced severe and barely imaginable threat and injury, a professional's judgement and decision-making can easily be affected by high levels of anxiety, any past experiences of abuse they themselves may have had,[13] vicarious (secondary) trauma, or current difficult life circumstances. At the same time, an attitude which is both compassionate and appreciative towards caregivers and children is essential in helping them regain their dignity. We should not take such an attitude for granted or presume that it will be prevalent among practitioners as a matter of course; it must be cultivated. As practitioners, we should hold ourselves, our teams and the organisations we work for to a standard, which continuously promotes and nurtures an attitude that values our clients, which deeply respects their human dignity – and our colleagues' and our own.

Notes

1 See Little (2011).
2 In co-authorship with his clients, Alan Wade (1997) retells their histories as narratives of resistance to violence and injustice. He attributes a healing effect to a client's recollection of their agency in resisting injustice and abuse, and the many meanings this recollection can be imbued with.
3 This book refers to all families or family-like groups in which parenting takes place. Most often, the word 'family' is used, but it can also mean social units such as the foster- or residential home. The principles and methods described here apply in certain ways to all groups of caregivers. Where it is not obvious from the text that only parents, foster carers or residential carers are being referred to, the term 'parents' refers to all kinds of caregivers and 'family' to all these different social units.
4 A notion that comes close to postmodern understandings in positioning theory (see Harré, 2015) and the concept of structural violence.
5 For an in-depth analysis of Douglass' psychological transformation and the intrapsychic as well as interpersonal determinants of this transformation, see Walker (2020).
6 Herman (2015) criticises the term 'borderline personality disorder', which has more recently been re-named 'emotionally unstable personality disorder' as an individualising diagnosis, which detaches a person's symptoms from the social conditions of their abuse. The disregard of e.g. sexual abuse in this descriptor in girls and women, with a high prevalence of such abuse, renders it in her view as a misogynistic concept. In a similar vein, Lannaman and McNamee (2020) have more recently criticised the diagnosis of PTSD as an individualising concept which disregards the 'social pathology' to which individuals respond with traumatic symptoms.
7 Child and adolescent mental health services.

8 For an extensive, in-depth analysis of shame regulation in NVR, including the distinction between 'righteous shame' and 'toxic shame', see Weinblatt (2018), also referenced in other sections of this book.

9 Verbally aggressive, transgressive or physically aggressive child behaviour patterns have long been referred to in the research literature as 'controlling behaviour' (Patterson, DeBaryshe and Ramsey, 1989; Eddy, Leve and Fagot, 2001). The use of this term relates primarily to the *function* or effect of such recurrent behaviours, generally meaning that parents or siblings submit to the demands of the young person who acts in such ways, rather than to an explicit intention of the child in question.

10 The Gestalt theorist and early social psychologist Kurt Lewin posited that, for change to take place, we need to identify the 'field' of social forces impacting on the individual and 'unfreeze' it, so that new forms of interaction can establish themselves (see e.g. Burnes and Cooke, 2013). Following this line of thought, it is important to identify the various social dimensions within which the family and family members exist, and find pivotal points for creating greater fluidity within them.

11 Where children or young people have been taken into residential or foster care, we should consider that, from the vantage point of the parents, residential carers or foster carers represent part of the larger system, while from the other caregivers point of view, the parents' communication belongs to the larger system.

12 'Child' and 'young person' will be used interchangeably, and at times may even be used to refer to young adults.

13 Given the very high rates of childhood sexual abuse and physical violence, domestic abuse and other forms of interpersonal violence in the general population, many professionals themselves have had past experiences they are likely to associate with their clients'. However, this should not be seen to disqualify them from working in this field. Adequate organisational support, without which they could take harm, can actually help actualise their lived experience knowledge and competence, to their own and their clients' benefit.

Part I

Systems that heal

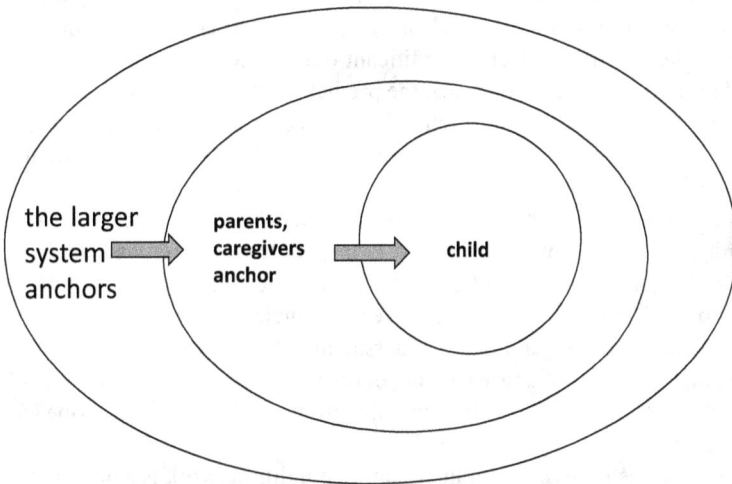

Figure I.1 Larger system anchors parents.

DOI: 10.4324/9781032717111-3

Chapter 1

How can the family, foster home or residential home become a healing environment?

In the process of healing from severe traumatic injury, the familiarity of our immediate social environment and of the larger interpersonal system around us becomes a key resilience factor: significant others, the customary social structure of our family or our circle of friends, the predictability of the behaviour of those we know well and our trust in their reliability and compassionate responsiveness can provide us with a sense of security. Omer and Alon (1994) have conceptualised this kind of resilience in the face of traumatic disaster as the 'continuity principle'; they stress the importance of preserving, among other things, interpersonal, relational continuity. A trusted environment can help people better regulate their psycho-physiological arousal and emotions. The communicated belief by significant others, that our clients will be able to recover with their self-efficacy restored, as well as the patience and compassionate understanding that the process of healing takes its time, that survivors of abuse cannot yet respond in autonomous ways at all times but that their ability to do so will eventually grow, can help generate hope and positive expectations.[1]

However, constructive communication within this network is a necessary condition for our familiar social environment to act as a *healing system* in the face of traumatic injury. On the one hand, we cannot simply expect that people who have had severe adverse experiences will be buttressed by family and friends; it is more likely that where there have been longstanding patterns of interpersonal abuse, supportive communication processes will not yet be sufficiently in place. On the other hand, we may also run the risk of underestimating the resource that their ecological social environment provides our clients with. This may be especially the case, where our own prejudicial stereotypes or lack of cultural understanding regarding 'complex cases', where families of lower socio-economic status, communities of colour or other minorities are concerned, obscure our awareness of the resources that are inherent in their social networks. Julie and Jonas' example illustrates the manner, in which some memories of interaction within the family can increase the burden of traumatic stress, while others become a powerful resource:

Julie's two children are subject to child protection measures. As a family, they are dealing with multiple challenges. In her therapy session, Julie tells me that she was injured in a severe car accident several years ago. She shares that the

DOI: 10.4324/9781032717111-4

paramedic's well-intentioned questions and comments at the time exacerbated her terror, rather than having a calming and containing effect. The paramedic had asked about her parents, spoken about Easter and had told her that she would soon see her mother again. For many people, such comments could have been helpful, as they would have maintained the expectation of continuity in the person who had just experienced such a terrible event – they would have re-directed the person's attention to the security they had felt as a child in their nuclear family, reminded them of the predictability of family rituals which re-affirm and renew close inter-personal relationships (Imber-Black, Roberts and Whiting, 2003) and invited the person to imagine a future in which there is normalcy. For Julie however, none of this was the case. Her father had sexually abused her when she was a child, and her mother did not believe her, when she later intimated that something had been seriously the matter. Her father and her mother's later male partners often beat her mother, and there were many terrifying situations. There were high levels of alcohol consumption in the family. Against this backdrop, it is unsurprising that the paramedic's comments did not have their intended effect on Julie and actually unsettled her.

Mother and daughter have become estranged and Julie, now a mother herself, is worried that her child could be taken into residential or foster care.

I ask her, who in a parallel universe would have comforted her, had the paramedic brought that person to her mind? She immediately answers: "Granddad".

She remembers her maternal grandfather, a farmer, taking her and her brother back to his farm when he had come on an unannounced visit and found the children unsupervised in the family apartment, while their parents were at their local pub. She tells me about the sweet milky tea Granddad made for her at bedtime, the feeling and the smell of the fresh sheets, the bedtime story he told the children, and the way they rode on the tractor with him when he ploughed a field. Her facial expression and posture appear relaxed and express feelings of warm comfort and happiness.

As we speak about this swift and unforeseen shift in her state of consciousness, Julie surprises me with a comment about her name: Her original name was different, but she now calls herself 'Julie' after her grandfather, whose name was 'Jules'. In this way, she feels closer to her grandfather, who died when she was an adolescent. The –internalised – relationship with her grandfather becomes pivotal in our work and influences the resource-oriented questions I ask:

"What strengths would Granddad see in you, even now, in this crisis? What would he appreciate about the way you parent your children? What advice would he give you about protecting your children from dangerous men? If your granddad could speak to your children's social worker, what would he tell her that makes him feel more optimistic you can succeed? What traps that you could fall into would he warn you about? Instead of calling Frank (her 11-year-old son Jonas' father, who is often under the influence of drugs) to support you in resisting Jonas' aggressive behaviour, who would granddad suggest you call? In your grandfather's opinion, who would be more suited than Frank and wouldn't hit the child or blame you for Jonas' behaviour?"

This example illustrates the importance of the nuclear and wider family for all family members – parents as well as children – as an interpersonal arena within which to heal from traumatic injury. It raises multiple questions: What if the mother's historic birth family was a place of severe abuse and neglect? What if, as in Julie and her children's example, men with a propensity for violence continue to violate the boundaries of the family? What if the son appears to reproduce the violence of men against his mother, his sister and himself, in his own response patterns? How can we work systemically to help protect the integrity of the nuclear family, so its members can begin to heal from trauma?

While in her childhood several men – first her father, then her mother's other partners – traumatically burdened Julie to a high degree by acting with sexual abuse and physical violence, she also felt abandoned and unprotected by her mother. Parents with such experiences of childhood adversity may be more vulnerable to intimate partner abuse during certain phases of their life trajectory, and this, in turn, can impact severely on their children. If a child then acts in aggressive and violent ways towards their mother or their sibling – ways which mirror the abuse by adults in the parent's earlier life – everyone in the family, including the child who is acting in this way, is likely to feel traumatised[2] or re-traumatised.

In Julie's example, her relationship with her grandfather was very different from the relationships in her nuclear birth family, and in spite of the difficulties they are currently facing, Julie's family of procreation is significantly different from her birth family.[3] It is now the task of the NVR practitioner to help a mother, who has experienced traumatic injury in her childhood and in intimate partner relationships and now feels re-traumatised by her child's behaviour, to transform her family of procreation in such a way that it becomes an emotionally safe social realm which will enable and promote her own and her children's healing. It is a tall order. In the above example, this was facilitated by 're-membering', a methodology drawn from Narrative Therapy (White, 1997). In re-membering, the 'inner' representation of significant others, as well as the actually existing external physical communities are revitalised by including people who have acted in ways that are supportive and emotionally safe, to help actualise both internal and interpersonal resources. The practitioner can help generate positive memories of the deceased, and the client can imagine how this person would respond to their current challenging circumstances. The deceased is thus 'reanimated', their support revitalised. Living individuals, whom the client has experienced as helpful or positive, are also approached to renew these relationships. In this way, the parent can once again come to feel connected with both deceased and living persons in a manner that encourages solutions for current difficulties to emerge. A necessary prerequisite for working with re-membering in this way in NVR, is the practitioner's openness for the perception of resources in their clients' interpersonal relationships, which they may not have previously been aware of. A position of 'not-knowing' or 'safe uncertainty' is necessary, helps becoming attuned to such resources.

Whenever people within the family's immediate social environment act in a manner that has a deleterious effect on parents – whether they are members of the ecological system or representatives of institutions such as social services or CAMHS – the family's social environment will need to incorporate more individuals who habitually communicate in an emotionally safe manner. It then becomes the practitioner's task to support parents in expanding their support network, and re-membering can serve a vital function in facilitating such an expansion for parents who have come to feel anxious or uncertain in the face of critical communication. In Julie and Jonas' example, the re-membering conversations helped move from the positive memory of granddad's caring responses and imagining how he would support Julie were he still alive, to dealing successfully with the challenges she is facing in the here and now, by augmenting her actual ecological support network:

In one of her sessions, Julie shares that she believes granddad would certainly like her friend Liz and approve of her. Liz and Julie used to occasionally take their children to their local library and afterwards, Liz would read stories to the children in the park. Often, a whole bunch of other children would gather around them and listen to Liz' storytelling. Julie feels safe around Liz, and Jonas trusts Liz, as well. Liz follows the invitation to attend the next therapy session and becomes Julie's very first NVR supporter, the nucleus of a newly forming support network around the family.

Repeatedly, Julie complains about the children's social worker's attitude. She relates the events around an incident, when she and Jonas had an altercation: Even after repeated reminders to switch off the computer and get ready for bed, Jonas became rude and verbally abusive, calling her a "f...ing c..." and a "f...ing b...", upon which she hit him in the face with the back of her hairbrush – in spite of the previously successful efforts at de-escalating she had been making over the course of the last few weeks. In a state of high arousal, Julie called Jonas' father on the phone, in spite of his propensity for violence and aggression, which is reinforced by his cocaine habit. He subsequently came to the family home, shouted at both of them and took Jonas with him over night. Jonas' social worker investigates this incident and tells Julie she believes that Jonas, at the age of 13, can no longer develop secure attachment to his mother. Julie responds to this negative prognosis and other, similar messages, by feeling extremely uncertain about herself as a parent and having very angry thoughts and feelings towards the social worker. To cope with these feelings, she avoids contact with the social worker and fails to answer her phone calls. The social worker, in turn, complains about her 'lack of cooperation', sees it as a personal trait of Julie's, and considers it to be a risk factor for the children, who are subject to a child protection plan.

Meanwhile, Liz has engaged two further supporters on Julie's behalf. The social worker accepts my invitation to a meeting with Julie and her three supporters. In the prior therapy session, Julie and I have carefully prepared the account she wishes to give her supporters and her children's social worker. In the meeting, she shares what feelings emerged in her, when she was called a 'b...' and a 'c', and she speaks about the background to these emotions in her own history of child sexual abuse, the guilt she felt after hitting Jonas, the way she felt completely alone and isolated in the world which led to her calling Frank in her distress, the fear she felt when he entered their home, and the worries and self-blame that took hold of her after Frank had taken the boy with him, not knowing whether he would hurt Jonas or how he would treat him. However – and this is of central importance in preparing the ground for inviting a change in the social worker's attitude, and to allow a sense of personal agency to emerge in her – Julie and her supporters report back about some of the significant successes Julie has achieved so far in her efforts with NVR.

We then discuss what Julie can do to facilitate the family's recovery from this setback, and what contributions her supporters will make in this process. In particular, we discuss the question of how Julie will be able to access safe support by contacting one of her supporters whenever she is in a state of high arousal, instead of calling upon Frank. Subsequently, Jonas' social worker expresses greater optimism about the family's future prospects and agrees to take part in a campaign of concern[4] herself. In the wake of everyone's efforts, Jonas' behaviour eventually improves again, the ruptures in the relationship between mother and son can begin to be repaired, and children's services[5] no longer see a need for Jonas to go into care.

If we want to see parental authority grow, parents should be anchored in an *ecological* support network. In a manner that is similar to the anchoring function of attachment, in which the young person's attachment to the caregiver becomes more secure, when the caregiver provides a deterrent from acting on their own destructive impulses without coming across as being threatening, the parent needs people within their ecological support system to provide deterrence in an emotionally safe way. Supporters within that system will need to cooperate in a manner that *the parents* require for their own sense of agency to grow. Being supported by a professional network alone will be insufficient to meet the parents' and family's needs (Omer, personal communication). This example illustrates that it is especially important for a mother who has had traumatic experiences to become anchored by people she feels safe with in her actual social environment, if she is not to be overwhelmed by feelings of fear, anger or rage and immediately act on those feelings – emotions that can emerge, when aggressive child behaviour or other threatening situations may have a re-traumatising effect on her.

Importantly, parents will only feel communally anchored in a supportive way if they do not feel criticised by the other adults. When parents report that communication by members of the larger family, friends, neighbours or professionals feels critical, I often ask 'what age' (developmentally) they feel in such a moment. They usually indicate an age from childhood or early adolescence. The ability of a father to remain connected with his sense of parental agency will be seriously constrained, if he feels *like 12* in the wake of criticism. A psychologically '12-year-old' father will struggle to respond competently to problematic behaviour shown by his 13-year-old daughter. Moreover, even well-intentioned criticism can revive traumatic associations, when they are 'made to feel 12' – which may have been a period in their life, in which they experienced significant abuse or neglect.

Re-membering (White, 1997) is suitable for working with NVR when parents, foster carers or residential carers and children have had traumatising experiences. It can be especially useful in helping members of the family, foster family or children's home feel emotionally connected to others once again. In work with NVR, we can use re-membering as a first step towards building a network of social support.

Method: Re-membering as a first step towards an NVR support network

Listen closely, when a parent discloses or gives an account of a traumatising experience in the past.

Act as a compassionate witness – speaking in the first person singular, shares how the parent's account has touched you. However, also remain attuned to the client's resilience and possible history of resistance to abuse: *Thank you for telling me all about that. I imagine it must have taken a lot of courage to remember that and share with me what happened back then. I feel very touched to hear that, as this little girl, you were able to carry on after this terrible experience and even look after your siblings, making them as safe as possible. I would have liked to have known that girl....*

Ask questions regarding people about whom the client has positive memories: *Who would have protected this girl and her siblings, if they had known what was happening at home? Who would have appreciated her courage, and her care for her brothers and sisters? What would your grandmother have said? What would she have done?*

You can create an imaginary scenario and 'revive' that person from the client's past: *How would he respond today, if he could see your efforts to protect your daughter from harm? What would he say if he saw your son pushing you?*

Ask about any of the parent's contemporaries, who may come into question as potential supporters: *Thinking about the people you know today, who would have protected the little girl you were back then?*

Introduce the possibility of actually reaching out to such a person to engage them as a supporter: *Imagine you would send... (the helpful person) a WhatsApp message or even call her, to let her know what's going on... How do you think she would respond?*

The more a family is burdened by external pressures emanating from their social environment, the more important it is for parents to become anchored in an ecological, emotionally safe support network. Should e.g. a parent feel threatened by another adult, it is essential that they experience a person who will position themselves in an emotionally safe way towards them, in order to counter-balance the traumatic experience of isolation, of being left alone to face threat. The felt connection to such a supporter can help facilitate a parent's emotional self-regulation. Julie's example illustrates how severely incapacitating acute threat by someone in the immediate social environment can be, especially when the family's life has already been burdened by uncertainty and fear.

Interaction in Julie's nuclear family of origin did not have the properties of a healing system. The road traffic incident represented type I trauma, an incident that does not occur within a close interpersonal relationship. Her adverse childhood experiences and the later adverse life experiences she and her children bore with Jonas' father and other partners however represented type II trauma. This kind of trauma occurs within close, usually intimate interpersonal relationships and is elicited by repeated, exis-tentially frightening abusive attacks or humiliation and degrading treatment. Such attacks, which occur in relationships that are marred by coercive control and violence against a non-offending parent, usually by a man against a woman, often affect the parent's relationships with her children in a variety of negative ways (Katz, 2022). Against this backdrop and the further traumatising experiences with her son's father, Julie now faced the challenge of transforming relationships with people in the fam-ily's social environment so that the nuclear family itself – she and Jonas – could become a healing system for both. As a very first step towards such a transformation, she identified people from her past and present, who interacted in emotionally safe ways. The possibility of involving them in an actual supportive community around both her and her son was raised in the client's imagination.

In this case, we can see the tension between constructive patterns of interaction on the one hand, and the kinds of problematic interaction on the other, which a nuclear family with the experience of severe traumatisation can find itself entangled in. When we evaluate patterns of current interaction that emerge between significant others in the family's social environment and parents and children, it can be helpful to understand how these significant others position themselves. Positioning theory dis-tinguishes between what an individual can or could potentially do under certain cir-cumstances, and what they may actually do (Harré, 2015). While there can be a great range of behavioural possibilities, only certain ones are routinely chosen, reflecting a position the individual takes or that is ascribed to them. The notion of positioning does not entail a fixed personality which would explain what behaviours an individ-ual chooses; instead, their position can be seen to reflect certain moral understandings of their rights or their obligations towards others, which, in turn, are influenced by the discourses in social networks and in society at large that they participate in.

Following on from this, we can surmise that an individual's repetitive behaviours towards parents and children express positions they occupy, rather than necessarily being based on fixed personality traits. I have found it helpful to distinguish three different kinds of such positions towards family members:

- a critical/prescriptive position,
- a dangerous/coercive position,
- an emotionally safe position.

These positions will be examined in the rest of this chapter; in the following chapter, we will move on to methods which can help parents distinguish the positions others take and find their voice in articulating their experience of them. Identifying such positions alone can begin to re-balance power.

Critical/prescriptive positioning

Criticism may feel like social rejection. This can be exacerbated when a person has been emotionally abused.[6] We experience social rejection as painful, in an almost physical sense. It has been demonstrated in fMRI studies to activate the same brain regions that become activated in conjunction with physical pain (Eisenberger, Lieberman and Williams, 2003). Many parents we work with feel socially rejected by frequent criticism; they tend to feel isolated, and their trauma-induced sense of not belonging to their community or social network may increase.

Receiving continuous criticism often correlates with high levels of stress hormones. This is especially the case in communication about parenting. For example, cortisol levels are highly correlated with the level of criticism between parents of adolescent children when they communicate about problematic behaviour in their offspring (Rodriguez and Margolin, 2013). We can safely assume that such an effect will be even greater in parents who have been exposed to emotional abuse by other adults, and subsequently by their own children, over long periods of time.

People, who repeatedly criticise someone's parenting and/or the person of the parent, prescribe certain ways of dealing with problematic child behaviour, admonish them for not following advice or directly intercede in dealing with the child without the parent's felt consent, occupy what I call a *critical-prescriptive position*. They communicate a belief that the caregiver lacks parenting competence. Their intercession in the parenting process itself, or their criticism of the parent's responses, is intended to serve a corrective function. They frequently attribute aggressive, self-destructive or self-harming child behaviour to the parents' ways of responding to the child and speak much more often about parents' current or past insufficiencies, than about their perceptions of 'what the parent has got right'.

Years ago, I was sitting in a beer garden in summer and looking after my twin sons who were toddlers at the time, playing in a sandbox. I waved back to a client who happened to be sitting a few tables away. The following week, in her therapy session, she mentioned seeing me and how annoyed she'd been at the "admiring looks" I received, simply for being a "bloke with kids", while she would merely be asked to "keep the pram out of the way". At that moment, I had not been aware of my own male privilege in this regard.

It is my experience that this 'bloke bonus' is still in existence today, while mothers bear the brunt of critical interaction in regard to their children and parenting. Critical-prescriptive positions do not simply emerge randomly. They are subject to a deeply embedded culture of parent blaming. Parent blaming is neither gender neutral nor neutral to race, social class, disability or other societal aspects of discrimination. For many parents, these dimensions of discrimination – and in conjunction with this, parent blaming – intersect. Women remain the hardest hit when it comes to parent blaming. For example, mothers, rather than fathers, specifically attract blame for childhood obesity in the media (De Brun et al., 2013). The overwhelming majority of parents ordered by courts in the UK to attend parenting classes in response to their children's anti-social behaviours are mothers (Peters, 2012). Jensen and Tyler (2018) investigate what they call a 'machinery' of parent blame that permeates all aspects of societal life, and which results in mothers being cast as figures of failure by people located in all manner of social networks, ranging from policy makers, cultural- and media producers and professional bodies to friends, members of the nuclear or larger family and members of the wider community. We can consider such a 'machinery' of parent blame to be a manifestation of institutional sexism, racism, ableism and classism. Dominant parent-blaming discourses in society are the substrate upon which critical/prescriptive positions grow. It bears no wonder that parent blaming in so many channels of public discourse invites people around the family to inhabit critical-prescriptive positions, especially when family members behave in ways that violate normative expectations. Yet, where parents, usually mothers, who are e.g. survivors of coercive control in partner relationships are concerned, living in a state of high anxiety in the face of constant imminent threat which could arise from conflicting with the perpetrator's wishes, is likely to create a psychological habit of self-policing. A parent develops this survival strategy in the hope that she can minimise risk (Katz, 2022). What then are the effects of parent blame, which is directed at her by other powerful adults, on a parent who has become self-policing in the face of anticipated threat – threat of dominance by someone who has held power over her, and whose behaviour she may feel is replicated in her adolescent child?

Where policy- and protocol-driven measures in agencies such as CAMHS or children's services reflect dominant parent-blaming discourses in wider society, professionals are implicitly invited to take up critical-prescriptive positions. Where this occurs, they risk becoming part of a system of structural injustice. Returning to the understanding that certain specific patterns of interaction emerge from certain kinds of positioning, we do not need to assume that professionals' or non-professionals' communicative behaviours in some way reflect deeply rooted personality traits. Such a notion would individualise critical response patterns and thereby distract from their wider structural nature.

Occupying a certain position vis-a-vis the family, and especially vis-a-vis the parents, will however provide the conceptual and perceptual framework within which that individual interprets the life of the family they are dealing with. Often, for a professional to *believe they know* can help alleviate some of the anguish one feels when confronted with child behaviour that is severely harmful or self-destructive, and with the corresponding helplessness their parents express. When people who are participating in the larger system around the family know that the children have been exposed to highly aversive conditions, they are more likely to attribute their current problematic behaviour in a linear, causal way to the impact of previous experiences and to current shortcomings in parenting.

Dominant societal parent-blaming discourses provide an easy answer to what seems so difficult to comprehend, and negative causal attributions can reduce the individual's own bewilderment and emotional discomfort. Often, the non-offending parent is blamed for the child's traumatic experiences, and in conjunction with this, their current parenting may be considered inadequate. Not only parents with histories of childhood and partner abuse, but also parents who have adopted children complain about parent blaming, which is often mirrored in the child's communication. Many adoptive parents report that their children have been automatically referred for child protection investigations when they have sought help from children's services, leaving them feeling outraged, highly stressed and feeling devastated that their integrity has been brought into question (Selwyn, Wijedasa and Meakings, 2014).

When some or many of the child's behaviours mirror the template of previous abuse the non-offending parent has experienced at the hands of other adults, parent blaming – which more often than not becomes mother blaming – turns into victim blaming. Victim blaming is especially pernicious when it becomes associated in the parent's experience with the kind of blame that was previously part of the pattern of abuse they were subjected to. It is likely to re-evoke the kind of negative self-directed beliefs that were formed historically, along with their associated emotions, such as shame and guilt; it will go hand in hand with deeply felt uncertainty and confusion, and deplete the parent's will to become active and persist in protecting themselves and their children from aggression.

Witnessing caregivers' helplessness and distress or thinking about the child's history of traumatic abuse or neglect, individuals may be easily tempted to form a two-dimensional, reductive image of the parent, consider them to be inadequate, and want to intercede and rapidly take measures that aim to bring about immediate change. Many individuals, who interact in a professional or private capacity with members of a family facing multiple challenges, manifest the critical-prescriptive positions they occupy explicitly in their communication with a non-offending parent. They may also communicate their disapproval implicitly, in their body language, facial expression, intonation, and by virtue of what they do not say or ask. Omission can inhibit certain relational possibilities.[7] For example, a professional who occupies a critical-prescriptive position towards a parent, holds her responsible for her child's current violent behaviour and perceives the parent as avoiding contact with her or not communicating openly, may struggle to find within themselves a compassionate response to the parent's distress. This will not only express itself in the professional's choice of words, but also in what they *do not* say to the mother, in their body language, facial expression and in the prosody and intonation of their voice.

Disapproval is communicated when there is no apparent adequate response to a caregiver's emotional burden. The following example illustrates the powerful effect such a discompassionate response can have, but it also demonstrates that changing what is centred in conversation can invite people to re-position themselves very quickly:

Providing consultation for the first time to a team of caregivers in a residential adolescent service, I feel great discomfort. There is a sense of emotional distance, a cold atmosphere in the room. Under discussion is an incident during which a teenage girl spat in her (male) carer's face. His colleagues speak about this incident in an unemotional way, while the carer himself seems withdrawn, almost psychologically absent.

He repeatedly says, in a formulaic sounding manner, that he will remain "professional" in dealing with the girl, will follow all procedures and carry out all his responsibilities. When I point to his tense posture and ask whether he might be feeling angry, the carer repeats, as a reassurance, that he will "stay professional". Asked what it may mean for him personally to have been spat in the face, the carer's demeanour changes, and he begins to express himself in a more emotional way, explaining that for him as a Romany Traveller, being spat at is a particularly humiliating experience: "We've been treated like that for centuries...".

The conversation becomes livelier, and some of the team members share that they feel affected by what they have just heard. One team member says they feel guilty not to have shown a reaction to what happened and not to have "done anything" in response to the way in which her colleague was humiliated. Another carer explains that they had not been taking their colleague seriously, having perceived him as overly sensitive, and that they now feel sorry for this response. This shift in atmosphere brings about a willingness to respond to the incident. Together, we plan how the team can cooperate in developing a 'campaign of concern' to respond to this and similar incidents and impress upon the young person that such behaviour is no longer accepted in the home, as it harms both the carer and damages her relationship with him. One colleague volunteers to support the girl in making reparation to the carer whom she spat at, or else make reparation on her behalf, should she refuse to cooperate. At this point, the team has become quite animated and the emotional atmosphere in the room has improved, with a greater sense of connectedness between the team members.

Eventually, the carer in question expresses an interest in what may have been going on inside the girl, when she spat at him. He explains that he hadn't been interested in this before, but that he now feels more open towards her. This becomes the new theme of the meeting.

This example illustrates that critical-prescriptive positions, such as those demonstrated by the colleagues in the residential home, can have an isolating effect on the individual caregiver and endanger the team's coherence. Importantly, once the carer in question felt both a compassionate response and experienced his colleague's willingness to take action, he became more open for and interested in the inner life and possible distress of the girl. This, in turn, created openings for greater attunement to her and potential better understanding of emotional difficulties which may have had their origin in her own history of abuse by male figures. Resistance to aggressive behaviour of the young person, and attunement to her vulnerability, did not posit themselves as binary opposites. Instead, the latter emerged in the wake of a conversation about the former. We will investigate the need for the caregiver's experience of strength as a prerequisite for the ability to attune to the child later in this book.

Earlier, I wrote about a referring psychiatrist who similarly took a critical-prescriptive position towards a mother who had had traumatic experiences. He qualified her as being incapable of change due to her traumatisation. In doing so, he implicitly expressed the expectation that I would share his description of the person of the mother, an inadvertent invitation to position myself in a similar critical-prescriptive way. In such a manner, apparent 'truths' about parents with traumatic experiences are spread within professional networks. Unquestioning and often unreflective conformity among professionals bears the risk of perpetuating negative assignations of parents to categories such as 'untreatable' or 'treatment resistant'. These assignations may also be hardened with diagnostic labels.

When narrative is thus mistaken for fact, when we absorb such 'truths' about parents who have had traumatic experiences into our thinking in an unreflected manner, they – and we with them – run the risk of missing out on a collaborative and mutually appreciative working relationship. As critical-prescriptive positioning spreads throughout the professional network, parents come to feel misunderstood, unappreciated, spoken to rather than spoken with, and instructed on how to behave. Communication between parents and professionals becomes superficial, and parents tend to show wariness of the professionals who deal with them, experiencing them as a growing threat to their own and the entire family's autonomy. Possibilities for change become overlooked in such an atmosphere, and parents feel even more isolated.

The very structure of service provision can mitigate against a trusting and appreciative relationship between parent and professional, by seeming to 'press' the professional into a critical-prescriptive position or closing down alternative areas of inquiry. Practitioners may find themselves under pressure, when they need to operate within a service structure that rations interventions. For example, when practitioners are required to provide extremely time-limited parenting groups for parents facing extraordinary challenges, they may feel mandated to achieve what they cannot be reasonably expected to. We are also well advised to attune to the experience of parents who are referred to psycho-educational parenting groups and be mindful of the circumstances in which they may feel they have been ushered or pressured into an intervention they would not have wished to take part in. They may take exception to 'being taught how to parent', and the inference that their child's aggressive behaviour is somehow the result of their diminished parenting capacity or other personal insufficiencies.

Furthermore, a look around the room provides empirical data: how many of the parents in a parenting group are women? What meanings do these mothers attribute to being held responsible for their children's outcomes? A further aspect of ensuring not to occupy a critical-prescriptive position is being reflective of whether, as practitioners, we use language in our communication with parents, in our internal dialogue, or with other professionals that reflects a normative expectation, language that articulates what we believe they *should* be doing, or language that expresses frustration at what they are not doing. Of course, the practitioner using NVR is not free from this risk at all; they may expect the parent to execute nonviolent positive action and feel irritated when this does not occur. Having suggested certain forms of direct action, they may ask, feeling irritated, questions such as: *WHY did she give him money AGAIN?* – a question which is not so much a question as a negative attribution. Becoming aware of responding in such a manner, they may attempt to reduce their cognitive dissonance by pathologising the parent: *He isn't capable of doing this… because of his trauma…* Showing such a response, they are nonetheless responding in a critical manner, albeit one that aims to direct attention to what are considered 'mitigating' factors. Reynolds (2019) stresses the importance of taking an ethical stance in clinical supervision and giving consideration to issues of social justice. We may wish to carefully scrutinise the institutional 'givens' we work under and ask ourselves pertinent questions about how our service structure may pressure us to occupy an unethical position, or how our organisation's culture may shape our thinking and invite us to adhere to counterproductive beliefs – beliefs that can result in the diminution of our clients' autonomy and sense of agency. Clinical supervision could then further serve the purpose of how we may – in solidarity with our colleagues and with service users – find ways to challenge such service structures and institutional cultures, in order to affect greater fairness towards and better outcomes for our clients. Where necessary, we may come to the conclusion that we need to proactively resist institutional pressures when they put us in an unethical position.

In Julie's case, the children's social worker originally assumed a critical-prescriptive position towards the mother by

- omitting to ask about how the obscene words her son used had affected her, and what meanings were associated with these words for her,
- communicating an assumption to know the reason for the son's behaviour by giving a theoretically based explanation and claiming expert knowledge,
- expressing a belief in an inability on the mother's part to contribute to a change in the nature of her relationship with her son and
- attributing pathology to the son, giving a negative prognosis of his ability to change within the relationship to his mother and characterising his 'insecure attachment' as a fixed trait.[8]

The mother responded to the social worker's communication with deeply felt uncertainty and high stress levels over a prolonged period of time. Such responses can then also reverberate throughout the relationships within the family. However, the conversation with the mother's supporters invited the social worker to shift to an emotionally safer position: not only were the mother's emotional responses to her son's behaviour centred in the conversation; her parental agency and the way she was anchored within a caring community of supporters became apparent to this professional. In this way, the social worker began to bear witness to Julie's efforts and the kinds of constructive parenting responses she was becoming increasingly able to show, in spite of setbacks in her and her son's process of change. She became able to perceive the mother as growing in competence, changed her prognosis and considered the son's propensity for change. Such re-positioning has a profound influence on how a professional communicates with family members. In this instance, as the social worker became less pathologising and developed more positive expectations, the relational rupture between the two women could be repaired. Her re-positioning went hand in hand with a reduction in the parent's sense of uncertainty. Feeling less threatened, the mother's embodied responses within the family began showing more confidence and less anxiety, which will have contributed to greater emotional security for her son, as well.

Professionals may feel institutionally obliged to occupy a critical and prescriptive position, which requires a belief in 'knowing' in an absolute sense. Certain social agencies or institutions tend to adhere to a single explanatory model for the issues that confront them in their practice. Such a theory base becomes part of the institutional culture, and professionals within such an agency will predominantly draw on this theory to develop an understanding of what can feel like bewildering phenomena in the client families they deal with. A professional who then draws from 'grand theory'[9] in this way runs the risk of letting their 'expert knowledge' override and crowd out their clients' perceptions of their own lives. Clients may then become even more voiceless than they had already been. Barthelmess (2016) speaks of the 'hubris of knowledge', the 'hubris of understanding', the 'hubris of distancing' and the 'hubris of suspicion', which professionals often manifest, especially when they are dealing with disadvantaged clients. The 'knowing' professional's message is: *I understand what motivates you. I know why you behave in this or the other way. I can determine whether and in what way you need to change.*

Ultimately, the 'knowing' practitioner, whose sense of absolute certainty is anchored in grand theory, communicates implicitly: *I know you better than you know yourself.* Structurally, this kind of message resembles that of an abuser who has been engaged in 'gaslighting' the parent, even if here, the intention is more benign. In my clinical experience, congruence with abusive communication structures can re-traumatise, regardless of the communicator's intention.

Thus, the power differential between practitioner and parent is exacerbated further. Mason (2015) proposed a quadrant with the dimensions of 'safe (vs) unsafe certainty' and 'safe (vs) unsafe uncertainty'. A therapist who wishes to work in a truly collaborative manner with family members who are entangled in complex patterns of controlling or coercive interaction, will need to bear a measure of safe uncertainty within themselves. Only then can they generate, together with their clients, relevant understandings of the family members' motivation and behaviours and encourage them in ways that make a difference in a pivotal or substantial way. If however the professional's attitude conveys a sense of 'unsafe certainty', the therapeutic relationship becomes ruptured, rendering truly collaborative engagement an impossibility. The professional's level of understanding will be insufficient to do justice to the systemic complexity of what they are witnessing and participating in.

An attitude of unsafe certainty is often taken on when individuals compensate for feeling especially helpless in the face of despair and suffering in family members with severe traumatic injury. When such an attitude becomes embedded in a critical-prescriptive position, we see dominant forms of interaction. These not only inhibit the process of change within the family; they may also add to the traumatic burden family members are dealing with. This is particularly the case, when there are already many individuals within the family's natural, non-professional or ecological social environment, who position themselves in dominant ways which are either critical and prescriptive or dangerous and coercive. Pressure builds on all fronts:

Everybody tells me what to do! I don't know what to think any more! And if I say anything at all, they tell me I'm wrong!

These words of a mother have an uncanny resemblance to the experience of a person who is exposed to coercive control by another adult in a close intimate relationship.

Sometimes, a parent with traumatic experience may appear to seek apparent certainty in another adult, however burdensome and even unsafe or outright dangerous this may be. This, to my mind, results from a relational logic that has grown from the experience of being dominated, whereby dominance and strength have become equated: the parent feels week and helpless, so the only person she feels can help her deal with her child's problem behaviour is someone who can dominate. Solid evidence of such a person's dominance – equated with strength in the parent's mind – is having felt dominated by that very person herself. At such times, when they feel overly burdened by their child's aggressive behaviour, parents may then signal a readiness to delegate their parental authority to other adults who communicate in a critical-prescriptive way. Nonetheless, the subsequent dominance and 'taking over' by the other adult undermines the parent's sense of agency and expectation of future efficacy.

However, when speaking with a parent and someone who has positioned themselves in a critical and prescriptive way towards her, we can centre the parent's need for the other adult to communicate with her, and with her child, in a manner that supports her own sense of agency. Such a conversation may act as an invitation to the other adult to re-position themselves. Rather than speaking about the parent's need on an abstract level, it is often best to ground their request in a practical example of positive NVR action, as the following example illustrates:

Mary's son often attacks her physically. She has asked her own father to become a potential supporter and has invited him to attend a therapy session with her to discuss his role in supporting her. He gets red in the face as we speak about his grandson's behaviour, slaps his thigh repeatedly and says in a loud voice: "Army cadettes! He needs to go into the Army cadettes! They'll teach him to obey orders that good-for-nothing! Just like his father! The apple doesn't fall far from the tree! Let me deal with him, I'll show him! You've always been too nice to that kid!"

Mary looks briefly at her father, buries her face in her hands, starts crying and shakes her head. In order to invite her father to compassionately witness her experience, I ask Mary to share first what emotions her son's behaviour, and then what emotions the grandfather's comments about her son bring up in her. Believing he had acted in a helpful way, Mary's father is surprised and feels troubled to learn about the difficult emotions his communication has stimulated: helplessness, shame and guilt. It is particularly shameful for Mary to hear how the grandfather asserts that her son is just like his violent father. This brings up a wish to protect her son from the grandfather's disapproval and disparaging comments, yet she feels unable to do so: caught between her loyalty to her son and her loyalty to her father, and feeling the need for her father's support, she feels immobilised.

To enable the grandfather to witness and appreciate his daughter's competence and agency as a parent, I ask her to speak about an occasion, when she took carefully planned positive action; in that instance, she gave her son a short message that she would no longer give him any more money over and above his weekly allowance.

We then go on to plan the next step the mother wishes to take. This is to ask supporters, including the grandfather, to send her son messages of concern the next time he threatens physical violence when she refuses to give him money. In this context, we have a conversation about what exactly the mother would like her father to say to the grandson, rather than interceding of his own accord as he has done in the past. She would like this new and different way, in which the grandfather would communicate with his grandson, to strengthen her resolve and help support her growing parental agency. We practice how Mary wishes her father to communicate with his grandson in role play. By expressing her wishes clearly, Mary feels able to protect her son's dignity by preventing him from being shamed by his grandfather. The grandfather makes a commitment to follow his daughter's wishes.

In the initial, heavily gendered communication pattern, we see many elements of a critical-prescriptive position. The grandfather appears, at least in part, to be well-intentioned: he would like to see his daughter protected from the grandson's violence. He assumes to know the solution; yet, his prescribed solution is as counterproductive as it is illusory: the mother is to delegate her authority to him, even though he does not live with her and her son, and to the military cadettes, which her son may never join. He implies that male dominance is required for dealing effectively with his grandson's aggression. The possibility that the mother could exert any positive parental influence is not part of his initial message. Having been subjected to coercive control by her son's father for many years in the past, the mother now feels dominated by her son. Within the relational logic of dominance by one person over another dominating person, in order to inhibit their aggression, the proposed and insisted upon solution is: male dominance over the domineering son. Male dominance has become central to the meta-narrative of problem and solution in this system, crowding out any notion of female, maternal agency. Inadvertently, the grandfather contributes to the very dominance which his daughter is struggling with, by further weakening her sense of agency, emphasising the primacy of male dominance and by perpetuating the illusion of control. Initially, the mother appears passive and seems to accept the grandfather's critical and prescriptive assertions and the way in which he implicitly defines his relationship with her: as one in which he has knowledge and relevant understanding and is in a position to determine what needs to be done. The mother is relegated to the position of helpless victim who cannot assert any relevant understanding of her own.

However, once conversational space is created for her own perspective – the question of what behaviours of his would help her to get in touch with *her own* embodied *sense of strength and agency*, she immediately knows what kind of support she requires from the grandfather. In such a dominance-saturated system, it is the practitioner's task to facilitate re-positioning. They can work towards achieving this by centring the parent's self-identified need for the kind of support that they feel will help to enhance their self-determined responsiveness towards their child.

Rather than assuming the parental resources must be wholly internal, I consider the growing parental strength to be grounded in the emerging *relational agency* (De Mol et al., 2018), between mother and grandfather, i.e. their ability to influence one another in a way that is constructive in the transformational building of their relationship. We can use therapeutic conversation to facilitate what Grabbe (2012) has called the 'language of alliance building'[10] and enable the emergence of supportive interaction. In the above example, this became possible when the grandfather was invited to show interest in his daughter's own aims and intentions and listened to what she needed from him in order to experience her own strength in relation to dealing with her son's problematic behaviour.

It would be unhelpful if the therapist, in an attempt to be 'non-directive', stood back from the communication between the parent and the person who has positioned themselves in a critical-prescriptive way. Instead, they can intercede in a manner that makes space for what has as of yet been unspoken and unheard in the parent's experience, and for the parent's *own will*. If we are to help a shift away from a critical-prescriptive pattern of communication, it can be useful to remind ourselves that even people who have had extremely traumatic experiences are still potentially able to develop self-determined motivation and request the kind of cooperation they actually feel they need. Instead of seeing their seemingly passive toleration of dominant communication as an inherent personality trait or as an inconvertible symptom of posttraumatic stress, we can understand this kind of response as a *temporary constraint* to perceiving and communicating their own internal experience. Often, parents with previous experience of domestic or childhood abuse have developed a communication pattern of outward compliance, when either flight or fight, or even immobility, would have enraged their assailant further, because what *he* required was *active* compliance. Outward compliance was thus an important survival skill. Appearing to agree with another person who is experienced as dominant, and the cognitive confusion that may accompany this, does not preclude the ability to identify one's own needs, one's own beliefs and knowledge, and one's own will. When the parent in question then communicates what kind of support they wish to receive, the language of alliance building has a chance take hold in communication processes both in, and importantly, outside of the therapy session.

If however no such shift towards the language of alliance building takes place, there may be a cascade of traumatic responses within the family. NVR theory and trauma theory can explain this process:

Symmetrical and complementary escalation: Omer (2001) describes two distinct escalatory processes that tend to take place, when a child or young person in the family displays aggressive behaviour. Where there is *symmetrical escalation*, both parent and child seek to gain control over one another, until one 'side' – usually the parent – gives in, or else a violent or otherwise destructive exchange ensues. Where there is *complementary escalation*, the child increases their controlling behaviour, while the adult attempts to manage the situation by giving in, appeasing the child, complying with the child's demands, showing submission or responding with physical or psychological avoidance of their child. Both forms of escalation may alternate, or one parent may predominantly be engaged in complementary escalation, while the other will be engaged in symmetrical escalation. In both forms of escalation, there are high levels of psycho-physiological arousal in both parent and child, which are commensurate with feelings of anxiety and fear or anger.

Threat responses – 'initial freeze', 'flight', 'fight', 'fright' and 'flag': under perception of threat, humans as well as other mammals show a particular arc of responses. From an evolutionary point of view, initial immobility – freeze – reduces visibility and enables an orientation towards threat signals, confirmation of the threat and determination of its nature. If the threat perception is confirmed and the nature of the threat identified, the individual shows self-protective responses such as 'flight' or attack – 'fight'. If however neither of these responses promise safety, the individual may show a 'fright' response, remaining immobile while having a very high level of psycho-physiological arousal. If fright lasts too long, it may give way to a rapid drop in arousal to a level far below the individual's normal baseline. This response is called 'flag' and has been likened to the organism acting dead or preparing itself for death. Immobility, dissociation, a total lack of self-protective physical impulses and apparent states of depression can be linked to such an extremely low arousal state. Females have also been known to seek protection or show protective responses towards others, especially their children, a so-called 'tend and befriend' response. In all these kinds of responses, with the exception of 'flag', adrenalin is distributed in high quantities, activating enormous energies throughout the body. As adrenalin is quickly absorbed, cortisol is distributed, in order to prolong high arousal, if there is a situation of ongoing threat.

Traumatic responsiveness and escalation: Parents and children who have had traumatic experiences often have chronically raised levels of psycho-physiological arousal. This exacerbates their propensity to feel threatened and respond accordingly, lowering their threshold for escalation. Parents' fight responses encourage symmetrical escalation, while flight or fright responses encourage complementary responses to aggressive or otherwise threatening child behaviour. We see parents showing fear, pleading, enacting submission or showing automatic obedience by immediately giving in to their child's demands, avoiding them or avoiding them psychologically if and when they move into a flag state.[11]

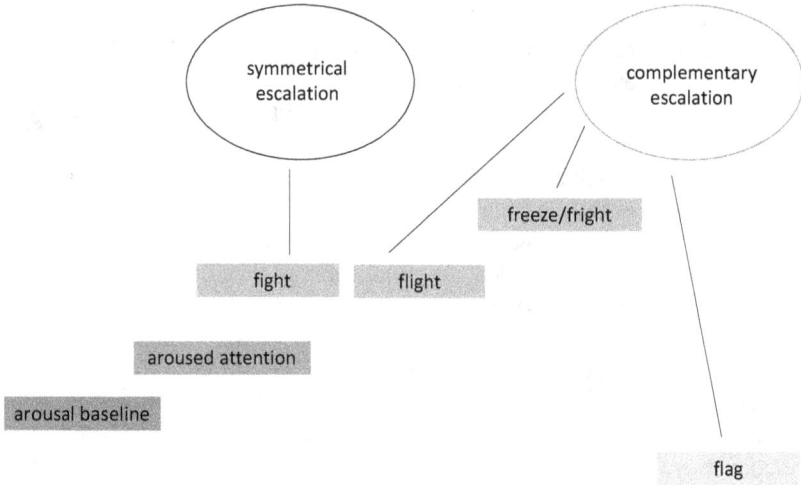

Figure 1.1 Parental threat responses and escalation.

Child behaviour which is perceived as threatening is not the only factor which can exacerbate traumatic responsiveness. Critical and prescriptive communication from people in the larger system around the family – either from within their ecological network or by professionals (Figure 1.1) is, in my experience, usually perceived by members of the family as accusatory and threatening. This additional source of threat further raises arousal, and with this, the propensity for further symmetrical or complementary escalation between parent and child.

Criticism, which in effect is tantamount to victim blaming for parents who have experienced domestic abuse, can elicit powerful feelings of shame (Haw, 2010). Frequently, fathers blame mothers, who bear the brunt of parenting responsibility, for problematic child behaviour. Criticism by professionals, and concurrent criticism by fathers, can have a powerful deleterious effect, leaving mothers anxious about the prospect of further shame being elicited in their communication with other adults. Such an effect can be even exacerbated, when the criticising other parent has exerted coercive control over the mother, when 'gaslighting' has undermined her sense of worth as a human being. Parents often report that criticism leaves them feeling socially isolated and feeling abandoned, resulting in their anxiety and/or anger intensifying. Fearing that they may respond with anger, anxiety or feel shame, they may in the future avoid seeking help from other adults, or shy away from offers of support. Such avoidance is often interpreted as a lack of parental cooperation, which, in turn, can exacerbate critical attitudes towards them, leading to a negative prognosis. The professionals' prognosis can become even more bleak, if the parent feels they need to pretend to comply with prescriptive demands by professionals or comply with demands of a coercive other adult who threatens to speak negatively about their parenting to child protection social workers: *I'll tell them how hopeless you are and make sure they'll take the kids away from you!*

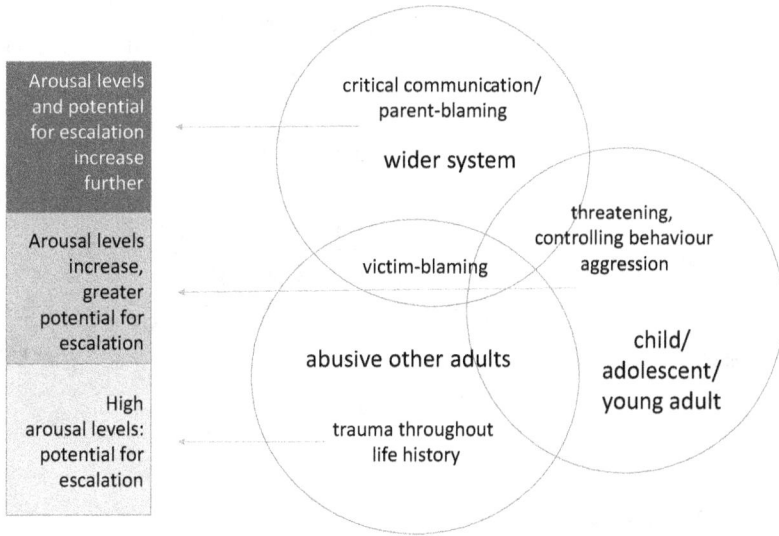

Figure 1.2 Arousal and escalation.

Taking these factors in account, one sees how isolation, anxiety and anger affect family interaction and lower thresholds for escalation within the nuclear family, especially where there are chronically high levels of psycho-physiological arousal in and between family members. Figure 1.2 illustrates factors compounding raised levels of arousal, and hence escalation.

Therapeutic experience suggests that the deleterious effects of arousal and escalation within the family are further exacerbated by the differential in power and social status between people in the larger system around the family and the parents. Figure 1.3 illustrates various aspects of social disadvantage which enlarge the power differential between members of the larger system and parents who have experienced often severe trauma. Being female and a single parent, belonging to a 'lower' social class and/or an ethnic minority, economic disadvantage – these and more aspects of disadvantage are often prevalent in families which are dealing with multiple challenges. Where there is intersectionality, the emotional burden increases exponentially. Figure 1.3 illustrates the power gradients between parents and members of the larger system around them at the intersectionalities of disadvantage and social injustice.

Children, adolescents and young adults who show aggressive or controlling behaviour often blame their parents or other caregivers intensely (Holt, 2013). Frequent blame directed at parents, residential carers or foster carers by young people who are exerting control over them can elicit intense feelings of guilt, which may result in giving in to their demands even further. This is also often the case, where there is entrenched dependency on parents (see glossary) and social withdrawal by the younger person (Lebowitz et al., 2012; Dulberger and Omer, 2021). When

institutional power   power of influence

coercive power   high social status

professional
qualification

shame

fear and anxiety

reduced knowledge of
the English language

refugee / migrant

ethnic/
religious   socially isolated
minority

psychological/
emotional
difficulties

lower social
class /
economic   single parent
disadvantage

LGBTQ

female

lower level of
educational
attainment

disability / neurodiverse

Figure 1.3 Power gradient.

members of the larger system blame caregivers or parents and the younger person becomes aware of such communication, it can give licence and encourage the younger person to blame the parent or parents even more and attribute responsibility for their own harmful or self-destructive behaviour to them.

While research purports to be objective, research agendas can reflect parent-blaming discourses in society. For example, Routt and Anderson (2011) take issue with the claim made by a host of authors who identify 'overly permissive parenting' (Charles, 1986; Agnew and Huguley, 1989; Micucci, 1996; Wilson, 1996; Cottrell, 2001; Cottrell and Monk, 2004) or 'parentification' (Harbin and Madden, 1979) of the child as causes of child to parent aggression and violence. They bring the fact that many parents in their own study of a child-to-parent-violence intervention have experienced abuse, and that this is likely to shape their responses to their aggressively acting child, into their critique of the *framing* of what these researchers have observed:

Many of the mothers of the single-parent families (…) are victims of domestic violence (n = 143, 53%) from their former partners or ex-husbands. In addition to confronting the challenges faced by any single parent, they are also reexperiencing domestic violence from their children, often in a fashion similar to their previous partner's abuse. These women often remarked that their children were using abusive language and behaviors similar to those of their violent fathers. (…) these single mothers are experiencing domestic violence a second time from their adolescent children. Battering in an adult relationship itself can have serious effects on parenting. When children see their mother as a victim of abuse, it affects their perception of her. A mother's authority is undermined because she is seen as ineffectual and powerless. Ongoing verbal abuse, such as humiliation, put downs, and criticism of her parenting adds to the image of incompetence. The emotional aftermath of battering, such as depression, withdrawal, and emotional volatility, can contribute to the image of a mother as unstable and difficult (...).

(pp. 12–13)

We can see how dominant discourses in society, which hold women to account for the violence they have been subjected to, also contribute to how research agendas and professional understandings frame the responses that are observed in parents who have experienced violence. It is an injustice, when a parent's fear or depression is not acknowledged as effects of the intimate partner abuse she has suffered; it adds serious insult to injury.

Parents raising children with histories of child abuse and neglect, but who have not experienced intimate partner violence themselves, are also frequently subject to parent-blaming communication. Research into adoption disruption has identified three key factors to which the adoptive parents attribute the familial difficulties that have led to the disruption. These are, in conjunction with each other, (1) actual violence instigated by the child towards the parents, (2) blame for this violence directed at the parents by the professionals involved and (3) a lack of the kind of support they feel they would have required, and which would have been useful to them and their children (Selwyn, Wijedasa and Meakings, 2014). I routinely hear parents complain about being blamed by professionals for problematic child behaviour, as do colleagues I supervise. For example, child protection measures may almost immediately be instigated in response to parents' requesting support from social services for dealing with their child's aggressive or self-destructive behaviour, or therapists in child mental health services may assume that parents wish to demonise their child, when they give detailed descriptions of violence or record aggressive incidents on their phone.

In therapy with these parents, it becomes apparent how, in their perception, such blaming messages by outside adults and by the focus child mirror blame by those adults, who have perpetrated violence against them in the past. Parents with histories of domestic abuse or child abuse have usually experienced victim blame in the past: *See what you've made me do? What's wrong with you?* Blaming messages perpetuate and reinforce the construction of negative narratives of parents' personhood, and become, often to a considerable degree, internalised by them. The parent's self is described in a one-sided manner by others, whose negative attributions of the parent bear key similarities; there is a truncated range of descriptions by others for the parent to choose from, and which often make the parent question their own perception and experience of self. Such a way in which definitional power over the self of the parent is exerted by others can exacerbate their uncertainty and increase their traumatic burden even further, by leading to greater inner fragmentation (Jakob, 2021).

The NVR practitioner may also run the risk of taking on a critical-prescriptive position. In particular, the offer of nonviolent methods for parents to use, such as the announcement, the sit-in or the campaign of concern, may be communicated by the NVR practitioner as *instruction* rather than as an invitation to consider *possibilities* for action and explore the meanings such kinds of action could acquire for them within the system they are moving in. Sometimes, NVR practitioners state that a father or mother is showing 'resistance to NVR' (!) In doing so, they position themselves hierarchically above parents. This can tempt them to go on to develop hypotheses about why such a parent may not be able or willing to follow what they have been advised to do. Such hypothesising *about* the client, which is not grounded in the client's own experience of self, represents an external determination of their personhood. In order to prevent risk to the emotional wellbeing of the client, which is inherent in the narration of self by others, it is helpful for supervision to be *"...informed by a spirit of social justice, practices of solidarity and an ethic of resistance"* (Reynolds, 2019, p. 2). Such supervision can also reduce the risk of so-called 'burnout', which could ensue with increasing helplessness in the therapist. Reynolds critiques the very notion of 'burnout' as an idea that is premised on isolated individuals: *"What I am contesting is the prescriptive, individualised accusations burnout levies against workers, which obscure the contexts of social injustice we work in, and blame clients for the harms we experience"* (p. 3).[12] It can be especially important for the practitioners' and their colleagues' reflections to enable them to view themselves as part of the therapeutic system. Doing so enables the professional to recognise when, in spite of their best intentions, they may inadvertently be limiting parents' autonomy – which may, in turn, have been the result of organisational pressures and of dominant discourses in their professional fields, that are based on the understanding that it is the practitioner's task – and justifiable right – to act as a corrective agent of social control, who is to 'cure' what 'is wrong' with their clients. Such reflections promote organisational learning (Grabbe, 2013).

Not only professionals, but importantly also friends, members of the wider family, neighbours or other members of the community or communities within which parents live often engage in parent-blaming communication and thereby position themselves in a critical and prescriptive way. This can be particularly the case, where parents are faced with multiple challenges[13] and may, in part, be the result of a relational logic, according to which the resolution of internal family conflict requires the control of the child which has been acting in a controlling way, as demonstrated in the case example of Mary and her father. Following such a logic, parents who are facing multiple challenges are perceived as incapable of living up to such an expectation. Of course, this very perception, and the resulting communication it feeds into, becomes part of the wider array of the very challenges the parents face. They are then instructed to *step up, get tough on him, let me deal with her* – instructions which may bring parents into conflict with professionals who, positioning themselves in a critical and prescriptive way, may instruct parents to do the seemingly opposite: *don't aggravate things, understand where he's coming from, he's been traumatised, try and mirror his emotions* – even if, at other times, the professional may tell them *you must call the police* (whom the parents may or may not trust, and who may respond either with further parent blaming and minimising, or with threatening behaviour towards the young person...). Even where the prescriptions do not differ, the very act of insistent prescribing reinforces the underlying, harmful sentiment that the parent is in some way inadequate. Differing prescriptions, in addition, put parents in the impossible situation of never being able to meet all the expectations of the other adults around them. Where communities struggle with socio-economic disadvantage, institutional racism and structural injustice, the stressful impact of such communication can be exacerbated by stress generated from exposure to the ever-present threat that emanates from high levels of crime and gang activity, while distrust of authorities – borne out of the lived experience of structural injustice over generations – leaves family members vulnerable and unprotected.

In summary, we can safely assume that critical-prescriptive attitudes, communicated by people in the wider system, contribute to the family's social isolation, leave parents bereft of the kind of support that would strengthen their autonomy,[14] undermine parents' sense of agency and raise the already high baseline of psycho-physiological arousal in parent and child even further, thereby lowering the threshold for symmetrical and complementary escalation.[15]

If interaction in the home is to become a healing system for adults and young people, parents and caregivers must be able to 'anchor' children, i.e. to use their personal presence to protect their child from their own harmful or self-destructive impulses, while providing emotional containment. Parents who have experienced trauma, adoptive parents and caregivers of children who have experienced abuse or neglect will be more able to do this if they themselves feel 'anchored' by people in the larger system in emotionally safe ways. To achieve this, it is necessary for a sufficient number of 'players' within the larger system to re-position themselves from critical and prescriptive to safe and supportive, as the social worker did in Julie's case. It is the NVR practitioner's task to help facilitate the conditions within which such a change in position is likely to occur. Next, we will explore dangerous-coercive positioning and emotionally safe positioning, and then in the following chapter go on to discuss ways in which conditions for a positional shift can be facilitated.

Dangerous/coercive positioning

How can we distinguish between critical/prescriptive positioning and the kind of dominance that is exerted from a dangerous and coercive position? While critical and prescriptive positioning of people around parents and children will have counterproductive or even harmful effects, these effects are inadvertent and unintentional. A second criterion for distinguishing critical/prescriptive from dangerous/ coercive positioning is the willingness to enter in dialogue about one's own position. Willingness to enter dialogue which opens conversational space for the parent's experience of one's own communication patterns conveys emotional safety and fulfils the parent's need to feel listened to and understood.

Where there is dangerous and coercive positioning, we can neither identify positive intentionality, nor an openness to dialogue. While critical and prescriptive communication generates dominance in a relationship, this is even more the case when someone communicates with the parent or caregiver from a dangerous and coercive position. We can often find the latter criterion missing in the positions some professionals take towards parents and other members of the family. In the following case example, we can see the positive effect of a parent's resistance to a professional's contemporaneous dangerous/coercive position:

Amanda is a single parent of two sons and a daughter. At the outset of our work together, the family are living from income support. In her first session, Amanda becomes tense and is unable to respond whenever I ask a question – any question. I start 'thinking out loud' to spare her the distress of being asked questions and observe her body language. Soon, it becomes apparent to both of us that her eldest child, a son, controls her by asking questions. Of course, these are disparaging statements about her, which are thinly veiled as questions, rendering her inability to 'answer' into a coercive trap: "Where are my football shoes? Are you too stupid to remember where you put them? You're not answering? You can't think of any answer, can you?" Sometimes, such pseudo questions are followed by a violent assault. On one occasion, he punches her in the face and gives her a black eye. Previously, Amanda used to be controlled coercively by her son's father in such a manner, and even earlier, in her childhood, her own father had used this coercive technique to humiliate her. When she first became motionless in response to questions I asked, Amanda was at the same time highly aroused, portraying a kind of reactivity akin to a traumatic 'fright response'.[16] Such responses are common when a person anticipates implicitly, on an embodied level, that any other possible self-protective threat response, such as flight, fight, tend or befriend, would be futile; Amanda becomes, literally, paralysed, albeit for emotional reasons.

Gradually, Amanda learns to distinguish between open, non-prejudicial questions and Toby's pseudo-questions. Instead of becoming mute and motionless, she now begins to remove herself, when Toby 'asks' disparaging and demeaning "questions". In this way, she can gradually preserve her dignity and protect herself, to a degree, from subsequent physical assault. Gradually, Amanda develops greater agency, by addressing such an incident of pseudo-questioning at a later point, when both she and Toby are calmer.[17] She impresses upon Toby that he will need to speak politely, if he would like her to meet a request of his. More and more often, she refuses any 'parental service' when he speaks to her in a derogatory way.

Toby's father's recently widowed second wife has been trolling Amanda on Facebook, and many others have joined in this aversive campaign. She also alleges falsely that Amanda has been abusing her children. A social worker, who carries out a child protection investigation, can establish that this allegation is unfounded. Nonetheless, he takes part in a supporters meeting involving Amanda's children's teachers, which I have called in. At the beginning of the meeting, he claims to have his agency's authority to take over chairing the meeting and starts asking Amanda questions about how she prepares the children for going to school in front of the teachers and myself. In spite of my polite and calm protestations, the social worker insists on chairing, and I decide to end the meeting prematurely at this point – I do

not wish to give in to this coercive behaviour, but at the same time feel it is neces-
sary to spare Amanda and her children's teachers the discomfort of further conflict,
which would be unproductive.[18] *Whilst Amanda says nothing during this exchange,*
unlike in past situations when she has had an impassive facial expression when
relating acts of coercion, her face now portrays her anger.

In her next therapy session, Amanda asks me whether I have read her recent email?
She has spontaneously written an 'NVR announcement' to the social worker. In it, she
articulates that she can no longer accept controlling behaviour, will not allow any
further contact between him and herself or her children, and uninvites him from the
pending family group conference. Together, Amanda and I write a joint complaint to
Children's Services. I also apologise to Amanda for not having sufficiently inquired
about her feelings regarding the social worker's participation prior to the meeting.

We can see many aspects of dangerous/coercive communication in this case
example. The father's widow and the social worker both overstep the personal
boundaries of a mother who can be perceived as vulnerable. Both utilise the children, in order to enhance their power: the widow by trolling the mother and making
false allegations, the social worker by asserting a claim to institutional authority
and power,[19] even though following the conclusion of the child protection investigation, he no longer has a remit in regard to this family.

Frequently, children's behaviour problems yield parents more accessible to previous partners who have been violent, as we can see in the previous case example
involving Julie and Jonas. In such instances, concern for the child is often a mere
ruse to regain control over the mother. Sometimes, it can appear that the mother also
'invites' a previous, coercive partner back into the family, when she feels especially
helpless and distraught in the face of extremely problematic child behaviour. However, we can normalise such 'inviting' behaviour by developing an understanding
with the mother of the ways in which it makes sense: parents who have experienced severe trauma may struggle to regulate their shame. Such a parent would be
likely to have heightened sensitivity to critical/prescriptive communication and,
anticipating such responses, avoid potentially supportive contact with other adults
in times of crisis, thus becoming even more isolated than before – especially if a
number of individuals in their social environment have been persistently positioning themselves in a critical/prescriptive manner. Not seeing any way out of a crisis,
such a mother may turn to someone who has been a significant other in her life,
albeit in an abusive way. The aforementioned relational logic, according to which
controlling (child) behaviour must be countered by reverse control, makes it seem
a reasonable move to involve a person who has acted coercively: *I myself am help-*
less (unable to control my child). The man who controlled me for so many years is
powerful. Only he can control my son, to keep him from controlling me. When this
relational logic informs the mother's actions, her parental authority is delegated to
a dangerous person who may proceed to violate the nuclear family's boundaries.

In Julie and Jonas' case, the mother was able to gain her child's social worker's
trust by planning, together with her emotionally safe supporters, how she would
counteract her inclination to involver her son's coercively behaving father at such

times when Jonas' behaviour felt especially challenging. The social worker was able to observe how Julie was learning to preserve the integrity of the nuclear family and develop greater agency in responding to even very challenging situations by involving emotionally safe, non-dominant supporters. This, in turn, enabled the social worker's own shift from a critical/prescriptive to a more emotionally safe position, thereby further reducing the risk that the mother would yield to the father's transgressive behaviour in the future.

Emotionally safe positioning

Parents with traumatic experience require a strong enough sense of belonging to a supportive community if they are to begin healing from trauma and develop a sense of agency in dealing with the challenges they face. They require the emotional security of a warm personal environment, solace when distraught, compassion and appreciation. It is essential that, when looking at themselves through the eyes of others, they can see themselves as competent, having agency, and acknowledge their own accomplishment. They need to feel listened to and understood by other adults when they share problems in the family. All this requires a sufficient body of other adults around the family, who take up emotionally safe positions towards parent and child.

What are the characteristics of an emotionally safe position? To begin with, it is non-judgemental, while at the same time, the person inhabiting such a position does not shy away from, express fear of or disgust over the difficult facts in the life of the parent or child. These characteristics form the bedrock of the emotionally safe position, on which the two essential forms of witnessing that were described in the introduction can grow: compassionate witnessing and appreciative witnessing. These proactive kinds of witnessing become the crucial prerequisite for parents with traumatic experiences to feel re-humanised, reconnect internally with their own parental agency, and to regain a sense of self-efficacy. Such witnessing requires dialogical forms of communication. Conversations should be free of all kinds of blame. Extensive 'psycho-archaeology', which seeks to solve current difficulties by unearthing reasons for them in past events, will focus the therapeutic conversation on the non-abusive parent's apparent failure, omission, inadequacy or pathology.[20] This would foment a narrative of parental guilt and inadequacy, leaving little or no conversational space for strengths, resources – both internal and interpersonal – for positive perspectives on the future and for solutions in the here and now.

Emotionally safe positioning can emerge, when people in the family's social environment *really* listen in a non-judgemental way, even when they have been emotionally affected by accounts of the child's behaviour or conflict within the family. They ask open questions that are motivated by a non-prejudicial wish to understand more about the situation of the family and each of its members. These are questions to which the questioning person does not assume a priori knowledge of the answers, and which do not aim to influence the caregivers in the direction of the questioner's favoured solutions. They are sensitive to the emotional boundaries of the parent whose predicament they are learning about, will not press for answers, and will abstain from offering their own causal interpretations of why the difficulties have emerged.

For eco-systemic interventions in families with aversive experiences to be effective, practitioners themselves need to assume emotionally safe positions. They further need to facilitate the growth of an emotionally safe support network; this is a caring community, in which the parents become 'anchored'[21] in an emotionally safe way. They will proactively facilitate the building of this network, as merely providing psycho-educational advice on how the parents could build such a network themselves runs the risk of leaving parents feeling overwhelmed and anxious about imagined negative repercussions in the responses of the people they would seek to recruit.

However, even if other adults position themselves in emotionally safe ways towards the parents and children in a family, a further step is necessary: family members need other adults, who communicate in emotionally safe ways, to become *proactive supporters*. Only then can these other adults help non-abusive parents to resist a child's harmful or self-destructive behaviour, while at the same time supporting them to strengthen the boundaries around the nuclear family. The therapist is also needed to help parents contribute to a shift in attitude by people who hitherto have inhabited a critical/prescriptive position. In this way, the practitioner who works in trauma-focused NVR goes beyond the parent-child dyad and addresses multiple vectors of intervention to help bring about emotional safety and willingness to act supportively in the wider social system around the nuclear family.

This raises the question: Why do we not simply remove all people who communicate in critical and prescriptive ways from the support network? Indeed, Ingamells and Epston (2014), whose 'family revolution' approach has been derived from NVR, explicitly recommend only including such people in the support network, of whom the parents do not expect a critical attitude. However, when working with families with multiple challenges, or with other families where children have experienced trauma, such as foster homes or families with children who have been adopted, this approach to building a support network can have its limitations. The social fragmentation they have experienced has left parents and caregivers too isolated, and the challenges they face are too great for us to expect that there would already be enough people in the family's social environment who are prepared to engage with them in an emotionally safe manner and support them proactively. In order to regulate themselves emotionally and feel less confused, many individuals around the family will have adopted reductive explanations for the bewildering problematic child behaviour they have learned about and thus come to occupy a critical/prescriptive position. The emotional bonds to people who are acting in critical and prescriptive ways can be very strong, and suggesting to remove them from the network around the family can run afoul of the parents' loyalty to these individuals. Therefore, the trauma-informed practitioner will *support parents* to:

- Communicate an expectation that individuals, who have hitherto communicated in critical and prescriptive ways, will shift towards showing emotional resonance and engage with the parents in a way that supports *their* own parenting efficacy;

- Invite individuals, who have already been communicating in emotionally safe ways, to become proactive in their support, and
- Use the methodology of NVR to resist transgression and detrimental behaviour by adults who act in coercive and dangerous ways.

*"Yes, but for **my** clients, that's impossible, they don't **want to** involve anyone else in their family affairs". "Well, I work with parents who are **too scared** to even step out of their front door, how are they even going to talk to other adults?" "This mother is **much too ashamed**...".*

Here, the parent's sense of helplessness has become mirrored in the practitioner reservations. However, we are not engaged in the practice of identifying and remediating inability. I prefer assuming that my clients are potentially able to form a sufficiently large, well-anchoring supportive network or caring community around the family, provided I offer them support in this process. It is *my* task as the NVR practitioner to engage directly with potential supporters together with the parents and facilitate the growth of a caring community around the family which will help parents or caregivers deal constructively with any challenges that may present themselves in the process.

Notes

1 The extensive research into 'growth mindset' has demonstrated the highly significant impact on people, when others communicate their beliefs that their traits are not fixed and personal growth is possible (Dweck, 2000; Dweck and Yeager, 2019).

2 It is possible to self-traumatise by virtue of one's own aggressive behaviour, especially when the person has previously been a victim of abuse or helplessly witnessed abuse against others. Such traumatic self-injury was first described in relation to US service personnel during the Vietnam War (Young, 2002). It is safe to assume that an attacking posture can raise the fear of retaliation, and thereby create a potentially threatening situation and stimulate traumatic responsiveness.

3 I am intentionally not including the birth father who acts in dangerous and abusive ways in this definition of the nuclear family, but locating him outside of the family unit, instead. His actions threaten the integrity of the members of the family, and to locate him within it in professional conversations could jeopardise their physical and emotional safety, dignity and prospect of recovery.

4 This constructive action method will be described in more detail at a later point. Originally called a 'public opinion intervention' by Omer, I now refer to this method as a 'campaign of concern' to express the underlying attitude, from which this kind of action is best taken – an attitude of concern for everyone who has been negatively affected by a particular incident, including the young person who has instigated it.

5 Child protective services in the UK.

6 Physical violence and sexual abuse also contain emotional abuse within them. The victim is humiliated, de-humanised, treated as a person of less value or not as a person at all. Physical violence and sexual abuse also carry the implicit message that their instigator considers the relationship with the victim of the assault to be of little value, or only of value by virtue of the abused person's objectification. In addition, explicit verbal messages and non-verbal or para-verbal messages may question the victim's value as a human being, their moral integrity, their intelligence, their ability to act with autonomy

or their physical attractiveness. Therefore, we can understand such emotionally abusive messages as extreme forms of social diminution and rejection.

7 See the 'axiom of communication': "One cannot not communicate" (Watzlawick, Beavin and Jackson, 2017).

8 See Dweck and Yeager (2019).

9 A theory on a highly abstract level that purports to fully explain all aspects of certain social or psychological phenomena.

10 German: 'Bündnisrhetorik'. Grabbe describes a manner of communicating, in which an open offer of cooperation in support of the other is made, without there being any pre-condition or one-sided determination of the nature of such support. For example, "I can be available at the weekend, what would you like me to do?" is stated in the language of alliance building, but not "I'll tell you what I'll do for you".

11 Parents who have the ability to dissociate may be in close proximity to their child while reducing their awareness of the child's presence; in other words: *if the body can't escape, the mind can.*

12 See also the critique of the concept of 'burnout' by Weingarten et al. (2020), who offers the alternative constructs of 'moral injury' and 'moral distress'.

13 The reader may have noticed that I have been referring to parents or families as 'facing multiple challenges' instead of using the terminology 'multi-stressed families' or 'multi-problem families'. This is to counteract the understanding of these families' difficulties as purely intrinsic traits, thereby contributing to a nosology of difference, and instead draw attention to the wider social factors which impact on family interaction and individual family members' behaviours.

14 Dulberger and Omer (2021) distinguish between 'autonomy' and 'independence'. The individual acting with autonomy is at the same time self-determined *and* requires interpersonal support for their self-determined action; they are dependent in a functional way.

15 In terms of trauma theory, we could see this as a narrowing of the 'window of tolerance', although here, the window of tolerance is not seen as a personal disposition resulting from past trauma alone, but instead, as subject to influence by social factors in the here and now.

16 See Figure 1.1.

17 Referred to as "striking the iron, when it's cold" in NVR, the deferred response is essential in preventing *symmetrical* escalation. "Strike the iron, when it's cold – but make sure to strike it!" however can be a reminder to act against a previously submissive parent's inclination to accept such behaviours, which would give way to further *complementary* escalation.

18 While such overtly coercive behaviour by professionals may be relatively rare, professionals who are willing to act in a controlling way are likely to target parents they perceive as vulnerable.

19 See Figure 1.3.

20 A more constructive way of redressing problematic parental responses of the past is discussed in Chapter 13.

21 The notion of 'anchoring' in NVR goes beyond the understanding of 'containment' or 'holding' in object relations theory. When anchoring another, the person provides emotional containment while at the same time practising 'vigilant care' and proactively withstanding the other person's propensity to act on their harmful or self-destructive impulses. When a parent 'anchors' a child in this way, it is seen as leading to greater attachment security (Omer et al., 2013).

Chapter 2

Anchoring parents

From a threatening or critical social environment to an emotionally safe support network

We can distinguish three ways of generating an emotionally safe support network – a growing, caring community which envelops a family, foster family or a residential home:

- *The exception principle:* After identifying other individuals who already appear to occupy an emotionally safe position towards family members, parents are helped to proactively engage them as supporters.
- *The utilisation principle:* People in the family's natural social environment or in the professional network around them who tend to communicate in a critical and prescriptive manner are invited to re-position themselves towards family members to become emotionally safer, and then invited to become safe supporters. The energies they have so far invested in critical responses are thus channelled into more constructive response patterns.
- *The resistance principle:* Non-abusive parents and their supporters proactively use methods of resistance drawn from NVR in a targeted way to protect their own integrity, and that of the entire nuclear family, from individuals or institutions that show dangerous or coercive behaviour.

The body's voice: Interoception as a 'diagnostic tool' for assessing relational qualities

Many parents who have experienced controlling interaction over the course of years or their entire life span will have become habituated to this kind of communication. It may feel normal, when other adults criticise them, instruct them on how to respond to problematic child behaviour, seek to control their actions or even threaten them. Often, they remain silent due to learned submission, which has been an important survival response in many relationships, because they do not feel entitled to their own autonomous views, or because they shrink back from the other person's apparent confidence. Their response may not appear to suggest that the other person's way of communicating generates discomfort in them; they may not even pay attention to their own discomfort. An observer could gain the false impression that such parents are showing indifference or mistake their apparent passivity for agreement.

DOI: 10.4324/9781032717111-5

Parents who have learned to protect themselves from violent attacks or emotional injury by showing gestures of submission – because submission was the enforced modality of response by an abuser or a series of abusers – can be prone to show body language that communicates apparent agreement to the demands of another, more powerful person. Often, professionals become frustrated when parents appear to agree with them but do not act in the expected manner. In some organisations, the professional culture is such that these parents may be discussed as demonstrating 'feigned compliance' and assumed to be manipulative and dishonest. The professionals will often be unaware of the pejorative nature of their attribution. The social field becomes marked by the simultaneous forces of critical/prescriptive communication by professionals, threatening or even re-traumatising child behaviour, and possibly dangerous and coercive threatening stances by other adults such as former life partners; parents are then likely to become emotionally overburdened. They may even show responses that oscillate between apparent agreement (submission), rage and withdrawal or avoidance. Diagnoses such as 'emotionally unstable personality disorder' or 'complex post-traumatic stress disorder' will tend to individualise the parent's difficulties and distract from an appreciation of the social nature of the emotional tensions they experience.

Reflexive obedience or submission to perceived threat signals is automatic and embodied; the person is often not fully aware of the manner of their own response. Ogden, Minton and Pain (2006) posit that this submissive tendency should not be misunderstood as agreement. The authors emphasise that transgressive or abusive individuals often use this embodied self-defence, in order to elicit automatic compliance. Pejorative professional attributions risk misunderstanding the drivers behind parents' responses and thereby perpetuating those very response patterns.

How can the various interactants in this social field begin to escape from what may appear to be an intractable conundrum? How can parents, who have developed such automatic apparent obedience to dominant other individuals begin to re-position themselves towards them? In a first step, the parent's use of language to discriminate between various positions of the other adults around them can be significant in regard to overcoming their sense of helplessness. Languaging the perceived positions of others, they can develop an awareness of and distinguish between emotionally safe and dominant response forms they encounter. Languaging is often a prerequisite for developing agency: If one can name it, one is more likely to become able to deal with it. Hearing and feeling one's own voice verbalise one's perception can already be a liberating experience. Rather than using the theoretical categories I have introduced in the previous chapter – emotionally safe, critical and prescriptive or dangerous and coercive – I tend to use the client's own emerging vocabulary, e.g. *He respects me* (for an emotionally safe position), *She makes me feel like s...* (for a critical-prescriptive position) or *He really scares me* (for a dangerous and coercive position): *So, you need to feel respected and not made to feel criticised by the people around you. You certainly have the right to be safe and not feel scared by anyone!*

When speaking about significant other adults who have occupied a critical and prescriptive position, it is important for the therapist to speak about this positioning as a *communicative habit* rather than a personality trait: *"So, you often end up feeling criticised by her"* rather than *She is a really critical person.* Critical and prescriptive positioning can spread easily within social contexts, and it should be remembered that this position should not be associated with ill intention.[1] Reframing the propensity for critical and prescriptive communication as a habit rather than a personality trait serves two important purposes: It helps avoid creating a loyalty conflict for the parent, especially if it concerns a significant other with whom they have a close personal relationship, and, importantly, seeing a certain position as a habit rather than a trait implies that the communication pattern could change quite rapidly. Inducing a loyalty conflict between parents we work with and their close significant others will often cause a relational rupture between therapist and client and damage the therapeutic relationship. The framing of the problematic communication as –changeable – habit, and the separation of person from the way they have been interacting with the parent around the interest child's problematic behaviour can engender hope: 'Habits' change more easily than 'people'!

Though some clients may initially find it very difficult to ascertain how another person positions themselves towards them, especially if they have little awareness of their own embodied responses, developing awareness of these responses can be especially useful in overcoming their sense of helplessness. By inviting the client to become aware of their embodied response, we can create conversational space for the languaging of their experience of the other's positioning. Social positions are inevitably reciprocal (Harré, 2015). By languaging the other person's positioning, parents can begin their own re-positioning towards this person. The method below aims to connect embodied experience with language; it enables parents to focus on their interoception while they safely ascertain the likely response of another adult.

Method: Giving the body voice

Using an empty chair, ask the parent to imagine they are sitting opposite the other adult. Ask the parent to imagine they are sharing information about a recent incident involving harmful or self-destructive behaviour. If the parent looks away from the imagined other person, you can inquire whether they are feeling shame or anxiety, and encourage them to 'look at' the imagined other person.

Ask them to imagine the other person's probable response to learning about the incident, based on their experience of how this person has previously communicated with them. Ask the client to describe the imagined body language – posture, movement, facial expression, the sound and volume of their voice, prosody of their speech and the content of what they say. Ask your client to use the unconditional present tense rather than the conditional when they describe this, e.g. *He's looking straight at me, sitting bolt upright...* rather than *He would be looking me straight at me...*, as unconditional language supports the suspension of disbelief, making it more likely for the client to experience their embodied response.

Ask the parent to first localise their embodied response (rather than immediately speaking about their emotion): *Where, in your body, do you feel a response to what you are seeing and hearing? You don't have to describe it, just tell me where you feel it, and notice what you're feeling in your body for a while.* Give your client enough time to develop their sensory awareness, as many people who have experienced abuse are not accustomed to this kind of intentional interoception.

(Should the parent struggle to localise their response, you can support their interoception but taking them through a body scan: What parts of their body feel warm, what parts cool? Where does the parent feel tension, where do they feel relaxed? Does the parent feel a motor impulse? Is this impulse pleasant or unpleasant? If it is pleasant, does the parent feel 'positive energy'? Is there a feeling of immobility or physical pain? Is the aggregate sensation in their body more pleasant or more unpleasant? Then, return to asking the client to localise their embodied response to the imagined communication by the other person.)

Once the parent has been aware of their localised embodiment for a sufficient length of time, you can ask them to describe the quality of their localised physical response – tense, warm and comfortable, relaxed, uncomfortable, hot, cold, etc.

You may now wish to explore the client's emotion and cognition that is associated with their localised interoception.

Reality check: Has the other person actually persistently communicated with your client in the imagined manner over the history of their relationship? This is an important step in the process, as parents who are prone to feeling shame may imagine adverse responses in the other person, when these are actually unlikely to occur in real life.

How does the parent generally respond to such communication? Does the parent wish to respond differently to this kind of communication from now on in? How does the parent wish to respond (in a way that is nonviolent, yet self-protective and protective of the integrity of the family)?

At the end of this exercise, ask the parent to name the position of the other person in their own words. This process may require some negotiation, if e.g. the parent minimises *"He's kind of, a little impatient..."*, it will be important to encourage them to use words that do justice to their actual experience of how the other communicates: *Well, it's like he knows it all and makes me feel I'm stupid if I don't do what he says...* If the client frames the other person's critical and prescriptive communication as a personality trait rather than a habit *She's a really nasty, unpleasant b.... who can only criticise...*, you can help them reframe this as a habit: *So, you're used to getting this kind of reaction from her… like she's used to talking to you like this?* Where your client has identified a dangerous-coercive position, it is vital to encourage your client to state this clearly *He gets really abusive* rather than *He gets irritated.*

Languaging the other person's positioning in a way that is congruent with the parent's interoceptive experience of their communication opens new possibilities for engaging emotionally safe support and protecting themselves and their family from transgressive, dangerous or coercive intrusion, using what I have called the *exception principle*, the *utilisation principle* and the *resistance principle* (Jakob, 2018).

The exception principle

For people who have become habituated to dominant behaviour by others in their social sphere and tend to occupy submissive positions towards them, a relationship in which another individual communicates in an emotionally safe way can often be seen as an exception to the problem, rather than the norm. In solution-focused models of family therapy, attention is paid to exceptions in family interaction (Nelson, 2018). Here, in a solution-oriented way working, we go further and pay attention to such exceptions between members of the nuclear family and members of the wider system, investigate the different behaviours a client has shown which are likely to have contributed to an exception, invite them to appreciate themselves for such different behaviour and encourage them to replicate the alternative behaviours in order to increase the frequency of the exception to the problem.

We create therapeutic possibilities when we aim to bring about a greater frequency of exceptions in the interaction between parents and members of the larger system around the nuclear family and, importantly, when we facilitate the re-positioning of individuals who have already been interacting in emotionally safe ways: from being an emotionally safe other to becoming an *emotionally safe and proactive supporter.* In Julie's case e.g., we were able to see exceptions to critical communication by the social worker and threatening, coercive behaviour by her son's father in the patterns of interaction between her and her friend Liz. The method of *giving the body a voice,* as described above, can help a parent identify whom they already experience as emotionally safe in regard to communication about difficulties relating to the interest child. Once such an emotionally safer relationship has been identified, the practitioner can create conversational space for exploring the nature of the exceptional communication. This alone can have a therapeutic effect, and the very simple therapeutic 'intervention' that can maximise this effect is simply the therapist's curiosity-driven: *Tell me more about it.*

The next step in working with the exception principle lies in encouraging and supporting parents in practical ways to invite other adults they already experience as emotionally safe to become active members of their growing support network – the family's caring community. By accepting this invitation, the other adults begin re-positioning themselves to becoming emotionally safe *supporters*.

However, parents, foster carers, kinship carers or residential carers may experience constraints to finding the courage to actually issue such invitations. They often worry about shame, fearing they could be seen as a failed parent in the eyes of the other adult. Therefore, they may wish to avoid a friend, neighbour or member of the extended family discovering just how aggressive, harmful or self-destructive many of the behaviours are that their child often displays. A parent may also feel that asking for help could be a sign of weakness. Researchers into interpersonal rejection speak of a finely tuned 'sociometer' which is believed to have developed over the course of human evolution, a fine-tuned capacity to ascertain the degree of acceptance or rejection or the valuing of the relationship by another person; perceived rejection has been associated with higher activity in neural regions that are also associated with physical pain. Investigations in clinical neuroscience further suggest that anxiety relating to interpersonal rejection can arise from people's perceptions that their relational value to other people could be in jeopardy, and may give rise to feelings such as jealousy, hurt, loneliness, guilt, social anxiety, embarrassment, and shame (Leary, 2015). These findings suggest that parents we work with in NVR may fear that the relationship could be undervalued by a potential supporter, and thus wish to avoid such an anticipated response. Clinical experience shows that parents who have experienced abuse in their own life history may be especially likely to fear they could be flooded with shame, were they to speak to the other person about non-normative child behaviour.

There are further constraints to approaching other individuals in spite of their likely emotionally safe position. Parents may wish to protect their child from becoming demonised or pathologised within the wider family, friendship group or community and face critical interaction. Whoever is not emotionally safe towards their child would not be felt to be emotionally safe towards them. Finally, parents who have been abused may be prone to feeling victim shame. They may anticipate the other adult perceiving them as becoming re-victimised and be anxious about the possibility of victim shame emerging were they e.g. to share that their teenage son has been hitting them. Pre-existing social isolation of parents who have been abused can often be attributed to parental shame-based avoidance of social contact.

In my experience, many evasive responses by parents to the suggestion they could seek to recruit a person as a supporter who will likely maintain an emotionally safe position can be attributed to this shame constraint. In such instances, it can be unhelpful to ask *whether* a parent would seek to recruit such a person – the answer will most likely be negative. It can also be unhelpful to name, investigate or analyse shame at this point in the therapeutic process (Weinblatt, 2018); this could be perceived as the practitioner viewing the parent as inadequate, which would only increase their potential for shame.

Instead, we can seek to escape the binary opposition of whether or not the parent *will* engage the other person as a supporter, and the binary opposition of whether or not the parent *can* (psychologically) engage them. We can do this by assuming that engaging one or more emotionally safe other adults as supporters evolves with the progression of the parent's shame regulation. We thus move from *whether or not the parent can accomplish this* into the realm of questions pertaining to *how, when, where and to whom* they will disclose difficulties, such as being subject to aggressive behaviour, or that their son is self-harming and threatening suicide, or their child has been running away from home and is being criminally and sexually exploited and misusing drugs within a gang or county line[2] environment. We can promote the parent's shame regulation by implicitly communicating our own belief that they will be able to meet this difficult challenge and accomplish a cornerstone of nonviolent resistance: breaking the silence around harmful or destructive behaviour. In this way, even parents with histories of serious abuse will generally be able to recruit at least one emotionally safe other adult to accompany them to a therapy session with a view to becoming a proactive supporter. According to growth mindset theory, our own hypotheses about another person's potential for growth in regard to a certain trait can have a significant impact on the degree to which actual growth takes place, if these are communicated to the other (Wolcott et al., 2021). It may therefore be useful to assume that if the therapist, counsellor or practitioner sees their client's shame-based avoidance of disclosure as a fixed personality trait and communicates this implicitly, the parent's shame regulation will be less likely to improve, than if the practitioner communicates a 'growth mindset', i.e. their belief that, in the right circumstances and with support, the parent will be able to meet this challenge.

To promote such change, it can be helpful for the practitioner to support the parents in the regulation of their shame. While in many therapeutic approaches this is undertaken explicitly, an indirect approach to this can convey the therapists' own belief in the parent's capacity for growth more powerfully. Weinblatt (2018, 2022) describes challenges to communication when individuals face strong feelings of shame. These are:

- We struggle to admit we feel shame;
- We are often not aware that we are afraid of feeling shame in a particular communicative situation;
- When we feel burdened by shame, we often do not know how to communicate effectively.

Weinblatt further elaborates on the risk of increasing shame within the communication system if we attempt to resolve conflictual interpersonal difficulties in conversation. There could be escalation, if a communicating individual avoids shame by feeling and expressing anger.

How can we then help parents overcome this constraint, regulate their shame and ask other adults for support? How do we avoid the risk of increasing their propensity for shame by speaking with them extensively *about shame*? One possibility is to guide the parent through an imaginary process, in which they can rehearse their interaction with the potential supporter. Research in imagined interaction theory

(Honeycutt, Vickery and Thatcher, 2015; Honeycutt, 2021) has established that rehearsal is one of the key functions of imagining future interaction. Imaginary rehearsal of disclosing their existing difficulties and asking for support can be a form of self-exposure to a previously avoided scenario. I believe that this process helps establish a parent's prediction that they will be able to regulate their feelings of shame and anticipate a successful outcome of such an encounter. Where another adult has already been experienced as emotionally safe in the past, a parent can imagine a successful interaction taking place without a loss of dignity, by anticipating an emotionally safe response. The practitioner can *implicitly* communicate their own belief in the parent's capacity to engage in such a conversation – imagination merely generates a future narrative; there is no 'whether or not', and the parent merely shares, with the therapist, a scenario in which, in their mind's eye, they can see themselves responding constructively to the exigencies of their own family situation by breaking the silence and seeking support. The 'imaginary support dialogue', developed by Willem Beckers (Beckers, Jakob and Schreiter, 2022) is one method that can help stimulate imagined interaction in requesting support. This can promote not only their perceived future relational agency, but also their self-determination, as they are not advised to do anything, but merely imagine it occurring.

Method: The imaginary support dialogue

If it has been ascertained that a particular individual will be likely to respond in an emotionally safe way to information about problematic child behaviour, the parent can imagine beginning a conversation with the aim of sharing the difficulties they experience and inviting the other person to become a supporter.

Ask about an ordinary, not problem-focused memory involving this person, in which the parent has felt emotionally comfortable. Use the present tense. Ask about the detail of the memory or typical scenario: What is the physical environment? The way they are used to greeting each other, their small interactional rituals? Who wears what? The time frame? What small talk? Help intensify the client's imagination by asking about sensory experience, e.g.: What do you see? What is the weather like?

Once your client has described the scenario in detail, guide them to imagine disclosing their difficulties to the other adult and asking for support, e.g.:

I would like to tell you what has been happening in our family. Some of this may be new to you. For several months, we've been really troubled by … behaviour. … has physically attacked us. Recently, I got hurt when he punched me. This has made us feel really uncertain and worried as his parents. We want to feel safe again and connected as a family. This is why recently, we've been seeing a therapist called …, who is helping us to overcome these difficulties. … helped us understand how important it is to tell certain other people around the family about what is happening and to invite them to consider supporting us. She asked us: "Who do you feel safe with? Who do you believe may be prepared to take part in a conversation among adults about supporting the changes that are necessary – and when she asked this, I thought about you".

Suggest to the parent: *Imagine that you are saying these things to ..., and you notice that they are listening to you. She looks at you and doesn't interrupt.*

At the end of your message, you ask the parent to imagine they are asking the other person: *Would you attend a meeting with me and ... (name of therapist)? And you hear her answer...*

Some questions you could ask your client after this rehearsed interaction: *I was wondering what it would mean to you to have asked ... to support you? What do you feel ... would have thought about you choosing them?*

If I asked ... at the supporters' meeting: What is it about (client) that made you decide to come to today's meeting? what do you think they would answer?

It is important not to advise or instruct your client to engage in this conversation with the other person, but merely communicate that this is a possible course of action they may decide to take. The purpose of this exercise is merely for the parent to experience greater inner freedom of choice.

For parents who have had an extensive history of abuse prior to their child's aggressive or self-destructive behaviour, it may be advisable to meet with only one or two potential supporters initially, rather than facilitating a meeting with a larger number of individuals. This can help parents with a significant experience of trauma process the complex emotional response they are likely to feel in the course of this challenging endeavour. Once the constraint of shame-avoidance has weakened and conversations have taken place with one or two prospective supporters, parents may find it easier to engage more supporters, and a larger supporters' meeting may become feasible.

A further constraint to engaging another adult as a potential supporter can be the wish not to burden them. Research into the experience of supporters in NVR has demonstrated, however, that individuals who have already been experienced as emotionally safe by parents, are pleased to have been asked to become supporters and engage proactively in this endeavour (Hicks, Jakob and Kustner, 2020). The research participants expressed a wish for proactive coaching by the NVR practitioner in order to meet some of the challenges associated with their re-positioning from emotionally safe other to emotionally safe supporter, but this need did not impinge upon their wish and their determination to support the family. They further reported that NVR corresponds with their values, and that they feel committed to proactively support the family.

Individuals usually speak of feeling *privileged, honoured* or *touched* to have been asked to support parents, rather than expressing a feeling that this is an undue burden. Parents often anticipate this kind of response when they imagine the encounter with the other person, thus reinforcing a positive expectation.

Similar constraints can present themselves in other caregiving contexts. For example, a carer working in a residential service may find it difficult to request support from another carer working in a different home, wondering whether the other person's involvement would be considered part of their remit, or whether it would be unduly burdensome to a colleague who may already feel a lot of work pressure. A more senior colleague, possibly a practitioner working across homes within the same residential organisation, may address such a constraint in supervision and help them feel encouraged to explore possibilities for mutual support in the NVR process. However, research into the experience of carers working with adolescents who have had severe or extreme traumatic experiences has demonstrated that some carers may indeed feel overburdened with the request to give NVR support, e.g. when they have had a very challenging shift (Mackinnon, Jakob and Kustner, 2023). This can become exacerbated if they have felt instructed to do so, but creating space in their duty rota can help ease the pressure. In my own experience, carers' willingness to support colleagues in another team will often be greater, if they feel the request has been made directly by a colleague to them and they are free to choose how they wish to respond to this request, rather than experiencing it as an instruction by a more senior member of staff. A carer from another team can be invited into a team meeting in the same way that a prospective supporter of parents would be invited into a therapy session.

Occasionally, a parent may experience a hurtful rejection of their request for support. This is however a much rarer occurrence that expected. In such a case, it will be important to help provide emotional containment to parents by compassionately witnessing the difficult emotions this has aroused, and at the same time encouraging them to keep looking for other supporters. This helps the parents to strengthen a key 'NVR virtue': persistence – or, in V. K. Kool's (2007) conceptualisation, the nonviolent trait of forbearance. A helpful motto is: "There are plenty more fish in the sea!"

The utilisation principle

The American psychiatrist Milton Erickson developed a resource-oriented form of hypnotherapy, which placed a great deal of emphasis on clients' motivation to cope with emotionally difficult or overwhelming life situations. He felt that 'symptomatic' behaviour can be understood as a person's attempt at coping with or mastering the challenges presented to them by such a life situation. Appreciating the efforts of clients is core to understanding responses which may be deemed problematic or counterproductive. The more energy is invested in such 'symptomatic' behaviour, the more energy can be re-directed into constructive solutions. Erickson called this process 'Utilisation' (O'Hanlon, 2013). Ultimately, *any* response a client – or in the case of NVR, another adult shows who is involved with the client in regard to overcoming a young person's difficult behaviour – can be utilised in a positive way.

We can consider critical-prescriptive responses by other adults as 'symptomatic' behaviours in this sense. They can be appreciated as efforts to cope with an emotionally highly challenging situation. In much the same way that parents or other caregivers initially feel a profound sense of helplessness when they first approach a therapist or NVR practitioner, other adults around the family, who have positioned themselves in critical and prescriptive ways, may be attempting to cope with a bewildering, discombobulating situation which they would like to change with immediate effect. The emotional charge of the situation they learn about can be even greater if they know of the traumatic experience family members have had. It can be necessary and desirable to help them re-direct their energy from criticism, prescription and interference to constructive support which helps to enhance parental agency. This is particularly important if the person in question is someone to whom the parents feel bound by loyalty or is someone who holds significant power over the family in a professional capacity. The NVR practitioner can help facilitate the re-positioning of such a person by generating a conversational context that is conducive to this transition.

The utilisation principle was brought to bear in some of the previously outlined case examples:

The initially critical grandfather listened to his daughter and learned to understand some of the distress his negative views of his grandson elicited in the mother. The ensuing empathy resulted in a greater willingness to help augment his daughter's own parental agency, rather than continuing to seek a solution to the family's problem by assuming parental authority himself or suggesting delegation of parental authority to a third party.

The social worker shifted from a deficit-oriented view of mother and son to a more resource-oriented attitude; this occurred as she became aware of the ways in which the parent was acting to obviate her risk of responding traumatically to specific incidents. She was especially impressed when she learned about the way in which the mother had been seeking and using support when she needed it: In child protection, making use of a strong support network is seen as an important protective factor and predictor of better outcomes (Pérez-Hernando and Fuentes-Peláez, 2020).

In both cases, the individuals had positive motivation and were open to dialogue, for which the therapist created conversational space. Subsequently, they both showed significant effort to support the respective parents' *own* solutions to their problematic family situations, thus re-directing their previously critical energies into activities that showed appreciation for the parent's self-efficacy.

When individuals are positioned in a critical and prescriptive way, they often fear that they themselves might be criticised. If the parent has a strong loyalty bond towards them, they could be drawn into a loyalty conflict if that person, expecting criticism, were to act defensively. To prevent this from occurring, it can be helpful if the practitioner develops a positive connotation[3] of the previously critical and prescriptive behaviour by, e.g., acknowledging – implicitly or explicitly – the prospective supporter's positive motivation to help bring about change, the energy they have invested in their attempts to do this, the concern they feel and express for the parent or the child, or the effort they have been making.

Once the practitioner has softened the defensive barrier by virtue of their acknowledgement and communicated appreciation, they will generally find that the other adult is open to showing greater interest in the experience and perspectives of the parent. It is at this point that we can centre the parents' painful experiences and those of everyone else in the family – including the interest child – in therapeutic conversation. This is then followed by centring their need for support of *their own parental agency*. I generally follow four steps in the utilisation process:

1   Positive connotation of the previous critical and prescriptive behaviour of the prospective supporter, as described above;
2   Creating conversational space for compassionate witnessing of parents' own distress, pain and difficult emotions that arise in response to the interest child's behaviour, as well as the distress of everyone else in the family, including the interest child themselves. This promotes *multi-directional partiality*;
3   Creating conversational space for appreciative witnessing of parental acts of resistance, as well as acts of care for their children, within the parameters of NVR and
4   Centring the parents' need for support of their own agency in the NVR process, by planning specific acts of resistance or relational gestures and designating the supporter's role within the planned action in a way that helps increase the parents' embodied presence.

We see in the last step both the invitation to the other adult to commit to re-positioning themselves and, reciprocally, we see the parent re-positioning themselves towards the prospective supporter, as a more self-determined individual and parent who will advocate for their own needs rather than remaining a passive recipient of unwanted advice, instruction or interference. Due to the 'tectonic shift' of both the parent and their prospective supporter re-positioning themselves towards each other, it can be advisable to carefully prepare a utilising consultation prior to actually inviting the prospective supporter into therapy. Careful preparation aims to help parents feel more confident about the prospect of inviting a person to attend a future therapy session with them, and it presages their own positional shift.

Method: Preparing a utilising consultation

It will be helpful to develop a positive connotation of the critical and prescriptive stance the other adult has taken thus far. This can help prevent the client from becoming anxious about a possible loyalty conflict, and conversely help them understand that the practitioner is not 'taking the other side' by developing a positive connotation of critical communication:

So, she overreacts and goes over the top, disses your son and tells you that you give in too much. I understand that's really not helpful. What do you think she's trying to achieve, even if she goes about it in the wrong way? What do you feel are her best intentions for you and Jamal?

Using an empty chair for the other adult, help the parent recognise their own spontaneous or automatic response to other person's critical communication:

Does the parent respond in a submissive way? Does this express itself by feeling lost for words? Does their body language express agreement – e.g. by nodding frequently, even if they do not feel comfortable inside their body (interoception)?

Does the parent feel passive, inert, motionless? Does this immobility feel flaccid (more akin to a traumatic 'flag' or shutting down type of response), or does it feel tense and rigid (more akin to a 'fright' response, where the activation of flight or fight is simultaneously inhibited)?

Does the client show a response associated with shame, e.g. by averting their gaze while looking at the empty chair?

Do they get angry and feel an impulse to escalate along with the other adult?

After identifying their own automatic response, you can invite your client to take part in an interactive experiment: While imagining the other adult's critical communication, the parent interrupts their own spontaneous response; e.g. by changing their body language to a posture that instils a sense of self-confidence if their automatic response has been submissive, assuming a posture of openness if they have felt an escalatory impulse and saying something conciliatory to acknowledge the other person's positive intentionality, or by making eye contact if they have avoided this for fear of shame.

Finally, ask your client to practise two specific messages for their prospective supporter:

… (specifically) what problematic incidents have taken place and how they have affected them, and how they believe these incidents have affected the others in the family, including negative effects on the interest child themselves;

… in which specific way they would like the other adult to act when they themselves will take positive NVR action, so their personal sense of agency as a parent is supported.

The imaginary preparation – consistent with findings that imagining interaction serves the purpose of rehearsal – is based on the principles of nonviolent resistance: Parents find that they can countervail their own impulses by an act of self-control. Parents with traumatic histories, who have developed the propensity to respond to critical communication by withdrawing, submitting, avoiding or angrily escalating, can in this way have an unusual, strengthening new experience. This experience opens the door to new behavioural options, while helping them to value their own integrity and personal boundaries more.

When we finally move to the actual meeting with the prospective supporter(s), it will be necessary to conduct the session in an unambiguously goal-oriented manner. It is *not* the purpose of this session to elucidate the other adult's perceptions of the problem or its resolution. The purpose of this session is to create conversational space for the parents' self-expressed need for support of their own agency. Its aim is to invite more emotionally safe communication on the part of the other adult and help motivate them to act in a way that will support the parents' agency.

If this session succeeds in bringing about emotionally safe, alliance-forming communication, a parent's level of psycho-physiological arousal will generally become lower and more functional. Often, one can see this leading to a general lowering of psycho-physiological arousal within the entire nuclear family. Parents become more hopeful and confident that they will be able to rise to the challenges they face and begin to feel anchored within the caring community that is beginning to grow around the family.

Often, a parent's life partner or co-parent is the 'other adult' who has been communicating in a critical and prescriptive manner, or there has been mutual blame, criticism, prescription and unwanted interference in dealing with the child. Where relationships between parents have been stressed and ruptured in such ways, working with the utilisation principle can not only help raise their efficacy to become a better functioning parental team, but also have the effect of helpful couples therapy – especially if their relational difficulties have primarily developed against the backdrop of the emerging problematic child behaviour. Such difficulties will often exacerbate pre-existing schisms in the parents' relationship. Utilising work can help ameliorate relational ruptures, by enabling each parent or life partner to feel empathically understood, treated with compassion and supported by the other in a manner they had not experienced previously.

The utilisation session enables the other adult, who has previously communicated in a critical and prescriptive manner, to

1 develop empathy for the parents and all others in the nuclear family and bear witness to their distress in a compassionate manner, thereby re-humanising the parent;
2 learn about the parents' successes in nonviolently resisting and reconnecting with their child, and appreciatively witnessing their agency and competence in doing so;
3 learn about the parents' need for support and how they will be able to meet that need;
4 make a commitment to become a member of the caring community around the family if they wish to become a proactive, emotionally safe supporter.

I will now introduce three stages of carrying out a utilising conversation. These will range from developing a conversational framework to enabling compassionate and appreciative witnessing and finally to using specific planning of positive action as a therapeutic vehicle which enables the parent to communicate their need for supporter responses that will help raise their sense of parental agency.

**Method: The utilising consultation
step 1 – Developing a conversational framework**

The first part of the session provides emotional reassurance to the other adult and establishes a clear structure for the ensuing conversation.

Many individuals who have previously taken up a critical position are likely to fear criticism by the parent or therapist. They need a welcoming atmosphere, appreciation of their previous efforts and their positive intentionality in regard to dealing with the difficulties in the family. This can be done in an implicit, indirect manner, which is conducive to lowering the possible shame the prospective supporter may feel if they were under the impression that they were seen to have 'done something wrong'. I prefer face to face sessions rather than online sessions for the purpose of such a consultation. You can e.g. create a positive connotation by welcoming them in a friendly way, asking where they have travelled from, the effort it has taken to get to the session, asking what their best wishes for everyone in the family are and expressing that you are glad they have decided to attend. The implicit message of such questions is: *You are accepted here; your motivation and your willingness to help are appreciated.*

Take on a leading role in structuring the session, by introducing a 'hub and spoke' model of communication: The practitioner speaks directly to each participant in the session alternately, rather than the parent(s) and the other adult speaking to each other in a free-flowing manner. This helps prevent dominant interaction and will enable a goal-oriented conversation.

Should the other adult start communicating in a critical or prescriptive manner, interrupt politely and develop a positive connotation of their critical communication. Once you have done this, the parent may wish to share some of the unintended negative consequences of the other person's critical communication; however, it is important to contain this and bring it to a close by e.g. summarising the parent's emotional response to the criticism and re-iterating that these are unintended consequences of the other adult's communication. It is important to stress to the other adult that re-positioning will be possible within this session: *I would like to emphasise that ... (parent) has said she really appreciates your efforts, and she knows you have only wanted the best for everyone. We will use this session to find out what will be helpful for bringing about change and what part you can play in that.*

Once a conversational structure has been established and a positive connotation of the other adult's previously critical/prescriptive communication has been given, the prospective supporter may be much more open to learning about the parent's experience of the child's problematic behaviour and about the parent's growing agency. The practitioner can now move on to the second stage in this conversation, in which competent compassionate witnessing, as developed in Weingarten's (2003) model, is brought together with appreciative witnessing of the agency which the parent has already experienced in the NVR process.

Method: The utilising consultation step 2 – Witnessing

Ask the parent(s) to disclose specifically what harmful or self-destructive behaviours the interest child has been showing. Where a parent uses euphemistic language, ask them to describe exactly what happens. If e.g. the parent says *He gets really angry*, you can ask *What does he do when he gets angry?*[4] If they indicate the actual behaviour in a more general, nondescriptive and thus minimising way, such as saying *She pushes me*, you can ask questions such as *Where does she touch you? How hard? Where does this happen? How often has this happened? How long has this been going on for? Have you been injured? How?* It is important to ask the parent's permission for asking such specific questions when you prepare the utilising consultation, and also during the utilising consultation itself. The specificity of the parent's account enables the other adult to imagine the actual kind of incident more accurately. This specificity of the parent's account and the greater accuracy of the other adult's imagination, together with the emotion that is often communicated in body language, tone and prosody of the parent's voice and their facial expression, help the prospective supporter to bear witness to the parent's distress.

Ask the parent(s) to share the deleterious effects of such recurring incidents in emotional and behavioural terms, e.g. *I feel so scared that he'll erupt, I'm always walking on eggshells. I'm too scared to wake him for school in the mornings. I actually worry about talking to him at all, because I never know when something I say will set him off. We can hardly be in the same room together. It feels like I'm losing my child. I miss the boy he used to be. He doesn't want me to bring anyone into the house. I don't see my friends any more; it's so embarrassing when he's rude to them, and I get it afterwards if someone has come round.*

Ask the parents to share their impression of the deleterious effects of such incidents on everyone else in the family, including the interest child themselves, e.g. *I can tell he feels ashamed when he's hit me. He's lost his old set of friends, and I think that his new ones are county line kind of boys. He seems pretty scared a lot of the time, but I think he makes up for that by acting macho. We found a machete in his room last week. He took it pretty hard when he got excluded from school, even though he wasn't going regularly anyway, but you could see him going from being upset to getting angry again.* It is very important to give space for the impact of the problematic incidents on siblings. Siblings are often overlooked due to the attention that the problem behaviour draws away from them. It can also be important for the parent to speak about the impact of such incidents on pets, especially when the interest child tends to threaten or hurt a pet in order to gain leverage over parents.

Ask the parent to share a memory of NVR action they have taken. It can be an account of resistance to harmful behaviour, such as an announcement,[5] or an account of the parent's effort to reconnect with their child, such as a particular relational gesture. It should be action they took in a well-prepared manner and preferably with the support of another person. Ask them to choose a memory which, when looking back, allows the parent to feel "*good about (themselves)*", strong, internally connected with their values as a parent and as a person more generally, and validated by the other person who supported them.[6] By asking detailed questions about what actually happened, the parent's internal state of mind, how they overcame internal constraints, how the other person supported them, what surprised them, etc., the other person again receives pertinent information that can help them imagine this 'positive incident' with greater accuracy. They can also perceive the change in emotional expression from when the parent(s) described a harmful incident to when they describe their own constructive action; this enables them to appreciate the parent's agency. It is important that success should not be seen as dependent on a positive response from the child, but as the parent having been "able to do something they never thought they could do before" (Omer, 2018).

You can now ask the prospective supporter to share their response to the parent's distressing account and to the parent's account of what they were able to achieve. Useful questions that invite first person statements (rather than comments *about* the parent) can be *What did hearing this bring up for you? How does it resonate with your own life experience?* If the prospective supporter only speaks about the parent's account of victimisation, it is important to ask them to also share feedback on the parental account of agency in the NVR process, as well.

The parent can then share their feelings about the other adult's feedback.

Compassionate witnessing by the other adult re-humanises the parents. The restoration of their dignity can help them feel that they have the right to resist harmful behaviour and that they deserve the support of the other adult in doing so.[7] The appreciative witnessing of their agency opens conversational space for the parents' request to receive the kind of support they require for increasing their sense of agency. The purpose of the next step in the utilising consultation is for the parent to articulate exactly what they would like their prospective supporter to do in support of their own sense of parental agency.

Method: The utilising consultation
step 3 – Centring the parent's support needs in
action planning

Instead of abstract conversation, specific planning and rehearsal of positive action becomes the vehicle for parents to express their expectation.

The practitioner helps the parent and their prospective supporter to plan a specific act of resistance and/or a relational gesture, which the parent would like to perform together with them. This can e.g. be an *announcement*, a *sit-in*,[8] or acting as a *stress-buffer*.[9]

Rehearse the act in role play. The therapist asks the parent to tell the prospective supporter, what kind of communication on their part they would like them to show, in order to help strengthen their own sense of agency. Helpful questions can be:

Where would you like ... (supporter) to sit, so you feel really supported? (It can, however, be important to negotiate this with the parent if you feel that their placement of the supporter expresses or symbolises a wish to delegate their parental authority to the other adult.)

What would you like ... (supporter) to say, if ... (child) asks her what she's doing here? What can she say, so that you remain in charge of the process?

In what way will it be helpful when ... (supporter) remains quiet during the sit-in, so you can focus on ... (child), while at the same time feeling assured of their support and presence?

At the end of the session, ask the prospective supporter whether they feel able and committed to respond in the way the parent has requested. They should only actually participate, if they can commit to acting in the way the parent has requested.

You can suggest that the supporter notes in which competent ways they observe the parent communicating during the act of resistance they take part in – especially if the young person responds in a provocative, rejecting, threatening or dismissive way or uses pejorative or abusive language. The supporter can discuss this afterwards with the parent or bring the notes along for discussion in a further therapy session.

In this third step, the utilising consultation creates conversational space for the parents' own knowledge of what will strengthen their agency. The observational homework assignment can enhance the resistance narrative in this change-determined system, by giving its account of parental strength and competence greater credibility. This, in turn, can be seen to support the shift in the supporters' social perception bias towards the parent.

Supporter meetings for families that face multiple challenges

While it is often advisable to gradually expand the caring community by including more supporters one at a time, it may also be possible to convene and facilitate a larger *supporters meeting*, especially when working with adoptive families, foster families or residential services. Due to the greater propensity for setbacks in these trauma-impacted systems, it can be useful to repeat such a meeting several times over the course of NVR-based work, or to conduct meetings for specific groups of people in one and the same case. Having experienced much relational rupture between themselves and other adults, including professionals, adoptive parents or carers can experience a carefully planned and facilitated supporters meeting as restorative and reconnective. This, in turn, will often encourage them to resist harmful behaviour, be it by the child or by adults who have positioned themselves in dangerous and coercive ways.

A wide-ranging UK study established that adoptive parents see child to parent violence and aggression as the foremost factor in adoption disruption and placement of young people in care (Selwyn, Wijedasa and Meakings, 2014). This study further demonstrated that adoptive parents often feel isolated from their social-ecological environment and unsupported by professional systems. They urgently require emotionally safe support. Sandra's example shows how compassion and appreciation can counteract a parent's sense of isolation:

Sandra and her husband Doug separated several years ago. Since then, she has been the single adoptive parent of now 15-year-old non-identical twin boys. In the run up to their separation, Doug had acted with increasing aggression and ultimately physical violence towards Sandra. After the parents' separation, the boys began developing aggressive behaviour towards their mother, and since the parents' divorce, this behaviour has worsened to the point of becoming unbearable. Sandra does not feel supported by their adoptive father and is afraid of him, yet until recently, she has seen his support as the only escape from her troubling situation, even though it has never been forthcoming. Both sons have attacked Sandra physically when she has attempted to refuse giving them money for buying class A drugs, and on one occasion, Robert punched her hard in the chest. She has no more influence on when they come home at night. Robert gets bullied at school by his brother John and John's friends and on social media for being gay, even though he has not yet come out. Robert and John often fight with each other, sometimes to the point of physical injury. Robert deals drugs in a county line. No-one in the family experiences joy or enjoys their relationships with one another.

Sandra shares a detailed account of this situation during the first supporters' meeting, which is attended face to face by six friends and her brother, while her parents attend online. She also gives an account of the announcements she has made to each of the boys with the help of a friend. Even though she had been very anxious beforehand, Sandra informed them she would no longer fund drug-taking and would not remain silent about their physical violence any longer. She further told them that she has thought a lot about how, especially as adoptive children, they will have been burdened by her and Doug's separation and divorce, but that drug taking and aggression are not helpful ways of dealing with this. The friend who acted as a witness to her announcements distributes paper copies of the text to each participant.

As previously decided by Sandra, I then interview her brother and another friend in front of the group. Both had known that there were difficulties in the family, but they had been unaware of the serious nature and extent of these difficulties. Sandra's brother shares how difficult it was when he himself came out as gay when he was a teenager. He feels very troubled by the violence towards his sister, but also by the fact that one of his nephews, whom he loves, has been acting in such a homophobic way against his other nephew, whom he also loves and whose predicament resonates with him. Sandra's female friend shares how troubled she feels as a woman by the violence Sandra has experienced from her divorced husband and from her sons. However, she also remarks that she is worried about the boys, whom she has seen growing up and is fond of. She is grateful that Sandra has asked her to become a supporter and says it must have taken a lot of courage to speak about these difficulties so openly.

At the end of the supporters meeting, the participants express their readiness to take part in a campaign of concern and any sit-ins that may be necessary, should there be any further violent incidents or threats of violence. One participant, a neighbour, agrees to come into the house if tensions arise, and Sandra decides to provide her with a house key. Sandra's brother volunteers to speak to each of his nephews separately about his own history of coming out as a gay teenager.

This case example illustrates some of the positive impact that witnessing can have. I carried out the supporters meeting, in part, as a form of 'outsider witnessing' as practised in narrative therapy (White, 2007): facilitating the witnessing of significant life experience of a person by individuals from outside of these events. Instead of asking for everyone's responses, I only interviewed two members of the group who had previously been nominated by the mother, as a form of what White called a 'definitional ceremony'. This procedure aimed to prevent her from experiencing an emotional overload. It further enabled us to intensify the emotional valence of the witnesses' responses and carefully scaffold layers of meaning that can be attributed to the parent's initial acts of resistance to her sons' harmful, but also self-destructive behaviours. The questions I asked the two witnesses aimed to elicit their personal resonance with the mother's own accounts; they were asked to share their response to what they heard against the backdrop of their own lived experience, rather than speaking in an evaluative way about mother and sons.

The structure of such a meeting creates a context for multi-directional partiality in absentia – the compassionate witnessing of some of the hardship and distress experienced by everyone in the nuclear family system, including those not present. We did not seek the boys' own perspectives on their problematic behaviours; this would probably have been counterproductive, as it would have given space to denial, minimisation and blame of their adoptive mother, who was already the subject of victim blaming by their adoptive father.

This structure further enables appreciative witnessing of a parent's growing agency and competence. The duality of the witnessing process is of central importance: would we focus on distress and suffering alone but leave moments of strength and success out of the conversation, we would only generate a victim narrative but not a resistance narrative.

The *self-told* victim narrative was developed in co-authorship between the mother, the members of the group, and the therapist. Sandra took back definitional power in describing herself. A self-authored victim narrative differs from previous definitions of the person of the parent which are issued by others (Jakob, 2021). Here, the mother became able to communicate the shameful details of the violence she experienced, the loss of her parental authority and her helplessness in protecting her sons from their drug use. By virtue of the group's non-judgemental, accepting responses, Sandra was able to regulate her shame. She felt connected to the others and reconnected, where there had been previous relational rupture with group members due to her avoidance of them. This process has supported the restoration of her dignity.

We can see that an effort at generating multi-directional partiality has been important for Sandra. Her sons are part of her 'extended self'. An absence of compassion for *them* would have felt injurious for *her*. Roger's homophobic bullying, the boys' emotional difficulties in the wake of their adoptive parents' separation and *everyone's* joyless existence were all shared at this meeting and influenced the two interviewees' responses.

In NVR, the systemic therapist faces a dilemma: it becomes necessary for the parent to take unilateral action in their resistance to harmful behaviour and self-destructive behaviour, when the young person does not cooperate or engage in a meaningful way in therapy. *One cannot resist a person's violence together with that person.* Individuals, even young people who act persistently in harmful and controlling ways and fail to amend their behaviour patterns, do not endorse or accept the resistance by the very people they target, even when such resistance is nonviolent. This necessitates parents and their supporters to form alliances against the harmful behaviour and act unilaterally. How can we then enable multi-directional partiality, an empathic and respectful acknowledgement of each individual family member's experience? This, going back as far as e.g. Boszormenyi-Nagy's (2014) conceptualisation, has been widely held as an essential ethical stance in systemic practice.

By creating conversational space for *indirect*ly witnessing the young person's distress and hardship – by virtue of their mother's account – we are helping to move the change-oriented therapeutic system *towards* multi-directional partiality. It can be hoped that multi-directional partiality may become a full reality once respectful dialogue without harmful interaction becomes possible. In this case example, the mother was not only acknowledged for maintaining an empathic and caring stance towards her sons, but the participants were invited to position themselves in an emotionally safe way towards them, and this, in turn, positioned the supporters in an emotionally safe way towards her. Their uncle came to feel even closer to his nephews as he learned about their own suffering and his sister's concerns for them. This would then contribute to shaping his responsiveness towards them, even when addressing difficult issues. He would implicitly and explicitly communicate powerfully that he sees them as belonging to the family and the wider community around it. In such a way, the connective impact of emerging but not yet fully formed multi-directional partiality, which is reflected in the narration of the family situation, can unfold. This was of particular importance in regard to the two boys' shame regulation. Shaming interaction has an exclusionary effect, while inclusive interaction can support shame regulation (Weinblatt, 2018). Moreover, perceived interpersonal responsiveness has been identified as a key component of satisfying close relationships (Reis, 2014; Reis and Gable, 2015), thereby, in my view, contributing to the experience of social inclusion.

A further central aspect of compassionate witnessing in this example lay in opening conversational space for the wider socio-political context of the boys' violent behaviour towards their mother, and the narrative was enriched by introducing the perspectives of gender and sexual orientation: the mother's friend shared how, *as a woman*, she feels affected by the violence that has been directed at another woman, the uncle shared his lived experience of homophobic abuse. In such a way, the lived while experience of the caring community can be threaded into a shared emerging narrative.

It is at this point that the self- and co-authored victim narrative can be augmented with a resistor narrative. Distributing the *announcement* text signalled the transition from witnessing victimhood to acknowledgement and appreciation of the mother's agency – an agency which was actualised both individually and in an interpersonal way. The mother's friend, her first emotionally safe supporter who took part in both announcements, shared her experience of Sandra's courage and competence in her acts of resistance. The resonance to this account within this solution-oriented therapeutic system has had an encouraging quality; through eyes of her friend-supporter, and the other people who are joining the caring community, Sandra became able see herself as someone who has interpersonal agency and competence.

My questions were aimed at inviting her to report her own experience of resisting in the course of delivering the announcements: *What motivated you to carry out the announcements? What did you learn about yourself, what did you learn about your sons when you were writing the text of the announcement? When you were delivering it to them? What was hard? What was easy? How did you manage to overcome the constraints to doing this? How did you manage not to get discouraged and stay the course, when your sons acted in dismissive and derogatory ways? What kind of competence did you discover in yourself? In what ways was... (friend's) presence supportive? How were you able to make good use of her support? In what ways did you embody the mother you want to be?*

In her resistor narrative, this mother has taken a further step in reclaiming her self-definitional power. She is not a mere victim – even one of her own description – but also an active agent. Rather than being a passive sufferer, or even someone who copes with what is inflicted upon her, she has become someone who impacts upon the environment which impacts upon her, as she moves through her social world.

For supporters, it becomes necessary to find resonance in themselves to the parent's self-efficacy. In my experience, merely experiencing a parent as helpless has a de-motivating effect on supporters. A one-dimensional victim narrative could render them feeling helpless, yet supporters need to feel their efforts will matter and bear fruit (Hicks, Jakob and Kustner, 2020). Frustration could result in some of the supporters falling into a critical-prescriptive position: *He should just go into care!,* while others may withdraw from the support network and avoid the parents. The introduction of a resistance narrative however can encourage the group to deliver a variety of proactive offers of support. A motivated caring community then becomes *activated.*

Method: First large supporters meeting
step 1 – Joining and witnessing

A large supporters meeting is only advisable for parents who are unlikely to feel overwhelmed by such a large gathering and may be more suitable for adoptive parents, foster carers, kinship carers or carers in a residential home. For parents who are still struggling with the experience of abuse and multiple challenges, a smaller meeting with one or two prospective supporters as previously outlined may be more suitable. The purpose of the first supporters meeting is to stimulate prospective supporters' motivation and generate an emotionally safe, caring community.

Joint preparation prior to the meeting: The persons who will be invited are carefully selected. No – one who has acted in dangerous or coercive ways should take part. The parent(s) should designate two or three people the therapist will interview for their witnessing response. Discuss, how the client can best invite prospective supporters. It may be helpful to agree on a script, or the NVR practitioner can provide a text for passing on to future supporters.

The meeting itself can take place face to face or online. Online meetings have proven to be practical, enabling people who could otherwise not attend to participate. However, a face to face meeting can have greater emotional valence.

Begin the meeting by greeting all participants and thanking them for their willingness to *actively* support the parents and the entire family. Discuss confidentiality – the parents will decide what information is shared and with whom. By staying in the meeting, participants commit themselves to confidentiality.

Use a hub-and-spoke structure of conversation: the therapist speaks with individual participants and the parents, i.e. is at the hub of the conversation. Participants and parents only address each other directly upon the practitioner's request. If a participant urgently wishes to comment on any issues, you can politely tell them that at a later point, two or three participants will share their feedback. This structure is necessary to protect the parents, who can be very vulnerable in this situation, from any unhelpful communication.

Ask the parent(s) to describe the difficulties in a concrete, specific way. It is important they avoid explaining or minimising the difficulties and use descriptive rather than abstract language, e.g. *When I told Fred I didn't have the time to drive him into town yesterday, he pushed me hard and I fell down the stairs. I got black and blue marks. This is the kind of thing that happens several times a week*, instead of using nondescript language such as *Fred gets upset when he doesn't get what he wants.*

Ask the parent or caregiver to describe the impact of the problematic behaviour on themselves, and, as best they understand it, on each and every family member, including the interest child themselves. It is important that this account is not primarily centred on the child who instigates problematic incidents, but that parents make sure to share their concerns for everyone involved, even pets. They can also express their concerns for neighbours or other people from outside the family who are affected. If there is a family history of abuse and aggressive incidents have a re-traumatising effect, it may be important to mention this, so that participants in the meeting develop a clear understanding of the harm that is being caused.

Next, ask the parent to give an account of an act of resistance they have carried out since they have been involved in working with NVR. This should be an act in which, looking back, they recognise their own parental agency, self-determination and strength. This can be an *announcement*, a *sit-in*, an act of *parental disobedience* or *de-accommodation*,[10] or a *relational/reconciliation gesture* the parent made to their child. If the parent speaks of such a relational gesture, they should also be asked to give an account of something they did to raise their presence that was difficult for them.[11]

Now, the therapist can interview the two or three previously nominated participants to share how they personally resonate with the parent's account: *You have heard, what (parent) has experienced, how this has affected them and perhaps others in the family as well, and they have shared what they have already been doing to bring about change. What does this bring up in you? How does what (parent) has experienced, and what they have done, resonate with your own life experience?*

Ensure that the witnesses speak not only to the negative impact of harmful child behaviour, but also to the parents' act of resistance.

The wish to be helpful, which has been stimulated in step 1 by creating space for both compassionate witnessing and appreciative witnessing, has prepared the ground for a thematic shift to proactive support. The caring community can begin to consolidate around a shared perspective on helpful, coordinated action.

Method: First large supporters meeting
step 2 – Action plan

Inform the participants about specific ways in which they can support the parent(s) and children in their resistance to harmful behaviour and reconnect within the family and to the larger community around them. It can be helpful to focus primarily on the 'positive' campaign of concern as a key method, as described below.

Discuss with the prospective supporters that they can participate with various degrees of involvement, and reassure them that it is legitimate for them to only commit to what they feel they can realistically undertake. Their involvement can be as little as a few minutes per week or far more extensive.

Address supporters' concerns, for example that the relationship with the interest child could be negatively affected. Some of these concerns can be dispelled by sharing the overwhelming body of experience in NVR that supporters and young people tend to become more closely connected to each other due to the inclusive nature of NVR action, especially if the positive campaign of concern and extensive use of relational gestures are brought to bear. However, the risk of a negative impact on the relationship remains, if only to a small degree, and it is realistic to accept that resistance inevitably entails taking risks.

Introduce the positive campaign of concern:

- Supporters will make at least three appreciative sets of responses for every one concerned set of responses about a harmful or self-destructive incident. I have also had good experiences with campaigns of concern utilising only appreciative responses.
- Appreciative responses are best subtle and avoid praise. They draw attention to the exceptions to problematic interaction, instead. Praise can create pressure for the young person and stimulate shame. Example of an appreciative response: *I heard you and your folks went camping on Dartmoor last weekend. Saw the pics of you swimming in that cold water! Here are some pics of when we went there last year.*
- Concerned responses are inclusive and express multi-directional partiality: *I've heard that you and your mum had an argument yesterday, and you pushed her down the stairs. I'm concerned for her safety because she could get seriously hurt. I'm also concerned for your relationship with her, because it's not good for either of you if she's scared of you or upset. Your mum and I have arranged that I can come round to your house when things get tense, so that things don't get out of hand. If you feel very aggravated about something and you need a break, you're always welcome to come over to our house and stay with us for a while until it feels better.*[12]
- Inform that the parent(s) will set up a social media group to share information with the group and that they will nominate certain individuals to

give responses to the young person after problematic incidents or after positive events. They should feed back to the parents how the young person reacted to their message.

- Messages can be texts, phone calls, face to face contacts or use any other media. A very helpful kind of message can be to send a video recording of speaking to the young person.
- Inform the participants that the young person is likely to appear to reject their efforts or remain unresponsive to them. This is normal and should not deter them from responding again. It lies in the nature of nonviolent resistance to persevere in spite of such reactions and gives the -ultimately reassuring, emotionally anchoring-implicit message: *We will not give up on you! We are here! We will stay with you!* The practitioner can introduce the notion of psychological polyphony: *A young person has many 'voices'. Some voices can be buried, like the wish to cooperate, wanting to act in a peaceful way, wishing to have mutually rewarding relationships. We don't often hear those voices in ... 's case (the interest person). They can be buried so deeply that a young person doesn't even 'hear' those voices themselves. Your persistent action will help, eventually, to bring those other voices back again.*
- Inform the participants that you will support the campaign of concern by following the communication in the WhatsApp group and will direct message the parents with your suggestions and ideas.

The last part of the meeting consists of a Q&A session. It is important to maintain the hub-and-spoke structure, to ensure that the conversation remains focused and supportive of the parents.

The resistance principle: Helping parents protect the integrity of the nuclear family

As Amanda's example illustrates, the nuclear family is unlikely to become an emotionally safe healing environment as long as family members encounter others who act in ways that are dangerous and coercive. Especially when de-stabilising events have affected the family, they become more vulnerable to intrusion by other adults who show a propensity to act in ways that are domineering, controlling and abusive. Such events can e.g. be illness, economic difficulties, a child protection investigation or a resurgence of especially problematic child behaviour. When such circumstances initiate a setback in the change process, individuals who position themselves in a dangerous and coercive manner are likely to exploit the family's vulnerability at this stage and violate its boundaries. These can be members of the wider family, a previous partner who physically, sexually or emotionally[13] abused the parent or the children, or other individuals who are in some way able to exert power. There can also be transgressions by professionals or officials who are involved with a parent or family, such as police officers, clergy, social workers or mental health practitioners. In such instances, parents who have experienced abuse may be prone to submission and feel unable to protect their own and their family's boundaries.[14]

Often, problematic child behaviour or the other adult's relationship with the child will be used as a vehicle to assert a sense of entitlement to or 'ownership' of the parent, (re-) establish control or sexually exploit them. This will generally cause severe distress and a resurgence of traumatic stress in the parent and their children, further de-stabilising the family and aggravating any setback they may already be experiencing. Here, it becomes vital to understand and practice NVR not only within the parent/child dyad, but to use its principles and methods of resistance as a possibility for maintaining the nuclear family's integrity.

It is vital to enable parents to disclose such incidents by communicating with them in a manner that is open, removes taboos to speaking about such issues, encourages them to share their experience and normalises their responses. Disclosures of such incidents are not a matter of course, even in therapeutic relationships in which the parent has been trusting of the practitioner. Shame about a setback, shame about having engaged 'yet again' with a dangerous person, fear of negative repercussions by agencies involved with the family or the fear of disapproval by others can be powerful constraints to the client's openness.

If, however, violations of the parent's and entire family's integrity are disclosed within an emotionally safe therapeutic relationship, possibilities for protecting parents and children by means of *nonviolent, multi-dimensional resistance* arise:

Christine is a single parent who lives with her 12-year-old son Liam in a small town. Following his abuse of a nine year old girl in the family's former circle of friends, her 15-year-old son Benjamin has been placed in a specialist residential therapeutic service for adolescents who have sexually abused children. Christine herself had been sexually abused as a child in her family of origin. The staff in the residential service, Christine and I cooperate in resisting Benjamin's refusal to accept responsibility for his offences and acknowledge the harm he has caused his victim and her family and, by extension, his own family. By claiming to have been seduced by this child and thereby blaming his victim, Benjamin continues to harm her and her family, his own mother and his brother in different ways. His denial of responsibility predisposes him for future sexually abusive behaviour and thereby increases the risk he poses to others.

Liam is being bullied at school in response to his brother's offences; the family has been ostracised by most of their former social network, and they are being trolled on social media. On his way home from school, Liam is beaten by other pupils. A police officer who has been involved with the family due to Benjamin's offences, sexually harasses Christine. This accumulation of pressure drives Christine to seek support from a previous partner, who moves back into the family home. In this enormously distressing situation – social isolation of the family, trolling on social media, violence against Liam, sexual harassment by a person with power over the family – Christine hopes that her previous partner's physical presence in the family home will provide a measure of protection. However, his controlling, dominant behaviour re-emerges quickly, and he attempts to determine how she dresses, whom she meets, etc. However, as Christine reports in her next therapy session, she is no longer prepared to accept such dominance due to experience in nonviolent resistance. In the course of an argument, her previous and now temporary partner throws her against the bathroom mirror, causing cuts to her back and continues to verbally threaten her.

Christine discloses this incident to me and to social services. Her 'partner' is arrested and spends the night in custody. She shares her fear of his return to the house. We plan nonviolent direct action. Upon his return home, he finds the living room full of Christine's newfound supporters, many of whom have joined her support network after learning about the family's isolation. They interrupt their conversation, look at him and greet him in a polite yet serious manner. They remain in the house for a further hour. Shortly afterwards and several times during the night, Christine receives phone calls and text messages from her supporters, to which she responds with a code word to indicate that she is not in immediate danger.[15] *The mother's 'partner' also receives messages, this time from the supporters' partners who ask whether he is "OK" and offer to talk to him if "everything gets too much", but that he needs to "leave Christine in peace".*

A few weeks later, Christine separates from him. Upon reflection, she realises that she had re-engaged with her former partner because she had felt overwhelmed by the enormous pressure on her, couldn't "think clearly" any longer and felt threatened from many different directions.

The recent experience of sexual harassment by a police officer and the violence by her 'partner' brought up severe anger at Benjamin in Christine. At the same time, she has felt immobilised, as she has not wanted to let her anger out on him. Christine cancels her next visit to Benjamin. However, her previous efforts directed at Benjamin, and her resistance against domestic violence have encouraged her to resume her resistance against Benjamin's denial of responsibility for his offences. The positive action she has taken has further emboldened Christine to seek a meeting with Liam's Headteacher and assertively demand that the school should take serious measures to protect Liam.

In a therapy session, we discuss whom Christine will contact should she feel overwhelmed again, and what she would like her supporters to do in such an instance to help protect her and Liam.

Christine's resistance to her "partner's" violence is significant in several ways:

- His threatening behaviour impacts heavily on her and on her younger son, violating the family's integrity. Her presence-raising nonviolent action, which entails proactive support by the family's caring community, affords them both real protection.
- There is an important gender aspect: Christine's friends show powerful female solidarity as they protect her and her son from male violence. While the woman supporters' male partners become supporters as well, they are responding to female leadership – the women involved, foremost Christine herself, are the

primary decision-makers. As Christine will report at a later point, this kind of female solidarity, empowerment and leadership supports her resistance to Benjamin's denial of responsibility and helps her not to resume the relationship with her previous, violent partner: "I don't need a man to protect myself!"

- The protective support from the women who have positioned themselves in emotionally safe ways around the family demonstrates to social services that Christine is cooperative and able to protect her younger son from having to witness domestic violence. This helps prevent critical and prescriptive positioning by professionals, whose considerable power may otherwise feel threatening to Christine and Liam and potentially raise the baseline of anxious-arousal in the family further.
- This example contradicts a particular understanding that mothers who have survived abuse would require long-term trauma therapy before becoming able to resist further abuse. We see a new possibility here: The parent's experience of nonviolent resistance and her interpersonal resources within the support network, her caring community, enable her to quickly shift from a traumatic state of mind to a more functional state.

Psychological literature generally distinguishes between 'traumatic' and 'normal' or 'functional' states of mind. However, we can be more specific in differentiating and describing alternate states of consciousness. We have described a particular kind of mind state as *presence mind* (Dulberger, Fried and Jakob, 2016; Beckers, Jakob and Schreiter, 2022). We can understand these to be specific mind-states that emerge more often and more easily by virtue of resisting. When parents shift into presence mind-states, they become more effective. A number of nonviolent resistance methods enable a rapid shift from a traumatic mind-state to one in which the parent is more in touch with those internal and interpersonal resources they need in order to access actual protection and maintain the nuclear family's boundaries. Such a mind-state is functional in a specific, resistance-oriented way. In contrast to such trauma-focused approaches which see people as generally impaired in their ability to function, I am suggesting a resource-oriented perspective. Feeling secure by becoming aware of the safety-inducing presence of a supporter can provide a counterweight to a trauma-induced sense of isolation. The parent gains access to psychological resources which become actualised in interpersonal processes that are perceived as emotionally safe and supportive. We can lay the groundwork for this during the therapy session while the parent's psycho-physiological arousal is lower than at other times. This is based on careful, pre-emptive preparation of future nonviolent positive action which will involve supporter action. Later, when the parent's arousal level threatens to become elevated above a functional level and there is a risk of major 'bottom-up' emotionality such as heightened anxiety or anger, the parent can find assurance in their awareness of the supporters' presence. For this reason, I call a method I use to this effect 'bridging states of consciousness in NVR'[16] (Jakob, 2018; Figure 2.1).

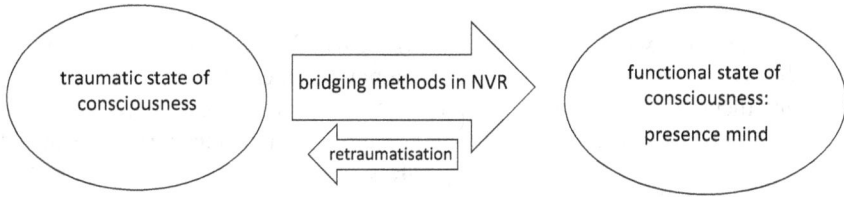

Figure 2.1 Transition between states of consciousness.

   The first step in bridging entails working with the parent to create the conditions in which they are more likely to facilitate the integration of emotionally safe supporters in their communication system.

**Method: Bridging states of consciousness
step 1 – Preparation with the parent**

- *Compassionate witnessing and normalising.* A pre-requisite for collaborative work with the parent at this stage is for the therapist to compassionately witness the parent's experience of threat. For example, a mother's patterns of reacting – even if at first glance they appear strange, nonsensical or counterproductive – make sense in the survival context in which they originally developed. The therapist discusses these reaction patterns with the parent, expresses empathy and, drawing on trauma theory, normalises their responses: *It must have been terrible to get threatened like that for so long. Many people who have had similar experiences tend to react impulsively in the way you have when they feel under threat again. The body just wants to protect itself, but sometimes there are reactions that afterwards you realise you didn't want. But that doesn't mean that you're doomed to always react in the same way. Shall we talk about some possibilities to interrupt or prevent your automatic reactions?*
- *Interrupting behavioural pathways.* When experiencing high levels of psycho-physiological arousal, parents may be prone to impulsively give a dangerous person access to or even appear to 'invite' them into the family. The further the parent has gone down such a behavioural pathway, the more difficult it can be to deviate from it. We can help the parent take precautions for times when their arousal levels will rise very quickly, while they are in a functional state of consciousness during a therapy session. These precautions make it easier for the parent to deviate from their traumatic behaviour response early on, bring their arousal down to a lower level and reorientate. For example, a parent can delete all telephone numbers of people who have acted in dangerous or coercive ways from their phone, write the numbers down by hand on a piece of paper and store

this in a place that is difficult to access. This will interrupt the automatic behaviour pattern. The parent can then put a sticker on their phone alerting them to an alternate behavioural possibility, such as *Call Olivia!*
— *Self-announcement.*[17] The following kind of self-announcement can enable the integration of emotionally safe supporters in the communication system, by directing the parent's awareness to their existence and creating a structure for the parent to make a commitment to get into contact with them in moments of distress. There are four themes for the parents to focus on in their written self-announcement:

"What I have learned to appreciate about myself as a parent since I have been involved in NVR". (It may not be advisable to ask a person with a severe history of abuse what they 'love about' themselves, as they may hold very negative self-directed beliefs);

What I won't do from now on when I feel distressed, why I won't do this any longer and what I will do from now on when I find myself in such a situation;

Who I will ask for help in such a situation;

In which ways the relationships in our family will change as a result.

It is important to name the new responses in a specific and concrete (operational) way, e.g.: *"I will delete Michael's number on my phone and block him, to keep us safe. I'll write his number on a piece of paper and put it on top of the cupboard. Instead, I'll set up a WhatsApp group with Monica's, Jude's and Marlene's numbers and call it HELP".*

While the self-announcement in step 1 represents a commitment to engage with their emotionally safe supporters, the parent turns the self-commitment into a social event by making it known within their caring community.

Method: Bridging states of consciousness
step 2 – Bringing in the supporters

Coaching supporters. The parent can make their commitment to seek help public, by distributing the self-announcement text within their caring community. In therapy or parenting sessions, the parent and the supporters agree on the code the parent will use to signal safety, and how the supporters should respond in the event of threat, such as come round to the family home, call the threatening other adult, or inform the police of a dangerous incident.

'Invasion' by interpersonal safety anchors. In a reversal of the way in which traumatic material can 'invade' a functional state of consciousness and evoke a traumatic state, safety anchors can help bring about a more functional psychological state. Trauma therapists help clients to do this by

using various intra-psychic methods such as the safe place technique. The difference here is that awareness of the protective qualities of their *relationship with an emotionally safe supporter* becomes the parent's safety anchor.

The practitioner can help make arrangements for supporters to approach a parent in an *unprompted* way during what may be a critical period. If e.g. a parent does not contact their supporters by a certain, pre-arranged date or time, they take action of their own accord, by calling, sending texts or other means of communication. If the parent does not respond using a pre-arranged code word, they may come to the family home or call the police. In a situation involving acute danger, a call-in might be used, which entails unprompted calls to family members which can serve a protective function by raising the presence of the family's supporters. Such calls can also be made at night. Not only do they afford practical protection, but, importantly, such measures counteract a trauma-induced sense of isolation when feeling under threat.

Acute risk mitigation. Once a parent has taken steps to resist e.g. domestic abuse or threatening behaviour by a former partner, she and the children will find themselves in a high-risk situation. A house occupation, during which supporters come to the family home and remain physically present for significant lengths of time, often taking turns, can mitigate risk to some degree. You can prepare such a nonviolent response by carefully planning the house occupation during a therapy session when a parent is experiencing a functional state of consciousness. As during a call-in, the parent is reminded of the presence of the supportive other, counter-balancing a possible trauma-induced sense of isolation. Parents have reported that they feel much less frightened and become able to 'think clearly',[18] which indicates a reduction in psycho-physiological arousal. In certain circumstances, such measures may be reported to social services or the police.

Not only parents, but also other caregivers may experience ongoing or acute threat. This can contribute to stress responses that are often identified as 'burnout', depressive states, or anxiety-related difficulties. In such instances, interpersonal resources can ensure emotional support and reassurance, as well. For example, going beyond mere physical presence during shift work in a residential home, such forms of interpersonal support can be an important psychological factor in bridging to more functional states of consciousness from which not only caregivers, ultimately young people also benefit.

House occupations can be put in place in residential children's homes, when e.g. young people are at risk from dangerous individuals in the drug scene who groom them for sexual exploitation or gang activity, or when a young person shows high levels of dangerous aggression within the home which cause harm to caregivers and could lead to becoming criminalised. A number of members of the caring community can visit the residential- or foster home over the course of several days. These may include parents, relatives, neighbours to the family home or neighbours of the residential home, caregivers from other group homes, 'old (previous) friends' of the young person who have been a good influence, professionals who have been involved with the young person, or any other supporter. Such a house occupation can be carried out in conjunction with measures that have been referred to as 'tailing', but which in NVR entail raising adult presence in more dangerous environments (Omer, 2021c).

A man who works as a waiter in a local restaurant has been selling drugs to an adolescent in a residential service. A group of adults, comprised of the parent, the keyworker and a service manager, pay a short visit to this man. The three women tell him they are aware that he has been selling drugs to this emotionally unstable young person and then leave. This is undertaken in conjunction with a house occupation in the group home.

Nonviolent resistance to harmful or self-destructive behaviour can be a serious, long-term struggle in any given case, and adults risk getting discouraged if they expect immediate behaviour change in the young person. The immediate outcome we are looking for here lies more in the impact the supportive connection with members of the caring community can have on the caregivers themselves, enabling them to reactivate their own psychological resources once their interpersonal resources help bridge to more functional states of consciousness. Supervision and team meetings can be a forum for careful planning and preparation of a house occupation in the group home. A roster can help plan who will be present in the group home or communicate with the young person at what time, in addition to caregivers on shift, in order to ensure a seamless presence of supporters over the course of several days. A supporters meeting can be used to discuss the specific kind of action each individual supporter will take. During the house occupation itself, it will be helpful for more senior staff or an NVR practitioner to communicate with each supporter, in order to learn more and reflect about their experience in communicating with the young person and adjust further action accordingly. Experience in residential care shows that, *in the longer term*, the frequency of serious aggressive incidents and the need for physical restraint or police call out, are greatly reduced by such NVR responses. Research within a residential service for adolescents with very serious traumatic histories and highly self-destructive and harmful behaviour has demonstrated that staff in residential care feel supported and emotionally safer (Mackinnon, Jakob and Kustner, 2023).

The starting point for the first part of this book was the premise that an emotionally safe and at the same time proactively supportive social environment is a necessary prerequisite for the family to develop into a healing system for trauma. The same can be said of other social environments such as a foster home or residential care. The next chapter will conclude this first part by outlining some ways in which working with parents on the basis of NVR can help a residential service and the family become emotionally safe environments for one another.

Notes

1 In an organisation in which I introduced the concept of positioning, some colleagues quickly adopted a new form of critical and prescriptive positioning: they acted in critical ways towards other professionals or members of the larger system around parents, who themselves had been acting in critical ways towards the parents!

2 In the UK, 'county lines' are subsidiary avenues for the distribution of illicit drugs from larger cities into rural areas or small towns, whereby inner city drug dealers tend to groom and exploit vulnerable local young people to carry out this activity on their behalf.

3 Originally arising from the practice of symptom prescription, which is no longer considered acceptable in systemic thinking. Here, I am focusing on positive *aspects* of an otherwise harmful or counterproductive set of behaviours and suggesting an appreciative response only to these.

4 It can be important to distinguish emotion from behaviour. *Feeling* angry is a common emotional response that emerges in virtually all human beings in certain contexts. However, in NVR we support parents to hold the child responsible for no longer *acting aggressively* in the future. Often, parents – and many professionals – believe that acting with aggression is inextricably linked to the young person's angry feelings, especially if the child has experienced abuse in the past. However, such a belief implies an inevitability of aggression and a complete lack of agency on the part of the child, which would render moot any expectation of the parent, that the child can and should exert self-control in the here and now.

5 The *announcement* is a carefully prepared, transitional ritual. Early on in the NVR process, parents or other caregivers tell the child in a formal manner that they will no longer accept their harmful or self-destructive behaviour, that they will no longer remain silent about incidents of such behaviour and that they commit to not acting in aggressive or humiliating ways towards their child (see Omer, 2021c). In working with families in which children have experienced serious trauma, I suggest using a form of announcement in which parents express the way they value the person of the child, emphasising and detailing their own commitment to nonviolence in order to address the child's need for a sense of emotional and physical safety.

6 Any NVR action the parent takes is, in a solution-focused sense, an exception to the problem. In narrative therapy, this would be seen as a 'unique outcome', a kind of sub-plot of the master narrative of problematic interaction and change.

7 See Introduction.

8 The sit-in is a form of protest which was developed by Omer (2021c). In the sit-in, parents can raise their presence with the child after a very serious incident, such as an act of child-to-parent violence, without becoming punitive or escalatory. A few hours or days after the incident, once their own and their child's level of arousal has reduced, the parents sit down in the child's room and ask for a suggestion how the child will solve the problem or make reparation for the harm they have caused. This act of resistance is carefully planned, in order to ensure that parents do not escalate with the child or act in any other way that could be hurtful or harmful. Instead of acting with rejection or social exclusion of the young person, caregivers seek to engage with the child while at the same time giving the message that they take the incident seriously and will not simply remain silent as they may have in the past. Facing and engaging them thus aims to facilitate the child's re-entry into the community of the family, foster family, group home or classroom, and can help them regulate their feelings of shame. In emphasising the importance of this latter aspect of the sit-in and expressing the importance of the connective quality of the caregivers' presence, my colleague Rachael Aylmer has suggested using the alternate term 'sitting-with' (the child) in some circumstances (personal communication).

9 A supporter acts as a stress-buffer when they enter the home by the parents' or caregivers' request in a highly tense or volatile situation, help calm the adults and children by virtue of their presence and become a deterrent from further aggression.

10 No longer submitting to coercion by physical or emotional means is the key form of resistance in NVR. Presence-raising protest, such as the sit-in, only becomes necessary in response to actual harmful behaviour. In this way, protest can free parents up to decide that they will no longer give in to coercion. This is especially important for parents with traumatic experiences, whose anxiety levels will tend to be very high in expectation of threatening child behaviour.

11 Omer (2018) speaks of acts, which parents originally would not have felt they could carry out as important milestones in the generation of their personal courage and which communicate parental strength.

12 This is an example of a supporter, possibly a neighbour, acting as a stress buffer. It further demonstrates the inclusive nature of an NVR response that expresses concern.

13 In patterns of coercive control, behaviours such as emotional abuse or 'gaslighting' are used to establish control over finances, dress, lifestyle, who the parent socialises with, etc. Demeaning communication undermines their self-confidence and dignity and leaves them more vulnerable to further subjugation. Coercive control was made a criminal offence in the UK in 2015.

14 See 'Giving the body voice'.

15 In a state of high psycho-physiological arousal, a person would be unable to remember an unusual or complicated code, and the absence of the code word is a trigger for previously planned, protective action.

16 See the states of consciousness model in Ericksonian hypnotherapy (Lankton, 1985; Schwarz, 2013). More recently, neuroscientists have been investigating the neural signatures of different states of consciousness in individuals (Cofré et al., 2020). While the method discussed here does not use a formal trance induction, it is informed by a states of consciousness model. In particular, it aims to generate specific states of consciousness by directing the parent's focus towards and generating internal awareness of the safety inherent in interpersonal processes between parent and supporter.

17 Heismann originally introduced self-announcements into NVR (Heismann, Jude and Day, 2019). Here, I am introducing a specific use of the self-announcement which has been adapted to working with trauma.

18 I consider this a form of 'social regulation' of the parent's level of psycho-physiological arousal and emotion. In addition to the more physiological kind of co-regulation, by which a person responds to the mostly implicit indicators of emotional regulation in the other person, we have here a clear awareness of the other person's readiness to act in a protective manner, showing strength and determination.

Chapter 3

New possibilities

Working with parents of children in care

Residential care workers, foster carers and social workers often express concern about difficulties in communicating with parents of children who are looked after in care. Often, parents appear to distance themselves, avoid contact with caregivers, express criticism or even open hostility. Some parents avoid contact with their children or become unreliable in regard to visiting them. It is worth considering that these are parents who have often experienced dominance, abuse, neglect, failure to support or protect and even threat to life and limb in various social contexts. Frequently, interaction with social services has become an integral part of the larger system the family is embedded in, sometimes for generations, and relationships with the – often changing – professionals in such a system can have been seriously ruptured. Our aim in such situations will be to promote trust and connection between professionals and parents, so that constructive collaboration can become possible. However, we need to deal with various challenges along the way.

In some cases, care workers or foster carers express their concern about escalatory conflict between parents and children during weekends at home, on the phone or via text. The fallout from such conflictual communication for foster carers or care workers in the group home is often an increase in the frequency and intensity of serious incidents they need to respond to, such as angry outbursts, damage to property, physical aggression, self-harm, suicidal behaviour or running away to places where dangerous individuals put the young person at serious risk. Such incidents cause pressure on relationships between caregivers and young people and have negative effects on the emotional and physical well-being of both. In supervision or consultation, care workers and foster carers often speak of feeling angry towards parents or disaffected with them. When they attribute problematic incidents to parents, caregivers take up critical positions which can lead to escalatory communication with parents, avoidance of contact with them, or both responses in an alternating pattern. Such relational difficulties between caregivers and parents will, in turn, have further negative effects on the child who, in spite of their conflictual interaction with the parent and their aversive experiences in the family of origin, feels nevertheless attached to their parents with a powerful loyalty bond.[1]

DOI: 10.4324/9781032717111-6

Connective work with parents

Wiebenga and Bom, in their conceptualisation of NVR as 'connecting authority' (2023), stress that instructive or prescriptive communication by therapists directed at parents is incongruent with a nonviolent position. In other words, telling the parent what to do, or explicating on what the therapist believes they are doing wrong, is inconsistent with the very position they would like the parent to take up in relation to their child. The same can in my view be said of professionals working in the care system, though their emotional involvement with the child renders it much more difficult to take up and maintain a horizontal rather than vertical position towards the parents. However, parents will often show more favourable responses to caregivers – and to their own child – when a collaborative working relationship can be established. Such a collaborative relationship can then provide a platform for a professional in residential care or a social worker to facilitate less escalatory and more connective interaction between parent and child, as Lizzy's example illustrates:

14-year of Lizzy is from another part of the country and has come to live in a specialist residential home for adolescents who are at very high risk. Her younger siblings are in care in different foster homes. Lizzy shows high levels of aggressive behaviour, especially towards female carers. Very often, she comes to the attention of the police. In the nearby town, she joins other teenagers in attacking others verbally and sometimes physically, vandalising public and private property and using illegal drugs. Often, her mother has told her not to "listen to them" (caregivers and social workers), that she needs to assert herself. On one occasion, Lizzy kicks, scratches and bites a care worker; another time, she punches her social worker. In response to this, some professionals wish to reduce contact between mother and daughter, to keep the mother from "undermining the placement". They feel she exerts a bad influence on her daughter.

Her mother Susan has experienced physical child abuse, child sexual abuse and domestic violence. Whilst she was actively drug dependent, Susan often acted aggressively towards Lizzy when she was experiencing withdrawal and coerced her into shoplifting to fund her drug habit. Following several rehab treatments, Susan has been drug free for a prolonged period of time.

The NVR practitioner in the residential service works on the basis of the assumption that Susan may see much of her social environment as threatening, even where this is not the case. She believes that Susan's advice to her daughter could be an attempt to protect her from harm. We also believe that Susan may experience shame due to her daughter's placement in care, feel marginalised and irrelevant to the care of her child. We further assume she may suffer from feelings of unacknowledged guilt and probably misses the physical and emotional closeness to her daughter. We conclude that Susan may need active appreciation and validation as a mother by the team.

To provide such validation, the care workers intensify their contact with Susan. They begin by sending her daily texts or making phone calls. Often, the carers ask

Susan's advice, as she knows her daughter better than anyone else. The manager of the residential service asks Children's Services for more train vouchers to enable Susan to visit Lizzy and cc's Susan into her emails. Susan is invited to take part in fortnightly parent consultations on Zoom; even though she misses these appointments, the NVR practitioner perseveres and persists in offering new ones. In order to be more enabling of Susan to cooperate in spite of any emotional constraints, we visit her at home, even though, including travel time, this takes up a day's work.

The care team send Susan an announcement. In the announcement, they carefully articulate their belief that Susan may wish to protect Lizzy. They also write about the positive effect that her drug abstinence is having on her child. However, they also point out that the message, Lizzy shouldn't 'listen to them' puts her in conflict with the care team, making it more difficult to feel settled in her current environment. They further elaborate that this message makes it difficult for the care workers to exert their authority and protect Lizzy from her own propensity to act with aggression, use drugs or get into trouble with the police. They emphasise that, as her mother, Susan is the most important person in Lizzy's life, and that therefore the team need her as an ally in giving Lizzy guidance and helping her to thrive. They close the announcement with a positive vision of the future,[2] in which Susan and the team have become mutual supporters in the interest of Lizzy's well-being and healthy development.

Gradually, better cooperation develops; the group home manager, the NVR practitioner and Susan write a joint announcement to Lizzy and deliver it in person to her. In it, Susan acknowledges that she is sorry for the way she often treated Lizzy while she was actively using. The announcement further elaborates that Susan and the team can no longer accept Lizzy's aggressive behaviour, and that Susan wants her daughter to become a happier young person in her daily life – including in the group home – and for her to develop more positive relationships with her care workers.

Lizzy is very moved by the announcement. Instead of angrily storming out of the room, she becomes tearful. Later, Lizzy thanks her mother for the announcement.

Lizzy and Susan are a family facing multiple challenges, while the group home also struggles with complex issues. In such circumstances, it would appear to be common sense to see the mother's current influence on her daughter, her past parenting and Lizzy's trauma as the causational factors in Lizzy's behaviour and therefore consider reducing contact between mother and daughter as a way of ameliorating her problems. Initially, social workers in children's services held this view. Instead, a different route was chosen that initially felt counterintuitive: the care staff proactively pursued the mother's inclusion in their efforts, aiming to establish an alliance with her. This did not preclude resisting her detrimental messages to defy the care worker's authority. Resistance and inclusion were not treated as binary opposites; on the contrary, they were seen as two sides of the same coin: *If we do not resist, we cannot engage with the person.*

While the care workers sought the mother's support in constructively resisting Lizzy's problematic behaviour, they, in turn, offered to support Susan when she had Lizzy in her own home. The shared aims facilitated a sense of 'we-ness', of coherence between everyone responsible for Lizzy's care. Several factors contributed to this interpersonal coherence:

- The residential staff generated trust by intensifying their own contact with the mother, instead of avoiding her or trying to reduce mother/daughter contact.
- The staff team's relational gesture – showing effort to help the mother see her daughter more often – made it more difficult to uphold an adversarial image of them.
- The caregivers' daily contact with the mother addressed her need to feel she matters to her child's development and care. Asking her for advice signalled that they took her knowledge as a mother seriously.
- The hypothesis that the mother's life experiences may have shaped her perception of much of her and her daughter's social environment as fundamentally threatening, enabled the team to consider that her initially problematic behaviour could be understood contextually as protectiveness.
- The positive connotation in the team's initial announcement to Susan – that she may have wanted to protect Lizzy from harm, when she told her daughter not to accept her caregiver's guidance and authority – represented an emotionally safe position towards the mother.
- The care workers validated Susan by expressing appreciation for her success in remaining abstinent and the positive effect of this on Lizzy.
- A practitioner who was associated with the group home, but not a member of staff, persisted in offering ongoing parent coaching, further emphasising the message that the mother was seen as mattering to her child.

All these ways of communicating with the parent represent invitations to join in a more connective relationship and building a caring alliance around her child. Where there is little contact with parents, daily, close engagement with a child and an awareness of their vulnerability will, in my experience, often lead to a critical position towards the parents. This positioning can be seen as the result of a structural artefact which is less bound to personal attributes of the individual caregiver, more the result of traditional ways of residential caregiving or foster care. It would be a mistake to assume that care staff default to an emotionally safe position towards parents. Even if they display a professional manner, their attributions towards them will generally communicate themselves implicitly to parents. Therefore, it is necessary to cultivate an emotionally safe position and internalise the kinds of attitudes that underlie it.

Madsen (2013) stresses that it is imperative for professionals to *generate* a respectful attitude if they are to work collaboratively with multi-stressed families. He suggests only to speak about the family in their presence. This is of course only possible in a purely therapeutic setting, but not in the context of a residential or fostering service. However, such an attitude can be generated by only speaking about family members in the manner in which one would speak about them in their presence. The central question is: *Would you say that, if the parents were here?* Such an organisational culture can be nurtured by agency-based training, team supervision and peer supervision. Ultimately, these modalities should be used in order to enable self-reflection, confront one's prejudices and develop an awareness of one's own privilege.[3] Thereby acquired respectful attitudes enable professional care staff to communicate with parents from an emotionally safer position.

Trust cannot be expected as an a priori condition of the working relationship with parents. However, cooperativeness on the part of the parent can be understood as the possible result of removing the constraint of negative expectations, and the efforts of staff and clinicians to establish close cooperation with parents are more likely to bear fruit.

The child in care: Constructive resistance and connective communication between parent and child

Relationships between young people in care and their parents can often be highly conflictual. Children and adolescents with traumatic experiences may have a high propensity for angry aggression towards their parents and act with emotional abuse, while parents may escalate along with their child, threaten to break off the relationship, or avoid frequent contact. Care professionals can help reduce the potential for conflict. Isla and Oliver's example demonstrates how parent work can support deescalation and strengthen the connection between mother and teenage child.

Oliver is 16. His adoptive parents have recently separated. Due to his drug misuse and his physical violence towards his adoptive mother Isla and the 10-year-old biological son Felix, he has been placed in a residential home. Isla routinely acts in an escalating way. On one occasion, e.g., she sends Oliver vacation shots with Felix and members of another family. In the lengthy text that accompanies the pictures, she writes that he misses out on all this fun because of his behaviour, and if he only changed his ways, he could enjoy being together with everyone. What she intends as a solution has become part of the interpersonal problem of escalation and estrangement. During their phone calls, Oliver often swears at his mother and blames her for his grievances, using misogynistic, obscene language. He also threatens to harm her. The normal sequence is for Isla to initially respond by begging him in a submissive way not to use such language, and a complementary pattern of interaction ensues. After a while however, she starts blaming Oliver for his own situation and her own emotional suffering, begins to shout at him and threatens to break off the relationship, resulting in a symmetrical pattern. For several weeks (and on one occasion months), Isla refuses any form of contact with Oliver; while he suffers greatly from this response, his anger is exacerbated and he continues to threaten his mother by text and voice messages. After any such cessation of contact, Oliver's behaviour in the group home becomes more problematic, including misogynistic attacks on female members of staff and a girl in the group home.

The residential service's NVR practitioner and I reach an agreement with Isla that we will support her communication with Oliver in a very specific manner.

From thereon in, she sends all messages and pictures which are intended for Oliver to the practitioner for editing first, who can then examine them for any escalatory or hurtful potential.[4] The practitioner then discusses amending the message with Isla.

We also practise a communication protocol with Oliver's mother in role play to help her protect herself from verbal abuse, without either acting submissively or escalating verbally. She commits to stop threatening Oliver with cessation of contact, and instead gets in touch with the NVR practitioner when she feels the impulse to do this.

Isla finds the discussion of her draft messages helpful. She learns to approach her son in a non-escalatory manner and becomes able to adhere to the communication protocol. Communication between mother and son improves in the course of several months to the degree that first visits back home become possible. During these visits, caregivers from the residential service support the family by being physically present in the family home, in order to act as a deterrent for Oliver from running away and protect him from drug misuse.

Oliver wishes to express his identity with a certain style of clothing and body piercings. His caregivers find Isla's attitude towards these wishes unnecessarily restrictive. He often rails against her attitude, but even when Isla doesn't express any opposition to his wishes, Oliver expresses anger when making a request. We discuss with Isla that it may be a lot easier for Oliver to have a sense of belonging to his adoptive family, if he feels free to express his different identity. We use an imaginary exercise which aims to support her empathic understanding of Oliver's identity formation.[5] Following this, Isla makes a series of relational gestures aimed at signalling a new openness towards his expression of identity. E.g., she gifts him a pair of "cool" trousers, and on another occasion, Isla gives her permission for him to get a small tattoo. Oliver knows that his mother finds these gestures difficult and responds enthusiastically to them, e.g. by showing the trousers around to everyone in the group home and emphasising that his mother got them for him. His caregivers note that in doing so, his manner comes across as quite childlike in a pleasant way, rather than expressing toxic masculinity.

In a crisis, when Oliver frequently absconds and uses drugs, Isla takes part in a sit-in in the group home, rather than threatening to break off contact. At a later point, Oliver agrees to avail himself of individual therapy.

In this case study, we can identify the mother's initial messaging to her son as a counterproductive attempt to control him, a fruitless way of trying to bring about better behaviour. Omer has described the attitude according to which controlling parent behaviour is intended to have a problem-solving effect as the 'illusion of control' (Omer and von Schlippe, 2016). We endeavour to facilitate a new pattern of communication which is both protective and connective at the same time, by discussing the futility of the mother's initial attempts at bringing about change by trying to control her son; at the same time, we offer a positive connotation of this problematic form of interaction by acknowledging that it was carried out with the intention of protecting her son from his self-destructive behaviour. In this way, it seems to become easier for the mother to recognise the inadvertently counterproductive nature of her attempts. In my view, such positive connotation of counterproductive behaviour supports shame regulation in family members and enables them to become more self-reflective and mentalise more productively.

Deescalating by virtue of using the protective communication protocol prepares the ground for further progress. By helping her to feel stronger in the face of verbal aggression, it helps the mother to reposition herself from being her son's victim back to feeling and acting from an authoritative parental position. This experience of strength enables her to become attentive to and engage with her son's emotional needs, and we are able to take steps towards child-focused practice, resulting in need-based relational gestures which aim to kindle caring dialogue.[6]

The protective communication protocol is easy to learn and practice. Its purpose is to enable parents to protect themselves from verbal aggression while avoiding escalating responses to their child, such as angry aggressive or demeaning communication or rejection. It can therefore be especially helpful where children or young people are in foster- or residential care and where parent-child communication is often fraught with high levels of anxious anticipation and tension. Its use can support NVR practitioners to help parents avoid serious relational rupture with their child.

Method: The protective communication protocol

Offer the communication structure to the parent, outlining each step in sequence and suggesting scripted verbalisations to avoid escalation and promote connection.

Hand the protocol to the parent in writing.

Practice communication following the protocol in role play. It can support the parent to empathise better if they initially take the child's role. Then switch roles, whereby the NVR practitioner interrupts the role play to give feedback to the parent at any point where the choice of words, tone or other conversational aspects feels counterproductive. It is important for all aspects of the communication to be connective rather than rejecting, but at the same time not to signal submissiveness.

'Rule of 1': The parent asks their child only once to refrain from using hurtful or abusive language. It is important for the parent to say this without admonishing their child, using first-person language and speaking in a calm ton of voice. It is also helpful to cultivate a non-aggressive, child-facing posture and body language. The message can be scripted: "Please don't say these hurtful things, they're upsetting and it's not good for our relationship. I would like us to have a really good conversation".

If the young person continues to act in a verbally abusive manner or returns to being verbally abusive at a later point in the conversation, the parent *slowly* (not abruptly) stands up and says: *I want us to have a good conversation. It's not working between us right now. I'll take a break, but I'll come back (call, send a text message) in about (e.g. ten minutes), so that we can carry on with our conversation.* At this point, the parent has already begun to turn around and begins to walk away at a measured pace.

Following their return, the parent resumes the conversation without any reference to the previous disruption.

Should the young person resort to verbal aggression or emotionally abusive language again, the parent again asks their child to refrain from this only once, but with fewer words: *Please don't use those words, it's not good for us.*

Should the young person continue to communicate in an unacceptable manner, the parent stands up again and says in a measure way: *It's not working between us today. I want us to get on well. I'll come to see you again (call again) tomorrow.*

This simple protocol is based on a fundamental principle in nonviolent resistance: not to accept the harmful behaviour of the other person, while avoiding acting in a harmful manner oneself. By signalling that they will resume communication at a later point, the parent avoids harming the child, who might otherwise feel rejected. This is especially important for young people experiencing attachment insecurity, who have been neglected or rejected in their earlier childhood, and who have become further sensitised to rejection by having been placed in care. We can see the use of this protocol as an act of inclusive care. Even where the protocol is used in face-to-face contact and the young person follows the parent, it is an alternative to remaining in contact under duress and coercion; various ways of interrupting the verbal exchange can be explored in role play.

Inclusive authority is especially necessary when responding to children or adolescents who have already been subject to harmful social exclusion, such as young people who have experienced trauma in close relationships, are socio-economically disadvantaged or discriminated against because of race or ethnicity. For example, the rate of permanent exclusion from mainstream education among children from a Caribbean background in the UK is 2½ times the average rate, for Romani children 3.9 times and for children from an Irish Traveller background 2.9 times the average rate (Department for Education, 2020). Traumatic experience in childhood strongly predicts later life socio-economic deprivation (Metzler et al., 2017), which, in turn, becomes a predictor for traumatic experience in the next generation (Doidge et al., 2017). Secondary school behaviour policies can be seen as protocols for escalating exclusionary practices. In spite of the existence of virtual schools or education inclusion services, 40% of care experienced children or children subject to a child protection plan are excluded at least once in years 7–11, while the overall rate is 12% (Jay et al., 2023).

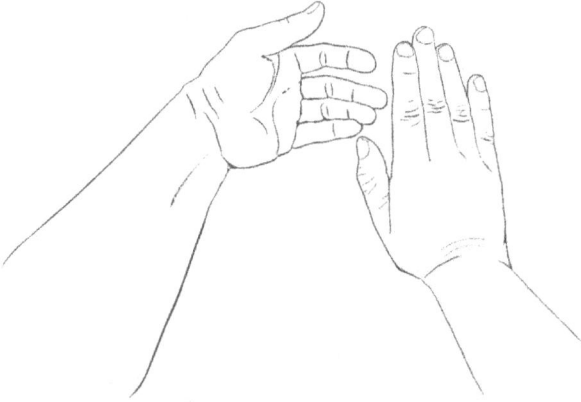

Illustration by Roberta Cramp

Figure 3.1 Both/and of parental presence: Social inclusion and deterrence.

Social exclusion and traumatising experience can form a vicious cycle. Figure 3.1 illustrates the need for adult responses to problematic behaviour that are at the same time calmly authoritative, acting as deterrent, and inclusive, child facing. Exclusion, rejection and disruption of relationships reinforce the trauma-induced sense in the young person that they do not to belong. Seeking a sense of belonging, some young people become exposed to dangerous social contexts in which they risk becoming habituated to their own propensity for acting with aggression, while being put at greater risk of further trauma, by virtue of sexual or criminal exploitation and physical violence. Placing a child in foster- or residential care, while undertaken in the interest of child protection, is in and of itself an act of enormous social exclusion. In order to deter a young person from acting in harmful or self-destructive ways, it is crucial to only use such interventions which can have an inclusive effect, in order to reduce their psychological, material and social isolation and help prevent further traumatic experience in wider social contexts.

Notes

1 See Boszormenyi-Nagy (2014).
2 In various systemic traditions, this is referred to as a 'preferred future'.
3 See Reynolds (2019) for further consideration of the use of supervision in the service of acknowledging structural injustice in clients' lives.
4 The mother's initial comments exacerbated the son's sense of not belonging, a particular vulnerability in an adopted child. See Chapter 13 for an examination of various vulnerability factors in children and young people with adverse experiences.
5 See Part III, Chapter 13/Section "Stimulating caring dialogue in the parent's imagination".
6 See Part III, Chapter 13.

Part II

Resisting the parent's trauma

"Between stimulus and response lies a space. In that space lie our freedom and power to choose a response. In our response lies our growth and our happiness."

Attributed to Victor Frankl

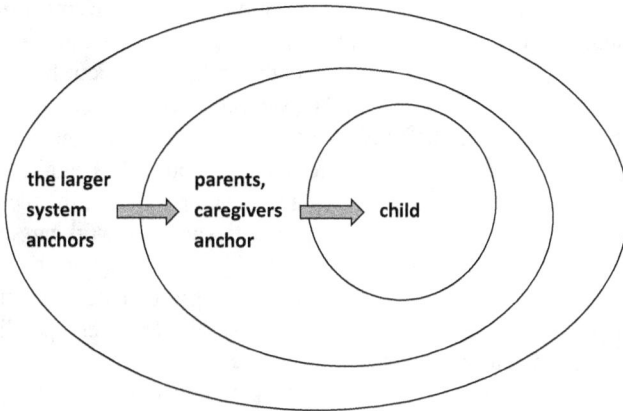

Figure II.1 Parents anchor child.

DOI: 10.4324/9781032717111-7

Chapter 4

Hope-generating therapeutic conversations

Recognising strength and agency

Generally, professionals take a child-centred view, especially when the young person in question has had a high level of adverse childhood experience. When trauma- and attachment theory become grand theory, this can individualise the difficulties that the young person is experiencing and distract from their parents' or caregivers' difficulties. Parents usually engage with an NVR practitioner from a position of having a profound sense of helplessness and only a vague expectation of an improvement in their situation. They tend to expect improvement 'from the outside', such that a professional should somehow be able to effect a change in the child's behaviour by working with them directly – but they will not trust in their own competence and feel they have little or no agency themselves. The helplessness of parents who struggle with their own traumatic experiences and a sense of erasure can be profound. In a parallel process, the professional working with such parents may also develop a sense of helplessness; they may very well become entangled in counterproductive ways of working, such as making suggestions which, when rejected as unworkable by the parents, are followed by 'even better' suggestions. It can seem as if parent and professional are getting sucked into the whirlpool of the same narrative of impossibility and inescapability, without being able to throw a glance above the surface.

It is a particular form of problem-saturated, pathologising victim narrative when parents are in their totality seen as victims of their child, the child is seen as the victim of their earlier life traumatisation, the family is seen as the victim of inadequate service provision (notwithstanding the fact that service provision is often inadequate), or the child may be seen as hitting their parent simply because they have been in some way victimised by this very parent. As previously discussed, one of the therapist's central tasks can be to help the parent generate *their own* narrative of victimisation, which is free from blaming, pathologising or devaluing attribution; a narrative that can help them restore their sense of dignity. In the transition from compassionate witnessing to appreciative witnessing, the focus of supporters who are members of the caring community around the family shifts to the parent's agency and competence, in order to strengthen not only their expectation of self-efficacy in the near future, but also to help generate hopeful expectation in the supporters themselves. I have called the kind of new narrative that can then emerge in co-construction between client, therapist and supporters a *self-narrative as resistor* (Jakob, 2021; Jakob and

DOI: 10.4324/9781032717111-8

Sarah, 2021). The parent becomes the protagonist in a self-told narrative which tells of how they influence the very social environment that impacts on them, as they move within it. It becomes a narrative of relational self-definition.

The structure of the resistor narrative

Resistor narratives and victim narratives are structured differently. One possibility for encouraging a resistor narrative is to introduce the linguistic structure of a resistor narrative into therapeutic conversation (Figure 4.1).

Thematic shift: From obedience to resistance

In the obedience theme, someone is or is not obedient, should be obedient, needs to be made to be obedient – e.g. a child *never* carries out parental instructions, parents *must* act in certain ways or there will be negative repercussions, the other parent, a social worker, someone *needs to ensure the child's obedience* by some means that are not at the parents' own disposal. Parents with experience of early childhood abuse or domestic violence who have learned to use submission as a self-protective strategy often employ language associated with obedience in reference to themselves and their child: *I'm not even allowed to invite my friend to our flat. I'm always walking on eggshells. He won't let me. Social services are making me...*

When the therapist first acknowledges the parent's feelings that are associated with their narration of obedience-themed interaction, and then introduces language that is associated with resistance, a thematic shift can occur, one which invites a parent to re-position themselves mentally as someone who can act with self-determination rather than simply being reactive, even if acts of resistance appear difficult to carry out.

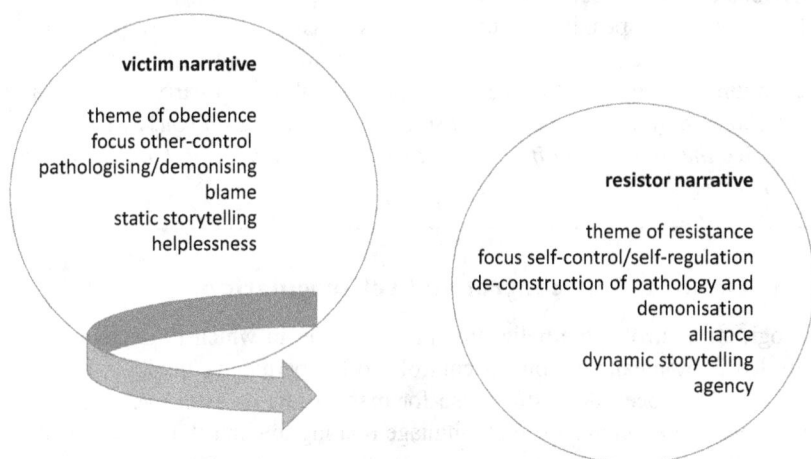

victim narrative

theme of obedience
focus other-control
pathologising/demonising
blame
static storytelling
helplessness

resistor narrative

theme of resistance
focus self-control/self-regulation
de-construction of pathology and
demonisation
alliance
dynamic storytelling
agency

Figure 4.1 Victim- and resistor narratives.

Method: Introducing the theme of resistance

Identify situations in which your client feels subordinate to their child or to another adult. Acknowledge the difficult emotions that are associated with this kind of subordination.

Ask permission to raise the question of how they could experiment with regaining their autonomy in small, specific ways. Ask them to identify one particular situation in a concrete way and describe to you what they would do, even if they do not believe they could carry it out at this point.

Invite them into role-play of this specific act of disobedience:

So you feel you can't even sit in your own living room and watch something you'd like to on the TV, so you go to bed early and watch it on your laptop, instead. You feel embarrassed that it has come to this. Can we speak about what it would look like if you took back just a little bit of personal freedom at home – even if just thinking about it makes you worry there could be an argument or worse? ... OK, so you'd sit in the living room for an hour longer, but you're worried he would start shouting at you and threatening... Let's just try out what it might look like, if you did it, and how you might deal with the repercussions, or even pre-empt what he does.

Acknowledge the client's fear of repercussions, but do not treat it as an obstacle to carrying out their autonomous act. If you were to speak about how the client could do this without fear, you would not only introduce an unrealistic scenario, but also give the message that they cannot act assertively if they feel anxious. However, self-regulation of their psycho-physiological arousal using grounding techniques or anchoring themselves in the presence of a supporter to effect co-regulation can be considered to help reduce their anxious arousal from an extreme to a more bearable level. Use conditional language when speaking about the child's possible negative response, but unconditional language when speaking about the parent's disobedience, to communicate your confidence in the parent's ability to carry out such an act:[1] *So he may start shouting and screaming. You've said you'll wait it out, or leave the living room if he doesn't stop or threatens you, but do it again the next day.*

Thematic shift: Self-control and self-regulation

The logic of control – the belief that the only way in which to overcome being controlled is by means of counter-control – often permeates thinking in families where there has been domestic abuse for many years or even over generations. When there is predominant use of language relating to control, the idea of control of the controlling person as the only avenue for change is maintained. This leads to a defeatist attitude due to the impossibility of counter-control, or into escalating cycles of interaction when counter-control is attempted. Abandoning the illusion of control can cause great emotional discomfort and be a liminal experience: the parent gives up what may feel like the only expectation for change and moves into an unknown relational space. At the same time, it can be a liberating experience, as the parent frees themselves from the compulsion to try to achieve the impossible: *I don't have to try to make him be polite to his teacher, because I can't make him do it anyway.*

Abandoning the illusion of control can open conversational space for possible solutions that are associated with parental *self-control* and *self-regulation*. Parents become more able to consider what they may do to raise their presence, how this might affect their child and their own state of mind, how they might protect themselves in constructive ways, provide guidance to their child or act as a role model and support their child in developing positive values (Omer, 2011). Self-control means to escape from a destructive behavioural pathway by resisting the impulse to either act with angry aggression or to yield submissively to the child's coercive demands.

For parents who have had traumatic experience, a further dimension is to resist the impulse to remain passive once a critical incident is over. Rather than 'letting sleeping dogs lie' or 'not rocking the boat', we can extend the motto *Strike the iron when it's cold* by adding *but make sure to strike it!* For example, instead of saying nothing when a daughter has used abusive language with her mother, a father can plan how he will bring up the subject of her verbal aggression in a way in which he will, as best possible, keep his psycho-physiological arousal within what trauma theorists call the *window of tolerance*. In other words, he can plan, together with the NVR practitioner, how he will practise self-regulation or co-regulation with another adult to develop a better prospect of constructive communication with his child, after resisting the impulse to simply avoid any kind of proactive response. This parent will be able to imagine – and later experience – that taking action will not necessarily result in yet another catastrophic encounter, if careful planning takes creating the right kind of conditions for their emotional self- and co-regulation into account. Eventually, this parent's arousal baseline will become lower, their thinking will be less threat-determined and their expectation of self-efficacy can grow.

Method: Focus on self-control, self-regulation and co-regulation with supporters

Specific questions relating to self-control can enable a shift from a control orientation to a self-control orientation. These are questions which invite the parent to imagine acting with self-control and psycho-physiological regulation, e.g.:

How will you resist your own impulse to avoid taking action, when you take the first step and make an announcement to your son? Which supporter's presence will be calming enough so you don't get overwhelmed by anxiety? What is it about this person that will help you to see this through? Once you've seen it through, what will it mean for you that you've achieved this? How will this encourage you to take the next step, even though it won't be easy?

It is important not to ask *whether* the parent might be able to act with self-control – this could invite an internal sense of inefficacy, but to ask *how* they will do it: *So you know that you're prone to lose it if he makes that face. What will tell you when you need to (leave the room, sit down, lower your voice)? How do you know you can do that?* Such questions normalise powerful affect, while inviting imagery of self-control, which, in turn, is more likely to modulate how a parent actually communicates in the real-life situation.

Always use *unconditional* language when discussing the parent's future proactive resistance, in order to communicate confidence in the parent's ability to raise their presence.

If the parent cannot answer your self-control-focused questions, this does not mean they will be unable to exert self-control; it merely means they have rarely imagined being able to act in such a way. Wait patiently and encouragingly until you get an answer.

Thematic shift: Deconstructing demonisation, de-pathologising families: parent and child as 'more than the problem'

In many systemic therapy traditions, problem-saturated narratives of the person are seen to maintain interpersonal and emotional difficulties. These are accumulations of stories that are often told in similar ways, and in which a person is cast as mentally ill, inadequate or fundamentally troubled. By defining the person in such a way, a narrative can be pathologising: the person looks at their image in the contorting mirror of these stories and becomes more likely to act in the manner they are depicted.

Many kinds of narration can elicit self-doubt and confusion, becoming a constraint to solutions. These are rife with descriptions of inadequacy, such as a disablist narrative of a person who has experienced trauma; they can demonise, such as when the person is cast as being intrinsically evil. All such narratives share common structural elements: they reduce the description of the person to very few traits, which are generally negative and derived from a kind of obscure 'essence'. This obscurity renders it impossible to actually investigate the credibility of the claims made about the person (Alon and Omer, 2006); they become a kind of reductive 'absolute truth'.

Members of the larger system around the family may be rendered in demonising attributions. For example, social workers involved in child protection may be described as *destroying the family* and *wanting to take children away*, or, conversely, as *doing nothing to help us....* In each case, there is an ascription of negative intentionality or an uncaring attitude.

The method of thematically shifting from blame to alliance does not entail challenging the claims made in demonising or pathologising narratives, but rather widening the framework within which claims about the person are made. In this way, the pathologising narrative loses a structural element, which is the reduction of the person's description to only a few traits. Widening the narrative frame can open space for new, encouraging stories of parents or children.

Method: Widening narrative frames

Ask the parent, caregiver or people in the immediate social environment around the family questions that open space for the investigation of previously hidden or hardly noticed aspects of the person, and which open space for richer descriptions, e.g.:

What do you love about your daughter, even if it hasn't met the eye for a long time? What will it mean to you when this trait of hers becomes more apparent once again? What will be the first sign that it is beginning to come to the surface again?

In what other way could the social worker talk to you? If she did, what would you notice about her more than you have done so far?

So, the psychiatrist has diagnosed depression, and you're asking yourself whether it's depression that makes you feel helpless? Someone asked once: Is it depression, or is it oppression?[2] If it's oppression, what difference does it make to how you feel about yourself? About how you deal with the challenges in your daughter's behaviour? What will feel different once you've called your supporters together to resist this oppression that everyone in the family suffers from? How will you see yourself in a different light, once you've taken this step? How will your image of yourself as a parent, as a person change?

Further open, curiosity-guided questions can thicken the de-pathologising plot.

Thematic shift: From blame to alliance

Self- or other-blaming statements are often an expression of the deep sense of helplessness parents feel who have been subjected to abuse for much of their life. People in the larger system around the family, including professionals, will also often show a propensity for directing blame at family members. Often, the interest child or their siblings will blame parents, foster carers, residential carers or social workers, sometimes by making false allegations of abuse (notwithstanding the fact that allegations of abuse made by children are generally credible).

Blaming communication is very common, where the narrator feels helpless and individuals who have genuinely or allegedly perpetrated some form of abuse or neglect remain inaccessible, such as one of the mother's previous partners, grandparents who have neglected a parent when they were a child, or, from the point of view of residential carers or foster carers, the parent they believe must have treated the child badly because they are showing problematic behaviour after having spent some time in the nuclear family. Blaming processes can spread throughout the family system and the larger system around the family and lead to increasing alienation between family members and between parents or children and other caregivers, teachers or further significant others. I consider this alienation to be the result of relational rupture emanating from the shaming quality of blame: too much blame designates the other person as deeply flawed, and when people are shamed, they tend to shame the person they have been shamed by when they feel unable to regulate their shame (Weinblatt, 2018). Shame is strongly associated with trauma (DeCou et al., 2023), and it is therefore reasonable to assume that parents and children with abuse histories will often risk feeling overwhelmed by shame, and therefore counter-blame frequently, leading to injurious escalation.

Instead of fruitless efforts at questioning the content of blaming statements, the therapist can invite clients or others associated with the family to shift thematically from blame to what Grabbe (2012) has called the *language of alliance building*. Grabbe sees the offering of connective alliances as generating resilience. These can be offers of support to parents, between parents, or from the parents to the child, whose harmful or self-destructive behaviour they are resisting. NVR practitioners can invite such a thematic shift by asking questions about past or present experiences of constructive alliances, or future possibilities of alliance building. It is important to note that here alliances are not seen to be formed against a person, but in regard to overcoming an externalised problem.

Method: Introducing the language of alliance building

The practitioner enables conversational space for the parents' need for support to be verbalised and heard. It is important to focus on these needs alone – they are not intended as conversations about anyone's opinions about anyone else. When working with two parents alone, the practitioner can ask each to parent to listen carefully to what the other parent needs from them. Where there is tension or serious disagreement between parents, such as after a difficult separation or when one parent is very critical of the other, it can be helpful to slow down conversation and use techniques which can generate empathic understanding and compassion, such as the interview of the internalised other (Tomm, 2014a).

Using questions focusing on alliance-building communication can help shift away from a blaming mindset: *So, you have sometimes been troubled by the feeling that something may be deeply wrong with Frank. You've told me that you often feel that his shouting, his threats and the way he blames everybody else (!) may have destroyed the family. Shall we speak about what steps you might take to help the whole family heal? I understand that you want to make it clear to Frank that you won't accept his harmful behaviour any longer and that other adults will support you in this. In what ways will you feel differently, once others stand by you in this? Who could this be? What is it about your neighbour that makes you feel, she might fit the bill? How will your neighbour need to talk to Frank, so that you feel strengthened and have greater freedom to act? How can your neighbour show Frank that you are no longer alone in this? How would you like her to show Frank that she likes him and values him, even if she doesn't accept his shouting which she can hear through the wall to her flat? What kind of relational gesture could she use to show Frank that everyone is on his side, too, that nobody wants to embarrass or expose him and that you have brought her into this so that she can help everyone in the family?*

Note that the questioning in this example moves on from acknowledging the parent's pathologising thinking and the associated feelings, to first elicit imagery of alliance building between parent and neighbour and then encourage imagery of alliance building between the neighbour and the interest child.

Thematic shift: From static to dynamic storytelling

Static forms of storytelling trap the mindset in an endless problematic here and now. They generalise and leave no space for the perception and appreciation of exceptions to the problem, for the possibility to learn from these exceptions and for the encouragement that comes with the appreciation of exceptions. There is no representation of change over time. In this way, static narration shows many similarities to traumatic memory, in that it represents always the same repetitive interaction sequences, with no before and after. As in traumatic memory, the sequences are not embedded in broader contexts and therefore appear to make little sense – like a GIF, static narration always represents an extremely brief, truncated version of perceivable reality. As in traumatic memory, there is a sense of inevitability to events occurring in the ever same manner, nothing new can be expected, no change effected. The most conspicuous linguistic markers of static, regressive narratives are the present tense and generalisation: *George **always** upsets **everybody**, shouts and throws stuff around. Even the dog **is** scared of him. He **never** puts his dirty clothes away, **I'm always** the dogsbody who does all that. **I feel** sick when he comes home from school.* The linguistic shading of this account closely resembles the qualities of a traumatic flashback in all its vividness and its sense of inevitability.

The generalising adverbs perpetuate this sense of inevitability: *He **always** gets angry. I can **never** say no.*

Progressive storytelling, however, has a wide narrative arc and is richer in description. The accounts that are given tell of change processes and the contexts that are relevant to change. From a social constructionist point of view, they not only portray reality of the family's and its larger system's social interactions in a new and often fresh way, but in a reciprocal process also impact on the social reality that is being depicted. In this way, progressive storytelling has the power to encourage new social realities by creating a perspective of change and new ways of responding to harmful behaviour.

Instead of challenging a static narrative, the practitioner can invite parents, caregivers and supporters to generate new and encouraging storytelling by introducing linguistic markers of progressive narration into the conversation.

Method: Generating progressive storytelling

While empathically mirroring the parents' experience, you can thaw frozen narratives by replacing generalising words with more nuanced descriptors:[3]

Parent: He **always** shouts at me if there's **anything** he doesn't like! I'm **always** like paralysed, I can't say **anything**!

Therapist: *He shouts at you **much too much**! That's really hard. **So many times** you haven't felt able to say anything.... You said last week something happened that was **different**. Can you **tell me more** about that? How you **resisted**?*

Stretch the time frame of the account by introducing past and future tenses, and ask questions which require answers that differentiate between past, present, near and distant future. When you do this and different content comes to light, you can ask about the parents' attributions of the differences:

I understand Marianne has recently been violent. When was the last violent incident? So that was about a month ago? That means that last month has been the longest period so far without any serious incident like that? How do you make sense of that? ... What have you done to contribute to that? ... What have you learned about yourselves, about your child, about nonviolent resistance, while you have been doing these things? How has Marianne reacted recently when she hasn't gotten what she wanted? ... So, not ideal, but she hasn't been violent. I wonder whether these are the first signs that she may be learning to deal with frustration better? What would you like to do in the coming days and weeks to support her learning to cope with frustration?

Thematic shift: Heroic narratives of resistance – from helplessness to stories of agency

The purpose of all the thematic shifts discussed here is to help co-create narratives in which parents recognise and experience, often in an embodied way, their agency in dealing with problematic interaction, gain confidence and develop a greater expectation of self-efficacy – in spite of the many setbacks they experience. Setbacks are common in most change processes, but can be more frequent and more severe, when there has been traumatic experience in the family.

Arthur Frank (2013) has investigated different narrative forms in relation to severe physical illness. Drawing on his personal experience of chemotherapy, he describes a so-called *restitution narrative* in which medical professionals are the protagonists within a curative framework, one in which all relevant processes aim at restoring physical health. The patient is not an agent in their own right, is not seen to contribute to their own healing. This narrative form provided no space for Frank's own experience of emotional and relational chaos at the onset of his illness, nor for the way in which, beyond patienthood, he shaped and influenced his own life and coping with illness. He writes:

> I increasingly resisted the restitution narrative, especially how it positioned the physician as the protagonist and relegated me to being the object of that protagonist's heroism. I was certainly part of this story, but it could never truly be **my** story.
>
> (preface, p. XIV)

Here, we see a parallel to the kind of narrative that is often imposed upon parents and caregivers. In such narratives, parents and children with traumatic experience are seen to embody an individualising diagnostic category of dysfunction, such as 'posttraumatic stress disorder', 'borderline personality disorder' (or, more recently, 'EUPD'), 'depression', 'substance abuse disorder' or 'attachment disorder'. Once such a category has been applied, it becomes the origin of the 'official' narrative of the family or the child, and the professionals who are dealing with child and family and are seen to be imbued with expert knowledge that is singularly superior to other forms of knowledge within the family- or within the larger system around it. Professionals become its heroic protagonists, who are engaged in the restoration of child or family. This is a psychiatric-psychological story of the family and their healers; it can, harking back to Frank, never be *their own* story.

Frank juxtaposes the restitution narrative with a quest narrative. It's form enables, in my view, several requirements to be met:

- It can describe how the parent or caregiver copes with chaos;
- It can capture how they contribute to the shaping of their life, and
- They can take back definitional power in their description of self.

A quest is a journey into the unknown, a search for a highly valued prize, in which the protagonist – in NVR, the parent – faces many challenges and constraints to their progress. There are many dangers along the way, which they are initially unaware of. The route is not a given; it must be established in the process of moving through unfamiliar territory. The parent-protagonist experiences recurring setbacks which they can learn from, and in the recovery from which they become more skilful and competent. Though the protagonist often feels alone, there are always other wayfarers who will come to their aid – in NVR, supporters. The strangeness of the terrain, and one's own uncertainty, are offset by increasing determination and personal strength, which grow with the experience of facing many challenges. The chorus of Rhiannon Giddens' song *I'm on my way* (2018) characterises the kind of orientation that is both required and generated by a quest:

> I don't know where I'm going, but I'm on my way
> Lord, if you love me, keep me, I pray
> A little bird is stretching out in the shimmering, shaking blue
> Don't know where I'm going. But I know what to do.

When in this book I discuss heroic resistor narratives, I see them as taking the form of quest narratives. For such a narrative to emerge, a therapist needs to practise deep listening (O'Hanlon, 2005), to create conversational space for the parents' experience of chaos and uncertainty, invite the parents to position themselves in their accounts of their current lives and their past as agents of resistance, to act as an increasingly trustworthy and trusted compassionate witness to the parents' emotional pain while becoming an appreciative witness of their growing resilience and agency – and to assure *themselves* of the support of emotionally safe colleagues in the process. In such a way, the NVR practitioner becomes a guide for the parent into and through what is as of yet unknown.

Notes

1 Growth mindset research demonstrates that communicated beliefs in the ability of another person to change in respect of a particular trait can predict the actual degree of change in that person (Murphy and Gash, 2020).
2 See also Wade (1997).
3 O'Hanlon, O'Hanlon and Beadle (1999) have called this method 'Carl Rogers with a twist'.

Chapter 5

Parental presence and self-perception

Parental presence lies at the heart of Omer's construct of new authority (Omer, 2011); raising presence is seen as quintessential to the NVR-based change process. For the purposes of working with parents who have experienced trauma, or parents or caregivers to children who have had high levels of adverse earlier childhood experience, I focus on three aspects of parental presence: *physical-spatial presence, systemic-interpersonal presence and embodied presence.*

Physical/spatial presence

Parents with traumatic experience will often avoid the physical space a child who is behaving aggressively inhabits. They may do this intentionally or automatically, with the purpose of lowering their often very high level of psycho-physiological arousal and avoiding the possibly extreme anxiety that can arise in the face of threatening child behaviour. As will be discussed later, reversing this behaviour by intentional, well-planned and carefully executed self-exposure to the threat of possible aggressive or dismissive child behaviour can help parents reduce their own anxiety to a bearable level and become more able to engage their executive functioning. Raising their physical/spatial presence in this way will have a positive, reconnective impact for parent and child, as it reverses the constant relational rupture that has ensued due to avoidance – which is particularly salient when a child has experienced neglect in the past. At the same time, it can promote the parent's own recovery – entering the child's room in carefully arranged conditions can become a therapeutic process for ameliorating the impact of trauma on the parent's emotional wellbeing. Crucial in this process is for the parents to develop an embodied sense of their strength and recognise their growing ability to provide guidance and support to their child by spending significantly more time in the young person's proximity.

Children with traumatic experience also need parents to raise their physical-spatial presence. Too often, such young people may have remained unprotected when witnessing or being subjected to physical or sexual violence when a non-offending parent was physically absent, had reduced awareness of the harm

DOI: 10.4324/9781032717111-9

done to their child due to self-medication with drugs or alcohol, did not have the capacity to protect them because of their own fear of a domestic abuse perpetrator, or was suffering from psychological difficulties that emanated from abuse by another adult, such as being depressed or even dissociative. Against the backdrop of such circumstances, a child will be prone to associate the physical absence of their birth- or adoptive parents or their foster- or residential carers with earlier situations, in which they experienced existential fear. Once the adults who have learned to fear and avoid the child enter re-enter their space, the opportunity for the child to begin to heal also emerges.

Systemic/interpersonal presence

The sense of threat emanating from angry-aggressive child behaviour can be even greater for parents who have had traumatic experience, while young people who have been abused may escalate at an extremely fast rate. While they may have initiated the escalation themselves, e.g. to gain a certain advantage over their parents, their traumatic experience can drive a flight or fight response very quickly and their level of psycho-physiological arousal will shoot up rapidly. Parents or carers often use images such as *He just sees red, She's like Jekyll and Hyde* or *He's blind with rage* to express how they experience the child in such situations.

To help ameliorate their – sometimes extreme – subjective fear of threat and experience a safety anchor, these parents may need the physical/spatial presence of an emotionally self-regulated supporter, in order to raise their own presence with their child. In the heat of the moment however, a parent who has experienced abuse may even lose their subjective, embodied awareness of the presence of the other adult, as we see in Rhianna's example:

Rhianna has invited her friend Jasmine to a therapy session, to prepare a sit-in with her 14-year-old son Damien following a violent attack on her.[1] Damien pushed her up hard against a wall, screamed in her face and threatened to punch her after she had refused to give him money. This incident left Rhianna severely bruised. Having in the past either yielded to Damien's threats, or apologised to him in a submissive manner and saying she had no more money, Rhianna had now decided to refuse his demands for money, apart from his weekly allowance, because she no longer wanted to be controlled by his threatening behaviour.

In the past, Damien had witnessed domestic violence against his mother, first perpetrated by his father and then by two further partners of his mother's, over the course of several years.[2] Early on in therapy Rhianna said that "he (has) the same eyes like his dad when he sees red". Damien is of Black-Caribbean heritage on his father's side, and Rhianna initially struggled with inviting her supporter to the session. Whilst we discussed and sought to discredit the racist assumption that Black teenage boys are inherently dangerous in the previous session, Rhianna nonetheless feels an intense sense of shame in this regard. Notwithstanding this feeling, she needed to "take the leap" and invite her supporter, in spite of her fear of shame. We discussed this as an act of resistance against the racist shaming of parents and their children of colour, by not allowing the racist infusion of shame to deter her from requesting support.

In the actual session with Rhianna's supporter, we undertake a risk assessment in regard to the planned sit-in; Rhianna still struggles to look at Jasmin. I ask her to imagine Damien is sitting on the empty chair while she says the opening words of the sit-in, and ask what response she expects. Rhianna answers that he will threaten or slap her. When I ask her whether he is likely to do that in Jasmin's presence, Rhianna appears surprised and admits, she has completely forgotten that Jasmin will be present – even though Jasmin is sitting next to her this very moment. She acknowledges that it is very unlikely he will show any violent behaviour in Jasmin's presence, but instead storm out of the room.

In this case, it was necessary to remind the mother that her friend would be present at the sit-in, to arrive at a *realistic* assessment of risk. Powerful internal forces were likely to have been at play in losing awareness of her supporter's physical presence: fear of shame, hypervigilance and a dissociative response to the internal expectation of threat.[3] This example illustrates the way parents who have experienced trauma may be prone to feel completely isolated and cut off, losing all subjective awareness of the presence of a supportive other.

Here, it becomes necessary for the practitioner to help the parent re-direct her attention to the physical presence of the supportive other person.[4] Interpersonal responses from within the support network can counteract traumatic responsiveness and provide moral support to the parents. The (literally) perceived presence of the supportive other liberates the parent, at least temporarily, from the overwhelming sense of existential threat and complete sense of isolation that emerge, when hypervigilance focuses their attention entirely on expected or real threat signals. Re-directing their attention can enable the parent to co-regulate their psychophysiological arousal with an emotionally safe supporter and thereby activate their social engagement system (Porges, 2011, 2015). This in turn can help them raise their presence with the child in a situation that is fraught with tension, so they do not act submissively, distance themselves by showing a *flight* response, *freeze with fright,* become dissociative, lose energy and surrender to fate as in a *flag* response, or show an angry-aggressive *fight* response. Instead, systemic presence enables very different kinds of embodied responses.

Embodied presence

When they do not respond traumatically, parents can communicate their agency not only explicitly, but also implicitly in their body language, facial expression, prosody of voice, choice of words and in their decision-making. Systemic presence supports such embodiment of calm and caring, yet decisive and self-assured parental strength.

Sensorimotor approaches to therapy are concerned with the impossibility of self-preservation and self-protection in situations that are experienced as threatening; the original traumatic experience gets locked into the very physicality of the person (Ogden, Minton and Pain, 2006; van der Kolk, 2014). These approaches seek to bring about change by promoting mindful attention to not yet consciously perceived action tendencies and by experimenting with different kinds of posture and movement (Ogden and Fisher, 2015). I would like to propose an integration of the sensorimotor mindful attention and the solution-oriented understanding of exception. By planning and then taking action in ways the parent has not yet felt capable of, focusing attention on the supporter's embodied presence in the room, and developing an interoceptive focus on one's own embodied response to the supporter, an exception to the problem is created in a solution-focused sense. In a given context, the parent not only demonstrates behaviour which is different from their previous response pattern, but can also become aware of a different bodily response. The therapist can help actualise the parent's experience of exception in the session, help the client anchor their experience, and make it available for future challenges. This in turn helps strengthen the parents' self-efficacy expectation in regard to the next step they wish to take – a step that previously may have seemed impossible due to their traumatic reactivity.

Instead of asking questions such as *How will you be able to switch the wifi off at night?*, the practitioner can express that they expect nothing else of the parent than to be able to take such action. They do this by bringing the embodied memory of previous parental agency in convergence with imagery of a future act of nonviolent resistance. An imaginary process is an implicit, analogue mental representation – there is no *if, whether* or *but*, no *yes* or *no* in the realm of imagination, only *that* – *a* concrete, anticipatory experience which diverges dramatically from previously encoded expectations (Beckers, Jakob and Schreiter, 2022).

If, as trauma theory stipulates, traumatic experience is connected with implicit, or embodied memory of a sense of having been unable to respond successfully to threat, then we should conversely be able to assume that implicit, embodied memory of responding successfully to threat exists and can be re-evoked in order to help parents imagine they will able to resist successfully in the future. In sensorimotor therapy, thwarted 'action tendencies', that are often not even yet felt as impulses, can create a sense of success in response to an experienced threat, once they are mindfully brought to the client's awareness and lead to motor action. We will explore the possibility of bringing embodied experience of success in resistance into convergence with generating imagery of success in a future challenge.

Method: The moment of strength

This method follows five stages:

1   Create exceptions to the problem by carefully crafting, planning and carrying out constructive resistance using methods designed for parents in NVR, such as the announcement, refusal to give in, a sit-in, or making

relational gestures. These must be acts of resistance that, while not easy to carry out, are nonetheless within the parents' reach;

2 Once the parent has carried out such an act of resistance in a real life scenario, ask them to bring up the memory of this exception and identify a moment in this memory during which they feel *good about themselves as a parent,* in touch with their values, experience a sense of agency, etc.;

3 Ask them to localise a body sensation that corresponds to their experience of self in this moment;

4 Ask them to imagine the next step they wish to take while evoking the body sensation associated with the previous exception;

5 Carefully plan the actual execution of this next, more challenging step.

When planning a future act of resistance or care, which a parent has not yet felt able to accomplish, use their embodied memory of previous, successful NVR action as a resource.

– Ask the parent to choose a memory that feels particularly significant in regard to the future challenge from their 'archive' of NVR action. Memories of action which the parent had previously avoided or never thought they could engage in are an especially valuable resource. If the parent feels 'blocked', you as the therapist can suggest a memory of constructive action they have carried out. Make sure that the chosen memory has similar situational features as the next NVR step they are aiming to undertake.

– The client should choose the moment within this memory, at which they begin feeling their own agency. Ask them to stay with this moment in their memory, e.g. by 'hitting the pause button'. Help the client intensify their experience by asking them to focus their sensory awareness, using the present tense: *Look around the kitchen. Notice the feeling of the chair you're sitting on. Is it warm or cool in the room? Notice how bright it is. What do you hear, what do you see? Look at Angie (supporter), look at Craig.*

– Continuing to use the present tense, repeat what the parent says as they recall this *moment of strength,* in order to strengthen its emotional salience: *So you and Angie are sitting in the kitchen and you're looking at Craig, and even though your heart is beating fast and you didn't think you could read the announcement to him, and even though you're scared he could start swearing at you Angie, the words start coming out of your mouth. You're surprised at yourself and you notice your voice getting stronger. This is the moment you realise: I can do this!*

Ask the parent to localise the body sensation that is associated with this memory of strength in the very moment. They may be able to describe the body sensation, but if they cannot, it is sufficient for them to simply tell you where they feel it and if it *feels good*. If the parent localises an unpleasant body sensation, ask them to search further until they localise the body sensation that is actually associated with the success. Continue to repeat, in the present tense, what the client tells you:

Notice where you feel something in your body at that moment, when you hear your own voice and you realise: I can do this! OK, so you can feel it in your chest. Stay with it for a while. Is it a pleasant sensation? Ok, so it feels good, like your chest has become flexible, you can breathe. Where else to you feel something? OK, so your shoulders, the back of your neck feels different. Do you feel it anywhere else? So, your throat feels open; you notice that you're sitting upright, not stiff or anything, but just upright. What's it like to sit upright like that?

Give your client some time to become more aware of their embodied experience of strength, so it can establish itself further. Now you can move on to *anchor*, i.e. to create an associative stimulus for this embodied experience, which your client will be able to evoke at a later point when it is needed:

Staying with this positive experience in your body .... What image, or what word, or what impression fits with this experience of your own strength? So, it's: BREATHE... OK, so you can think: BREATHE, and you can be aware of yourself breathing. Good, notice yourself breathing right now, and notice how your breathing is connected to the sensation of strength in your body, your throat open, your chest can move, sitting upright... good, OK.

Ask your client to evoke the embodied sensation of strength by themselves, using the *anchor* they have associated with it. Repeat this a few times, until the parent feels they can do this easily.

At the next stage, again using the present tense, ask the parent to envision the challenge they will face, while at the same time evoking the body sensation of strength. Ask what in their mind's eye the parent sees themselves doing – It is important to ask what the parent sees or finds themselves doing, rather than asking what they need to do or could do:

You've decided you don't want to give Craig extra money any longer... So, think BREATHE... let the breathing bring back the experience of your strength in your own body... It's ten o'clock, and you're refusing to give Craig extra money, just like you told him you would. What do you find yourself doing? How do you find yourself talking to him? What do you notice about yourself? So, he's shouting at you and threatening you, and your heart is beating fast, but you notice that you feel determined. Do you find yourself saying anything else, or do you remain silent? So, you're saying: I have to do this, it's for the best, for both of us ... So, he storms out of the room. As he storms out of the room, you find yourself saying: good night. What does your voice feel like?

At this point, it would not be helpful to ask *Do you believe you could do this?* Using conditional language could communicate doubt or uncertainty rather than a firm belief in the parent's ability to carry out their intended action. We have discussed earlier how growth mindset theory stipulates that communicated positive expectation of growth in regard to a specific trait in another person often predicts such growth (Wolcott et al., 2021). It is more productive to end this imaginary sequence with a comment such as *Tell me about it next week.* In this way, the context markers of your communication with the parent frame the conversation in the unconditional realm of *that*, rather than the conditional realm of *whether or not*. As the practitioner, you implicitly communicate your confidence and trust in the client's agency.

Working with the moment of strength can help parents rapidly shift into a functional state of consciousness when previously, conflictual situations have stimulated powerful threat responses. This functional state is not one in which the parent experiences *no* emotional discomfort. However, while they may still feel anxious, afraid of being shamed in front of another person or fear physical aggression, their level of psycho-physiological arousal will have been reduced sufficiently for them to become able to draw on their internal and interpersonal resources. It is therefore important to create therapeutic space for the expression of unpleasant emotion and heightened psycho-physiological arousal *in spite of which* the parent will be more able to act decisively and with an experience of personal strength.

Neuroscientific research has demonstrated that extremely high psycho-physiological arousal is associated with deactivation of the medial prefrontal cortex, while other brain regions become highly activated, especially within the limbic system. Siegel (2012) outlines the functions of the medial prefrontal cortex as (27-2 to 27-3):

1   *"Body Regulation* – keeping the organs of the body and the autonomic nervous system coordinated and balanced.
2   *Attuned Communication* – tuning in to the internal state of another.
3   *Emotional Balance* – enabling internal states to be optimally activated: not too aroused, not too deflated.
4   *Response Flexibility* – pausing before acting to reflect on available options for response.
5   *Fear Modulation* – reducing fear.
6   *Insight – self-knowing awareness* that links past, present and future. This is a mindsight map of 'me'.
7   *Empathy* – imagining what it is like to be another person, to see from another's perspective. This is a mindsight map of 'you'.

8 *Morality* – imagining, reasoning and behaving from the perspective of the larger good. This is a mindsight map of 'we'.
9 *Intuition* – having access to the input from the body and its nonrational ways of knowing that fuel wisdom."

Siegel further elaborates that these nine medial prefrontal functions go hand in hand with neural integration – the very opposite of the kind of psychological fragmentation or disintegration we see in traumatic reactivity. In my clinical experience, reducing psycho-physiological arousal using the *moment of strength* seems to help reactivate these functions of the medial prefrontal cortex. What does that mean for the relationship between parent and child?

Well, attuned communication with their child, empathy and morally motivated caring responsiveness for their child require a parent to become liberated from their subjective experience of existentially threatening, pervasive victimhood; they need to feel they are not fighting for sheer survival. As we will see in Chapter 12 in more detail, parental self-regulation, which utilises imagination and embodiment as well as co-regulation between parents and supporters, can promote co-regulation between parent and child and eventually better self-regulation in the child themselves. A child who has experienced or witnessed abuse in their own right, will respond with great sensitivity to any dysregulated behaviour of their caregivers, automatically associating the adult's response with anxiety or hostility. When however the adult becomes anchored in their embodied experience of strength, it modulates their expressed emotion in such a way that they no longer communicate anxiety, fear or aggression as they did before. When they repeatedly experience their caregivers as unthreatening, and able to convey protective strength, children can begin to feel more emotionally secure. This, in turn, prepares the ground for more successful co-regulation between adult and child.

The moment of strength can create a greater expectation of self-efficacy in regard to specific parenting challenges. Bandura (1983) established on the basis of numerous studies an inverse relationship between anxiety activation and self-efficacy expectation: if a person believes that they will be able to act competently in certain situations, they will be less anxious in anticipation of their challenge, more likely to expose themselves to these very situations and act with greater success – thereby lowering their anxiety further.

Parents have a right to become liberated from a victim state of consciousness. At the same time, this liberation can promote embodied parental presence – a prerequisite for better attunement to the child at a later point, and the ability to eventually engage in dialogue that is concerned with care of that child.

Notes

1 A majority of parents who suffer violent attacks by their adolescent offspring are female, while the majority of young people instigating such attacks are male. Police reports demonstrate that single parents are disproportionately affected, though it is uncertain whether this is representative of the general population (Holt, 2013).

2 Witnessing male partner violence correlates highly with later adolescent violence against mothers, but not against fathers. Some studies only show a correlation of witnessing male partner violence with male, but not female violence against mothers (Holt, 2013).

3 Perception of the actual physical environment, self-perception and memory can all be affected during a dissociative response.

4 Chapter 9 introduces an imaginary, sensorimotor-based method for supporting this process.

Chapter 6

Hope and self-confidence

An NVR trainee complains: *That moment of strength thing looks pretty good, but **my** clients are **much too traumatised** to even trust themselves to risk an announcement. How can they build up their sense of agency if they have **no self-confidence at all**?*

The emphasis on *my* clients seems to tell of isomorphism, a parallel process between parent and practitioner, in which the helplessness of the NVR practitioner mirrors the helplessness of parents who have experienced abuse in their own life history, or adoptive parents, foster carers or residential carers, who are struggling with secondary traumatising experiences relating to children in their care.

We can look for answers to this colleague's question in solution-oriented and narrative ways of working. Both focus on expanding the client's self-efficacy and sense of agency. While a solution orientation foregrounds immediate self-efficacy in the here and now, narrative ways of working also create conversational space for re-storying past life experiences. In this way, they can enable a transition from narratives of the parent as victim, which are constructed by others who are in different positions of power relating to the parent, to a self-told narrative of victimisation and the person the parent feels they are. Beyond that self-told narrative of victimisation and person, they can finally move on to construct narratives of self as resistor (Jakob, 2021; Jakob and Sarah, 2021).

Solution-oriented questions in NVR

Parents who have persistently experienced an external locus of control over their lives often struggle to recognise their own impact on the social environment around them. Similarly, the experience of parental erasure, which emanates from an internalised sense of no longer mattering, will undermine the awareness of their own parental agency. Nonetheless, a parent's agency can be identified, if they and we look closely. As mentioned before, *any* nonviolent act of resistance as a parent, *any* act which a parent has carried out and which they may not have thought possible, constitutes an exception in a solution-oriented sense. Active listening by the NVR practitioner is important. The therapist very simply asks parents to speak more about the exception that they believe to have identified, however insignificant it may initially appear.

DOI: 10.4324/9781032717111-10

Parents, and many professionals, often measure a parent's success by the immediate reaction a child shows. This can be even more the case with parents who, due to their past experience of abuse and their sense of erasure, feel highly determined by external events – for them, it will feel they have failed, if the child expresses displeasure in any way in response to constructive action the parent has undertaken.

With this in mind, it becomes important to attribute success to the parent's ability to act in a new, presence raising way. Once a parent has been able to persist in showing constructive resistance, *in spite of anticipated negative reactions* from the child, they have been successful. The attribution of success to the parent's ability to respond constructively in the face of aggressive, dismissive or otherwise harmful child reactions creates a more internal locus of control: the parent can feel more self-determined, when they exert self-control under duress, self-regulate and interact in the manner they have prepared rather than reacting in an anxiety-driven or anger determined way. NVR practitioners can invite parents to appreciate themselves for these achievements, and exceptions gradually become a more normal part of the parents' repertoire.

When parents more frequently act in such self-determined ways, children are more likely to begin accepting these new parental behaviours. With Tomm (2014a; 2014b), I see emerging new forms of interaction within a family as 'transforming interpersonal patterns': patterns that mark a transition from a previously established more problematic form of interaction within the family to a new, not yet fully established modus vivendi. It lies within the therapist's power to stimulate such transforming interpersonal patterns (TIPs) by cultivating in themselves an openness to perceiving and appreciating even the most apparently insignificant small signs of difference in the parent's response to their child. We, as professionals, are part of the changing system, and our sensitivity to and appreciation of difference can powerfully promote positive change. Like a tiny green shoot of a tender plant breaking ground, such a new TIP can be nourished by our constructive inquisitiveness and appreciation. Eventual and more positive child responsiveness can be explored, once the unilateral difference in the parental way of communicating with their child has been thoroughly established.

His adoptive parents having divorced several years ago, 13-year-old Julian lives with his adoptive mother Agatha and her partner Christian. Julian has refused to go to school, has played games on the internet at night and slept during the daytime. Neglected by his biological parents in early childhood, Julian witnessed his birth father's domestic violence against his birth mother and became a victim of physical violence. Later, he acted with physical violence himself; e.g. when Agatha attempted to regulate his use of the internet by no longer providing round the clock wifi access, Julian attacked and injured her. This sort of physical aggression even occurred in Christian's presence, who felt unsure how to respond whenever Julian would begin to show angry-aggressive behaviour, but would then restrain him when the aggression reached a dangerous level.

For quite some time, Julian has no longer been exhibiting this sort of physical aggression and has overcome his day/night reversal. He is also attending school more regularly. However, as the therapist's supervisor, I am initially more interested in differences in the adults' response patterns and differences in their perception of Julian as I interview Agatha.

Agatha: *I think, Julian has been feeling better, more secure in himself, and we haven't been punishing him, we absolutely haven't been punishing him.*

Author: *How have you managed to help him feel more secure in himself without punishing him?*

Agatha: *By telling ourselves, we can do something about it, we can do it, and this is what's going to happen.*

Author: *What's the biggest difference in what you and Christian do?*

Agatha: *That we just turn the wifi off at night, that's what's been making the biggest difference.*

Author: *So you've noticed that as adults you respond differently now than you used to. You've persisted in turning the wifi off at night. Is that difficult?*

Agatha: *It used to be really hard, really scary, but it isn't that hard any more, he's used to it now.*

Author: *So you're doing some important things differently now, and you can even see changes in Julian?*

Agatha: *I think, he must have, he must have been ashamed you know, and I think he's not so ashamed of himself any more. We just have ... you know, we've always had good moments, they never disappeared altogether. But now, you know, there are a lot more of them, more than the not so good moments. He doesn't have the same kind of temper tantrums like he used to, I mean not so extreme. He hasn't attacked me for a long time. He still gets stressed, doesn't regulate himself well, but now he's been learning to find his own solutions, like when he gets stressed because of school. I think he's got more confidence, and that's good for our relationship.*

The conversation with Agatha illuminates several important aspects of the emerging narrative of change within the family:

*   Change is attributed by the parent to her and her partner's *persistently* different responses to the young person. Determination and a positive expectation are described as the main factors that have enabled such different responses, and one can infer that these attitudes communicated themselves to the young person in an embodied way.
*   The different responses by the parents are initiated in spite of the apparent risk and the fear of negative repercussions. The narrative outlines a process of the young person's habituation to the new parent responses. This, in turn, helps reduce the parents' fear.
*   The mother distinguishes between her refusal to give in to self-destructive behaviour – staying on the internet at night – and threatening punitive measures. She merely '*disobeys*' by de-accommodating his day/night reversal, but does not threaten any '*consequences*'.

- Increasing parental agency, determination and reduction of fear are described as being commensurate with an improvement in the young person's own emotional wellbeing and increasingly constructive behaviour, such as facing stressful situations at school rather than avoiding them. Having previously coerced his mother and her partner to accept his school avoidance by threatening violence, he is now exposing himself to stressful situations.
- Parental agency seems to be commensurate with parental attunement – the mother expresses her sense that her son has had to struggle with feelings of shame, but also that he now appears to be less overwhelmed by shame.

In the above narrative, unilateral parental action is described as seminal in bringing about change. Change in the young person's responsiveness is described as resulting from the difference in parental attitude, behaviour and emotional self-regulation – the young person is described as 'getting used to' this difference. His 'temper tantrums' are no longer as severe or dangerous as they were before. The mother does not believe that *she* needs to change the child – he finds 'his own solutions'. She expresses not only greater confidence in her own ability to withstand threatening behaviour, she also communicates greater confidence in her son's propensity for transformation, and sees his own, more constructive behaviour, as 'good for the relationship'. It is at this point, not earlier in the process, that we see reciprocity emerge between mother and son.

Most important in this vignette is the emphasis on the unilateral action by the parent and the invitation to construct a narrative of *interaction in transition*. This requires centring exceptions to the previous problem patterns that have been brought about unilaterally by the parents in our therapeutic conversation: *How have you managed to help him feel more secure in himself without punishing him?* It does not require great therapeutic acumen to help facilitate further growth of a TIP. Simply asking the parent to speak more about their unilateral action clarifies what has already been achieved, however small or insignificant it may have appeared until now. This clarification, in turn, can help build parental confidence and growth. What is examined under a magnifying glass proves to be a lot larger that it seemed.

Method: Storying acts of resistance as exceptions to the problem

- Treat *any* constructive act of resistance that has been planned in the NVR session and later carried out by a parent as an *exception to the problem* in a solution-oriented sense, and create ample conversational space for this exception in the therapy session.
- Ask open, curiosity-driven questions, focusing on how the parents were able to exert self-control and eventually practise self-regulation. When asking such questions, refer to traumatically induced or reinforced

constraints to self-control and self-regulation, *in spite of which* the parent was able to act in the way they had planned to, e.g.:

How did you manage to walk into your son's room in spite of feeling so scared he could get violent?

You went to town with your supporters to look for your daughter at the usual hangouts, in spite of having felt so hopeless earlier on. What motivated you to do that?

How were you able to wait until the next day, after you'd spoken to your friend about it, to tell your son in that calm but firm way that you're going to subtract the money he's stolen from his allowance, without getting drawn into an argument?

When you felt so utterly distraught, you called your supporter instead of your son's abusive father – did that happen all by itself, or did you remind yourself to call her instead of him?

You told me that in the past, you were too ashamed to tell people what happens at home, and that you didn't want to be a burden. How come you told your supporters this time that your daughter spat at you and hit you? And asked them to talk to her about it?

For months you felt helpless when your son attacked you, and you were too scared to go into your own living room – and this time, you had a sit-in after he pushed you the day before. How did that come about?

So your mother told you you've got to punish him hard, but you told her in a polite but firm way that you need something else from her than that kind of advice? In the past, you would get very quiet when she'd tell you how to parent, and you would remember the way you yourself got hit when you were a girl. How did you find your voice this time?

- Ask the parent to identify their success by their own ability to act, in spite of traumatic and other constraints, before you explore any possible different responses from the child.
- Clarify with parents that it is unrealistic to expect not to feel any traumatically elevated emotions any longer, in order to be able to act. Normalise traumatically elevated emotions. Here, it can be helpful to introduce a new perspective:

It's normal to feel scared (angry/ashamed) after what you've been through. But you can still resist, in spite of this feeling. Eventually, the fear will get more manageable, as you stop avoiding doing what you need to do and don't give in to it.

- Be observant of anything that indicates a parent has spontaneously initiated a transforming interpersonal pattern and explore this with them thoroughly. When there has been an in-depth description of this event, you can ask the parent what the next step in line with this act will be.

- At a later point, you may wish to elucidate different kinds of child responses to *repeated* or persistent exceptions in the parents' unilateral action. Two common ones are:

  1 The child begins to tolerate a parent's refusal to give in to controlling behaviour, or the parent's acts of resistance against harmful or self-destructive behaviours, and
  2 The child shows first small signs of thriving that superficially do not appear to be linked to the reduction in harmful behaviour, e.g. an indication of being more confident in a particular lesson at school or an act of kindness towards another child. It can be helpful to make sure to contextualise exceptions in child behaviour by associating them with exceptions in the parent's behaviour:

You went to see the teaching assistant and apologised to her for your son spitting at her the day before, even though he refused to come along, and you recorded your conversation to her and sent it to his phone. The following day, he helped her get over a stile during the class outing. You've told me both these things in the same breath. Where do you see the connection?

- Ask about interpersonal support from within the support network/caring community. Several perspectives on interpersonal support can be helpful:

  1 How did the supporter contribute to the transforming interpersonal pattern you are discussing?
  2 What quality or aspect of the relationship may have motivated the supporter to act in this way?
  3 In what way was the parent able to constructively make use of the supporter's contribution? For example:

How exactly did your supporter talk to your daughter about this problem? It was pretty involved, coming over to your house to talk to her. What is it about you and your family that made her want to talk to her? How have you been making good use of her conversation with your daughter?

Re-authoring the life stories of parents who have experienced trauma

The colleague whose misgivings were shared at the beginning of this chapter is not yet satisfied:

But I have a client who has never been self-determined. All her life, everyone in the family was dominated by her father, humiliated and physically abused. And now, she's being controlled by her children. How can there be a resistor narrative in such circumstances?

O'Hanlon (2005) has drawn attention to the way in which therapeutic models and the mindsets they generate limit our possibilities for helping clients, referring to this as 'theory countertransference': our expectations of a client are strongly influenced by the theoretical perspective that underlies our therapeutic work, and these expectations, in turn, modulate and restrict how we interact with and perceive that person. Such an orientation guides us to focus on certain aspects of a client and their relationships and draws our attention away from others. It thereby shapes the structure of the therapeutic relationship and the forms of interaction that become established between therapist and client.

'Trauma' concerns the dynamics of psychological injury. Freud's conceptualisation of this medical construct in his sexual aetiology of 'neuroses' has been roundly criticised as pseudoscientific (Cioffi, 2022). Nonetheless, the notion of the need for 'repair' of traumatic injury has become a paradigm of theory building in the mental health field. We can see some justification in trauma theory's endeavour to identify psychological injuries as precedents of later emotional problems. However, we can also be mindful of the risk of becoming oblivious to factors which underlie healing processes yet are not problem focused, such as internal and interpersonal resources and new experiential possibilities in relationships. None of these aspects are concerned with the 'repair' of original trauma. Olthof (2017) emphasises that we need a therapeutic framework which can generate multiple narratives of the reality of clients' lives. He sets forth that none of these narratives should be seen as truth or valid per se, but that each one of them contributes to our depth of understanding. He quotes the Dutch cartoonist Toon Hermans (2010):

> I think that if you can muster the patience to spend your entire life painting pictures of potatoes, and only then, you might end up learning what a potato is. Every day you will see new shapes and colours. The potato will look different each time, not because the potato changes but because you yourself are constantly changing and constantly comprehending that potato from within a different inner world.
>
> (exhibition placard)

While Hermans can draw new perspectives on a single potato over the course of a lifetime, we can take things even further from a social constructionist point of view. The potato is a fixed entity; we change, not the potato itself, but the therapeutic relationship is a subject-subject rather than a subject-object relationship. Unlike a potato, the parent we work with is not located outside of this relationship as an entity unto itself, but influenced in a dynamic interplay with their therapist, who, in turn, is influenced by them. Perceptive constraints and new perceptive possibilities become part of this dynamic interplay. Without constructing the therapeutic frame Olthof proposes, we run the risk of privileging just one single perceptive possibility that originates from a theoretically restricted inner world, and thereby severely limit the array of relational responses the practitioner may develop. We risk closing down many different options for change if we remain rooted in trauma theory alone, when hitherto unrecognised resources in the parent, caregiver, supporter and their relationships with one another remain outside of our awareness. If we observe a parent and interact with them merely from within the perspective of their traumatic injury, we only see and position ourselves as towards a victim with little agency. In doing so, they and we – inadvertently – miss out on becoming aware of a magnitude of possibilities of change. It is as important to open oneself to a multitude of facets of healing, as it is to understand psychological injury and emotional wounds.

One aspect we can add to our observational framework is the history of resistance in a parent's life, it's understandings and interpretations, and how it presents openings for further inquiry. While their resistance may not have been recognised and appreciated by people around them – including professionals – even parents who have suffered from severe abuse in their life histories can be seen to have resisted. These stories need to be told.

To illustrate how a new storyline of resistance can emerge, I will return to Amanda, whose resistance to a transgressive professional was described earlier.[1] The events below preceded her resistance to the social worker's dangerous and coercive communication.

Only after a peer supervision session it becomes apparent to me that I have paid little attention to an important aspect of her life history: Amanda became pregnant at the age of 16, giving birth to her eldest child at 17. It is only at this point that questions come to mind about Amanda's potential ability to cope and resist: How will her abusive father have reacted to her teenage pregnancy? How will she have dealt with his reactions? What strength did it require of her to carry and give birth to a child in such circumstances? How did she find such strength?[2]

As the story unfolds, I begin to see a new and very different Amanda. We co-construct a new narrative of her life and person, as she tells me about the events of that period. While pregnant, Amanda 'ran away from home'. At first, she understands this as an account of personal weakness and cowardice – attributes which reflect the definitional power her father and later her partner have held over her. However, I am curious about her motivation to leave the family home as a teenager. Eventually, Amanda appreciates that questions around this are not aimed at undermining her sense of self and no longer stimulate traumatic reactivity:

"I'm sure you had a good reason to leave. What made you want to take this on yourself, as a teenage girl, and pregnant?"

Her answer articulates a caring, protective attitude towards her unborn child, and her resistance against her father's emotional and physical abuse:

"I didn't want my child to grow up in this atmosphere and have to go through what I did".

Her response to my next question shines a light on Amanda's resilience:

"How difficult was it to do that, for your unborn child?" to which she responds

"I was scared, really scared".

"And nonetheless, you did it. That must have taken a lot of courage? How did you find the courage to see it through?"

"Because I didn't want my child to have to go through the same things I had to".

"Did you do this all by yourself, or did anyone help you?"

"I talked to my friend about it, and she told me to get out. That's where I stayed the first few days".

The case example illustrates the idiosyncratic way in which we can generate new perspectives. Taking Olthof's understanding of a multi-dimensional therapeutic framework into consideration, this is neither the 'correct' perspective nor the 'true story' of my client, but simply what followed on from an opening of my own mind. It appeared to have been linked to my own family history: after speaking about my client's teenage pregnancy in peer supervision, I remembered my own mother's survival in war-torn Czechoslovakia as a single young woman with an infant born out of wedlock. This spurred my curiosity and the questions that I then asked my client. Another therapist's inquiry may have gone down an entirely different route and could have been equally or more productive; my opening perspective merely proved to be a *useful* one. From a pragmatic point of view, this client's act of self-determination may not have been seen as successful – external circumstances soon dictated her return to the parental home – but we became able to co-create a new historic narrative of her as a person: she had been able to act towards her unborn child in a way that was caring and protective, she showed courage and resisted abuse, and she had been able to utilise an important interpersonal resource in her friend and her friend's parents. Such an understanding of oneself can motivate new acts of constructive resistance in the here and now. In this client's case, she felt encouraged to resist emotionally abusive and physically aggressive behaviour by her son, but also verbal abuse by a neighbour and by certain members of the larger system around the family: *I'm not a pathetic stupid woman. I'm someone who can do what's necessary!* This re-generated confidence also contributed to her resistance to the social worker who had been acting in a dangerous and coercive manner towards her.[3]

From an NVR perspective, the relationship with her friend and her friend's parents, who allowed her to stay in their home, is especially significant. We see here an early pattern of an interpersonal resource; their moral and practical support had an encouraging effect on my client as a young person. This is a template for the growth of personal agency in interaction with others who have positioned themselves in emotionally safe ways. The client's self-efficacy is not just an individual trait, but also a dynamically growing, interpersonal attribute. If in trauma-focused work with NVR we carefully facilitate the expansion of a well-structured caring community, we can maximise such an effect.

Re-storying one's life history as a narrative of resistance was first introduced by Alan Wade (1997) into the canon of systemic therapy. Wade's premise is that resistance against threat or ill treatment is fundamental to the human condition. Patriarchal interpretations of 'resistance' can obscure resistance that does not conform gendered norms. These can narrow our understanding in such a way that we frail to interpret important historic acts of resistance as such. As a result, we are less likely to form resistor narratives relating to people who face structural and societal injustice such as women, members of LGBTQI communities, differently able people, people with economic disadvantage, people belonging to ethnic or racial minorities, children and adolescents. It becomes our therapeutic task to widen our own perspective, so we can recognise acts of resistance and create space for these in therapeutic conversations, generate previously untold stories (Rober, 2017) and thicken the plot.

Historic narratives of resistance can make valuable contributions to the re-telling of personhood. A parent can move away from being defined by others who have held power over them; eventually, they can migrate to becoming the protagonist of a self-told survivor narrative and eventually, of a self-told resistor narrative (Jakob, 2021; Jakob and Sarah, 2021). Beginning with such a historic narrative, resistance can become part of the framework within which valuable descriptions of the person are generated. Constructive acts of resistance can then become a substrate upon which such descriptions begin to feel more credible to a parent who has previously been wracked by self-doubt and beliefs of personal insufficiency.

A fusion of various frameworks can be useful in developing understandings of the person-in-change within their family and the larger interpersonal system of which it is a part. I would like to suggest some perspectives that have proven to be helpful:

1 A trauma-informed perspective, which can do justice to the parent's previous life experience of abuse and its psychological impact in the here and now, along with the impact of re-traumatisation by child behaviour, which has become associated with earlier abuse;
2 A systemic perspective, according to which there can be structural isomorphism, or mirroring, between pathologising interpersonal processes in the family of origin, the current nuclear family, and the larger system the family is embedded in;
3 A resource- and solution-oriented perspective, which can illuminate resilience on the personal and interpersonal levels in the here and now;
4 Wade's framework, which re-stories parts of the person's life history as a narrative of resistance, and
5 A perspective embedded in principles and understandings of nonviolent resistance, which helps recognise how personal resources become actualised in interaction with supporters in the growing caring community. This perspective offers concrete methods of resistance that can inform the planning of constructive action, and such acts, in turn, become a learning environment for future resistance while reinforcing the credibility of the resistor narrative in the parent's own eyes and in the eyes of others (Figure 6.1).

Integrating such different theoretical perspectives, rather than privileging one alone as grand theory that promises to explain everything can help avoid, in the words of the writer Chimamanda Ngozi-Adichie (2009) 'the danger of the single

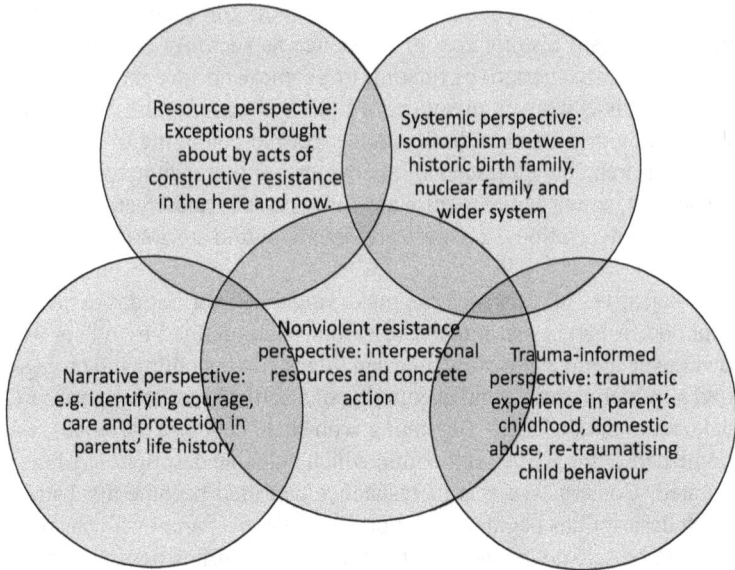

Figure 6.1 Therapeutic perspectives.

story': a narrative that would merely yield a two-dimensional image of the parents and their process of change. If even a potato can be depicted in a myriad of ways, how many images of a changing person in all their social dimensions are possible! These are images that influence and shape our expectations of parents. Our expectations, in turn, modulate the ways in which we interact with them and influence their capacity for change.

Co-creating significance: Attributing meaning to constructive acts of resistance

White and Epston (1990) put forward a foundational, existentialist premise in narrative therapy: the meaning of what clients do in the course of therapy is not a given, but rather becomes co-constructed collaboratively between therapist, client and the wider social environment. Many parents who have experienced ill treatment struggle with an existential absence of meaning in significant relationships. This can induce a kind of inertness or apathy which manifests itself in what are often diagnosed as 'depressive symptoms'. The lack of reciprocity and mutuality in the relationship with their child can reinforce their sense that they do not matter either to their child, or in themselves – yet such a sense of mattering is a large aspect of what shapes their identity and gives meaning to their lives (Beckers, Jakob and Schreiter, 2022).

When parents do not feel validated by their child's responses, in particular, the child's acceptance of their care – when *caring dialogue* between parent and child

(Jakob, 2019)[4] does not flourish – it can be necessary for parents to attribute meaning to their *unilateral* acts of care and constructive resistance. Here, meaning-generating questioning becomes a valuable therapeutic instrument for supporting clients to escape the profoundly discouraging feeling that their parental, and perhaps their entire existence is senseless.

Method: Meaning-generating questioning

Associate questions that elicit a sense self-efficacy, with questions that invite parents to attribute meaning to their action, e.g.:

Self-efficacy questioning: *This time, when you visited Ben at the therapy centre (a residential centre for adolescents who have sexually abused children), you found that you were able not to act as if everything was ok when he blamed the girl he had abused. You didn't raise your voice or put him down but, if I understand you correctly, you just said that you can't accept it any longer that he blames the girl for what he did, and that, if you just went to MacDonalds with him and went to buy him new trainers, you'd just be acting as if nothing had happened. But, you stayed with him at the centre, for the whole length of the visiting time, even though he scowled at you and swore under his breath. In the past, you found it really difficult to respond in the way that you just did, because you were afraid of Ben rejecting you, and you were afraid of getting angry at him. How did you manage to act in the way you did on this occasion, in spite of the anxiety you felt, and keep doing it in spite of Ben's reaction?*

Meaning-generating questioning: *What do you think Ben can learn from the way you firmly but calmly resisted when he denied his responsibility? ... You yourself endured this kind of abuse by your brother. What message is this kind of resistance against Ben's denial giving your sons about how girls' and women's dignity must be respected? How are you helping them to grow into respectful young men? How is your resistance against sexual abuse changing you as a woman? Do you see a way in which your efforts might help the girl heal from Ben's abuse? Ben is suffering from a lot of the repercussions of his own acts. How do you think your resistance against him denying his responsibility could help him lead a happier, more fulfilled life in the future?*

This kind of meaning-generating questioning[5] emphasises the desired longer-term effects of the parent's constructive resistance. Bringing self-efficacy questions and meaning-generating questions in conjunction with each other raises the likelihood that the parent will attribute positive meaning to their own action. The questions need to reflect the parent's values; in this case, as a survivor of child sexual abuse herself, the mother holds a strong value that it is important for girls and women to be treated fairly and with respect. She cares about her sons' wellbeing and wants Ben to eventually live a better life than in the residential unit, and she wishes to feel close to him once again, but for this to come to fruition, she needs to be able to see him as an upright young man who respects the dignity of girls and women.

Meaning becomes embedded in one's own righteous behaviour, not in the immediate reaction of the young person. Success is attributed to the capacity for such *meaningful* action, which is carried out in spite of the constraints that pave the way. An attitude, whereby a person can feel free from needing an external or pragmatic success in their persistent endeavour has been explored by Kool (2007), who researches nonviolent personality characteristics. Following on from Hindu philosophy, he calls this attitude 'anasakti', and considers its formulation to be a therapeutically valuable concept: most of our personal difficulties are seen to emanate from not attaining external goals or worrying that we will lose the fruits of our efforts. If we can liberate ourselves from this urgent need, we can become more emotionally balanced and healthier. In fact, Pandey and Naidu (1992), who operationalised anasakti, were able to demonstrate that high levels of this trait are associated with better mental health. This is of course of particular importance for therapists who work with parents who have experienced severe abuse, or are struggling with what Weingarten calls common shock.[6]

I would like to highlight what I consider to be three important ingredients of meaning-generating therapeutic conversation:

1 An openness to the parents' perception of their own agency as they carry out nonviolent constructive action. This is expressed by using questions motivated by the practitioners curiosity, which, in turn, can support parents to evaluate their own action in a positive way.
2 Targeted, meaning-generating questions, that accord with the values of parents or caregivers, can help them to attribute meaning to their action and encourage them to persevere.
3 To attribute meaning to their actions can help caregivers develop fortitude even, or especially, in the absence of immediate external success, i.e. changes in child behaviour. An attitude of freedom from the need to see immediate changes in child behaviour can help promote better emotional balance and mental health in parents.

More strongly motivated, persistent, determined and emotionally balanced parents and caregivers will be in a better place to anchor young people who act in harmful or self-destructive ways, especially those who have experienced abuse or neglect in their own right. They will be even be in a better position to do this when they face serious setbacks.

Notes

1 See Chapter 1.
2 At this point, we see a shift in perspective, from a trauma-oriented to a particular resource-oriented viewpoint.
3 See Amanda's resistance against her son's social worker's intrusive behaviour, Chapter 1.
4 See Part III.
5 See also the case example of Christina, Benjamin and Liam in Part I.
6 See Introduction: PTSD or 'common shock'?

Chapter 7

Overcoming setbacks

Many people who have had traumatic experiences are likely to suffer setbacks in their process of change, especially if functional states of consciousness have not yet become well established; they may be prone to fall back into traumatic reactivity when things get difficult. Setbacks are, however, not only individual events, but manifest themselves on different levels of the system, ranging from anxiety- or anger-driven behaviour of individual family members to the reenactment of previous problematic or pathologising interpersonal processes (PIPs) in the nuclear family, to attitudes, beliefs and decision-making in the wider system, including professional networks around the family. These latter attitudes can lead professionals to position themselves in ways that are critical and prescriptive, or even dangerous and coercive. We can then see the emergence of what St George and Wulff (2014) call socio-cultural interpersonal patterns (SCIPs), which can work their way into the family's own interaction and subject parents and children with institutional injustice. Morgana, a therapist, was negatively affected by the critical-prescriptive positioning that re-emerged within the professional network at the point of a setback within the family:

"NVR remained ineffective in the case of the Brown family. The trauma-induced aggressive behaviour of 13 year old Leon has further deteriorated and his mother's depressive symptoms have returned. We are convening a professionals' meeting for the purpose of developing an alternative new care plan for the family".

Morgana, a therapist in our service, receives this invitation, which reflects the language used in a report by a local consultant psychiatrist. She had previously closed the case due to improvement. Like a stone thrown into water, the effects of this message seem to spread out in concentric circles. In our team meeting, we discuss that there may be an isomorphic process at work, in which certain difficult emotions felt by family members are mirrored in emotions experienced by professionals in the network around them. However, this mirroring results in professionals assuming to 'know' about this family that 'belongs to the social underclass' and communicating about them in pathologising ways. In response to the tenor of the invitation, Morgana feels disheartened and incompetent. She comes across as low and powerless in our team session, and we ask ourselves whether her response may mirror feelings that her previous client might experience during this setback, but which may be exacerbated by responses of professionals around the family?

DOI: 10.4324/9781032717111-11

We hypothesise that there may be several motivating factors involved in bringing about this kind of reaction within the professional network. One of these could be a medical-psychological discourse, according to which it is taken for granted that a very senior professional should have knowledge about the clients which is deemed superior to their own. Therefore, this professional is seen to objectively evaluate the mind-states of the family members 'from the outside' and 'from above'. We believe that the vertical power differential has resulted in a determination of family members, and the privileged voice of the senior professional is set to gain prominence within the wider system, leading to prejudicial decisions that pre-empt any discussion not only about, but also with the family and with all professionals who have had experience in their care. Such a kind of discourse can feed into a restitution narrative, according to which senior professionals hold the power to heal and the people who are receiving treatment do not figure as protagonists in their own narrative.[1] We believe that the setback has been understood as a setback by and in the family alone, and that it is, in an un-reflected way, seen to be indicative of their underlying, untreated, severe pathology. Morgana feels that the narrative, which is expressed in the invitation to the professionals meeting, along with the attached psychiatric report, has had a discouraging effect on her, because it denotes the family itself as having failed, as well as the work she has undertaken with them.

In our team meeting, we begin to deconstruct the narrative offered by the invitation, by focusing on unquestioned assumptions and 'untold stories' about the family and the therapeutic process:

- The invitation makes no mention of any improvement in the course of therapy. However, our case notes indicate that the case was closed after three months without any aggressive incidents, while there had been near daily incidents prior to referral. Further reasons for closing the case were that Leon had increasingly shown signs of thriving, and his school attendance had become more regular.
- *The phrase "...his mother's depressive symptoms have returned" raises a number of questions: If the symptoms have **returned**, there must have been some initial improvement. What improved? When did this improvement occur? How did it manifest itself? Which measures and responses supported this improvement? The case notes indicate Leon's mother had reported feeling much better and was reducing the doses of anti-depressant medication and her consumption of alcohol and cannabis significantly.*
- *The conclusion, that "NVR remained ineffective..." is drawn from the unquestioned assumption, that 'real improvement' is only assured, when therapeutic gains have been fully maintained. This assumption can be seen to be rooted in a curative view of therapeutic care, according to which only the absence of 'symptoms' is indicative of the restoration of mental health.*
- *The purpose of the meeting, stated as developing an "alternative, new care plan" implies an agreement among professionals that the work with NVR and associated interventions such as NVR-informed family support work have been*

unsuccessful, thus marginalising the information our team holds and which has come from family members themselves. Our conclusion is that NVR has proven to be effective, and we do not accept the un-reflected assumption, that a new care plan with alternative measures is necessary.

In our tentative conclusion, there appears to have been a temporary setback within the family and professional network around them. Therefore, there is no need to assume that Morgana's therapeutic efforts, and those of the family members, have been unsuccessful.

First in our team meeting, and later in conversations within the professional network, we investigate the information we hold within an understanding that the family are likely to have been experiencing a (temporary) setback. A phone call with Leon's mother informs our thinking. It appears that the setback began after Leon, who is on the autism spectrum, learned that his father, who had been convicted of inflicting grievous bodily harm, was soon to be discharged from prison. With fear cascading within the family, and Leon finding it difficult to express his emotions, his own fear was quite likely to have become channelled into aggression, which, in turn, will have further exacerbated his mother's already high level of distress given the father's pending release. In this phone call, she also expressed that she had gone back to avoiding Leon's physical presence because she was scared of his controlling behaviour and was again "walking on eggshells", i.e. acting submissively.

Given the precedent of the father's pending release to the re-emergence serious difficulties within the family, it is plausible to assume this a temporary setback. Rather than seeing it as 'rooted in deep pathology', we can instead consider that this may be an understandable response to violence. In the professionals meeting, we are able to shift the focus of the conversation from what have been seen to be immutable personal characteristics, to an understandable resurgence of pathologising interpersonal processes. We share our view that, while the new transforming interpersonal processes may not yet have been established well enough to weather the storm of a violent perpetrator's imminent release from prison and the threat this poses to the family, more productive interpersonal processes could re-emerge, if the family were to receive the necessary support, and if professionals were to acknowledge that their current reactivity is normal to the context of domestic abuse. Our conversation moves on to what measures may help the family weather this crisis, and how certain members of the professional network could take on protective roles and help mother and son reduce their arousal levels. Leon's social worker discusses this care plan that has been informed by previously marginalised information and understandings with Leon and his mother, who also agrees to a fast-tracked re-referral to Morgana.

Let us consider that in different contexts parents are likely to inhabit different states of consciousness. For example, they may be able to quickly shift from a traumatic state of consciousness to a more functional state of consciousness, in which they are able to raise their presence, when there is a change in context, such as that proposed to the professional network in the case example above. We can then safely assume that the nuclear family may very well be able to move quickly from PIPs, which are characterised by symmetrical or complementary escalation, back to their previous transforming interpersonal processes. When parents have, at least at times, already been able to de-escalate more, resist controlling child behaviour constructively, make good use of support by members of the caring community and make relational gestures to their child, contextual change in a setback may support the resumption of such responses. The child may also begin adapting to these changes again, albeit more rapidly that was the case earlier on. The nuclear family, and with it the professional system around them, can thus begin to recover from a setback. Setbacks offer family members, parents in particular, the opportunity to learn about recovery from crises, which may be more frequent for families that are surrounded by threat or disadvantaged in a number of ways. Finally, more 'healing interpersonal processes' (Tomm, 2014b) may begin to establish themselves, and the nuclear family can start becoming a healing environment for the recovery from trauma.

Back to square 1? Brief resumption of NVR support

There is an assumption in solution-oriented therapeutic work that what has been shown to be successful should be repeated and built upon. This can hold true for overcoming trauma-induced setbacks: when parental responses based on NVR have been successful, a resumption of the NVR intervention is probably indicated in a setback. The re-referral of the family to the service which has provided the previous intervention becomes a first step in setback recovery. It is therefore imperative that services establish rapid re-referral routes for brief resumption of their interventions. When funding is limited and services rationed, this will often not be the case; here, we see structural injustice at work: socio-economically more disadvantaged families will not be able to receive the professional support they need when they need it, while more affluent families will be able to access services privately. In the absence of a rapid re-referral route, we can expect that interpersonal problems within the family will become more chronic and transforming interpersonal processes more difficult to reestablish. Instead of counterproductive socio-cultural interpersonal processes between family members and the professional networks around them, which are based on problem-focused, and possibly discriminatory perspectives, feeding into a setback, rapid re-referral and a shift in multi-agency responses can facilitate rapid improvement.

In the case of Morgana and the Brown family, rapid re-referral was part of our service structure, and Morgana was able to resume work with the mother and consultation to the family support worker from another agency quickly. After three sessions over the course of two weeks, we can see clear signs of recovery. Morgana is able to facilitate Leon's mother's reconnection with supporters, and as a result, Regina feels more confident that she will be able to access protection from Leon's father, should he attempt to act in threatening ways. While Leon's father will have supervised contact with his son, the family's social worker raises her presence with the family by increasing the frequency of her visits and phone calls. In this way, she is able to practise 'vigilant care' (Omer, Satran and Driter, 2016; Omer, 2017), a practice by which levels of attentiveness are flexibly adjusted to perceived levels of risk, and call in additional support when required, in order to provide a more protective social environment for the family.

It should be noted here that the focus of setback support was mainly directed at securing greater protective re-connection with, and vigilance by members of the ecological and professional networks around the family. It was this focus, not any attempt to 'repair' the relational patterns between mother and son, which brought about a recovery from the setback. This follows a principle which I call *identifying the relevant vectors of resistance* (Jakob, 2023): rather than seeking to alleviate the presenting difficulties in a problem-focused manner, we establish with our clients what their support needs are in a given crisis situation, and focus resistance on the constraints to their recovery – in this case, the resurgent isolation of the family in the face of anticipated threat from a parent, who has predictably acted in very dangerous and coercive ways. Choosing the salient vector for resistance can thereby shift the family's social context to one which allows the transforming interpersonal patterns that were established earlier on to re-emerge.

Getting back on track: Solution-oriented questions for dealing with setbacks

We have explored the way that a so-called 'quest narrative' can, unlike a restitution narrative, facilitate the telling of the chaos experienced by a seriously ill person, and enable them to formulate how they themselves are agents who are central to treatment (Frank, 2013). Such a quest narrative can also enable parents find a way back to transforming interpersonal processes out of the chaos of a setback.

To help contribute to the reactivation of these processes, we can use question sequences to explore the painful, traumatic experience of parents and other family members, while also illuminating any possible improvement during the period of crisis. Derived from solution-focused (De Jong and Berg, 2012) forms of therapy which can generate hope (Franklin, 2010) and adapted to the NVR process, such question sequences can help parents reconsider the resurging difficulties in a setback as a normal part of change, and feel that they may be able to ameliorate or overcome them, rather than seeing their current situation as an immutable result of unalterable personality traits in themselves or their children.

In traumatic states of consciousness, there is often a restricted perception of the past and the future; the person exists within an all-encompassing sphere of the here and now. When this in the case, parents become temporarily unable to access the necessary internal and interpersonal resources for overcoming their current difficulties – when they need them the most. Questions that expand the time fame of consideration can be helpful; by expanding the time frame, parents can become aware of having retained some of the progress they have made. They can further realise that they now are potentially more resilient than earlier on in the therapeutic process. Restoring an awareness of their internal and interpersonal resources and the synergy between these, their expectation self-efficacy can return. They can begin to imagine change in the near future. Such imagery, in turn, widens the scope of action parents or caregivers and the practitioner can recognise and plan for. At the end of such a question sequence, when clients begin to imagine what it will be like when they've overcome the setback, they can further imagine 'looking back' at how they and the entire family will have recovered; this end to the question sequence can not only help to build hope, but, importantly, enhance parents' knowledge and understandings of their own process of change and recovery.

Method: Solution-oriented question sequence for setbacks in NVR

Begin by developing your own empathic understanding of the parent's experience of 'chaos'; be a compassionate witness to their disappointment and despair.

While parents will often initially describe the setback in terms of the child's resurgent problematic behaviour, keep an open mind for the resurgence of problematic interpersonal processes (PIPs) between parents and children, for counterproductive socio-cultural interpersonal processes which feed into the PIPs, and for critical and prescriptive re-positioning around the family. Acknowledge the difficulties associated with these processes.

Once you feel that you have listened closely to the parents' account of the resurgent difficulties and conveyed an understanding of these problem-inducing patterns, you can punctuate this part of the conversation with an empathic, compassionate summary. However, this summary can already begin stretching the time frame and countermand generalising language: e.g. (based on the case example of Leon, Regina and Morgana):

If I get it right, Tom has recently (!) started threatening you again (!) and pushing you, when you've been saying 'no'. He started doing this after he found out that his dad is about to be released from prison. I can't even begin to imagine what that must be like for you, and for Tom. You've said that the old feelings come up again, the fear, the helplessness, that you feel paralysed a lot of the time (!). This has been happening far too often recently.[2] You've found yourself giving in to Tom when you know you shouldn't, and you've been blaming yourself for that.[3]

To expand the time frame, ask when the setback has begun, and repeat how long the family have been in setback:

What started this setback? When did that happen? So, the setback started last Friday. Today is Friday, so you've been going through this for a week now.

Ask a series of questions which focus on the parent's experience of the setback, but then move on to elicit how progress has been maintained. Move on to questions about the process of recovery from the worst phase of the setback to the present moment. These questions punctuate past, present and future:

When has the setback been the worst? OK, so that was Sunday. What happened? On a scale from 1 to 10, if 1 indicates what things were like when you started coming into therapy, and 10 would indicate you don't need this any longer, where were things on Sunday, when they were at their worst? OK, so things were at 3. What nonviolent responses of yours helped keep things from getting below 3? How did you resist/de-escalate/protect your other children?[4]

Which of your supporters has helped prevent things from getting worse? How did you make use of them doing that?

If you look at your own nonviolent ways of preventing things from getting even worse during this setback ... when you look at the contributions of your supporters ... when you remember how you resisted to prevent things from getting even worse... (pause for reflection) ... how does this setback begin to look different?

You can now move on to exploring the recovery process so far, i.e. between the worst scenario and the present moment:

Where on this 10-point scale are things right now? OK, so things are at 5. They were at 3 on Sunday. What's different now from the way it was on Sunday? What have you found yourself/yourselves doing since Sunday that you weren't doing between Friday and Sunday? Who else has contributed to making this difference? What have they done? How have you been making use of their contributions? Who supported you in taking constructive action? Who comforted you? Who encouraged you to stick by your decision not to give in to your child's threats? How have they helped you feel safer? How have you helped your child feel safer?

After exploring the recovery process so far, you can move on to a focus on future resolution of the setback:

What will be the first small sign that will show you there's light at the end of the tunnel, that you will be able to overcome this setback? Can you tell me more about that?

You can then move on to questions that help your client plan their next concrete steps:

When you come home today, when you're dealing with the difficulties that will confront you tomorrow, what do you see yourself doing to resist your son's aggressive behaviour/protect your other children/protect yourself/protect the family?

Who will you ask, today or tomorrow, to support you in this? What will you ask them to do?

At the end of the question sequence, you can ask the parent(s) to take an imaginary perspective: that they have already overcome the setback and are looking back at this process:

Imagine you've overcome this setback, and you're looking back at how it started, what you did and what others did to get things back on track, and what you've experienced along the way. Looking back, what have you learned about resisting harm to your family/in your family? What have you learned about your own capacity to do this? What else have you learned about yourself? What have you learned about your child? What else have you learned?

The second-to-last set of questions in this sequence pertains to the fact that the parent or caregiver will need social support to deal with the challenges they will face in the very near future, while the last set of questions pertains to a somewhat more distant future. The question sequence can enable a helpful integration of different experiences of personal agency, which create a balance to the client's traumatic experience:

- Memories of pre-setback self-efficacy in the pursuit of NVR,
- Current self-efficacy in the course of the setback,
- Interpersonal agency during the setback,
- Anticipated future self-efficacy and interpersonal agency.

In my clinical experience, the juxtaposition of personal and interpersonal agencies – before, during and at the end of the setback – is pivotal to rapid recovery. Instead of seeing a setback as an indicator of pathology, we can co-constructively re-story it as an important further learning process in our client's liberation from harm or destructive behaviour.

The body holds the answer to the setback

Some parents literally lose their voice, when they are in a traumatic state of mind. Others struggle to express their internal experiences due to early childhood attachment difficulties, because they are on the autism spectrum or differently able, or because mentalising was simply not part of their own family of origin's interactional repertoire. Losing one's voice is usually associated with a profound sense of helplessness and the difficulty to imagine resistance against harm. The body loses its energy or feels paralysed, while cognitive difficulties result in a seeming inability to even think about solutions to the threat of harmful or demeaning behaviour by their child or others; 'empty-headedness' takes over. Trauma therapists are familiar with the embodiment of traumatic experiences which have formed the substrate to such reactions. These modalities of trauma-induced biological regulation can be understood as traces of ill-treatment in the body's memory, which have been described at length, e.g. by van der Kolk (2003, 2014).

However, we do not need to assume that these are the *only* possible modalities of biological regulation that are available to a parent who has experienced severe and traumatising ill-treatment in their earlier life, even when they are facing challenges that would in the past have stimulated implicit (embodied) traumatic memory. From a solution-oriented point of view, we can ask the question whether there may be previously unrecognised, and therefore not yet utilised embodied responses, which could form the substrate of overcoming trauma-induced setbacks? This question gains salience, when parents have already had tangible success by using nonviolent methods in similar contexts – experiences, which in their own right have left traces in the body. By actualising these traces, we may be able to help parents who have lost their voice. A specific way of using family sculpting can bring this about:

Method: Resistance sculpting

Sculpting is an adaptable method commonly used in systemic work. Perceptions of interaction in close or significant relationships are demonstrated sculpturally, either with actual people or with the use of objects such as dolls. Sculpting methods have always felt somewhat unsatisfactory to me because they generate static images of interaction patterns and therefore do not lend themselves easily to progressive narratives. I have therefore added the elements of

1 embodied responses to memories of exceptions;
2 following on impulses to move, and
3 arriving at sculptural manifestations of transforming interpersonal process.

This particular sculpting method is suitable for working with parent groups, in which other participants can stand in for children in the family or for people in the family's wider system, while parents demonstrate the way they perceive their own positions in the sculpture. It can bring movement into a traumatically 'frozen' social system in which there has been a setback to traumatically induced experience, behaviour and interaction. Its purpose is for the parents or caregivers to experience themselves again as being engaged in a process of change and thereby discover new or rediscover previously attained behavioural options. Therapists or supervisors who use this method should have previous experience in sculpting work. The entire process takes about two hours. The sculpting work can be videorecorded and shown to supporters, other family members or professionals at a later point.

You as the therapist, and the parent(s) you are working with, collaboratively decide which persons in the nuclear family and from the larger system around the family (or foster family or group home) should be included in the sculpt. Choose people on the basis of their relevance to the setback and to the recovery from it. Do not hesitate to include professionals in the sculpt if relevant, including yourself. Also consider supporters in the caring community whose position, skills, experience, knowledge, etc., may be important in regard to recovery from the setback.

Other participants can stand in for family members or members of the larger system (or for you as the NVR practitioner), but the parent(s) should represent themselves. The parent chooses who should represent whom.

Ask the client to first sculpt a representation of the PIPs that they feel have reestablished themselves during the setback. It is important to emphasise that this is not a representation of the 'family per se' – the family, and each individual within it, are much more than the problem.

The client decides where to place each participant in the sculpt, using all the available space in the room, and then shapes their posture in order to make the sculpt as expressive as possible. This should be done without any interpretation of the postures.

Once all postures have been sculpted, the client puts themselves into the sculpt and takes on a body posture that expresses how they experience their own position.

All participants in the sculpt remain motionless and silent for about a minute, while you ask them to notice their body sensation, emotions, thoughts, memories or associations and what they notice around them. (It is important to start with body sensation and then pause before continuing to speak, so the sculpt participants have enough time to become attuned to their body sensation in this position.)

The participants can then relax, but should stay in their place. Starting with the parent or caregiver, debrief every participant, asking them what they experience in this position, beginning with their body sensation. Their feedback relates their own experience of interpersonal process that has been sculpted, but (with the exception of the parent) it is important to emphasise that this is just subjective reality and not necessarily what the actual person who they are representing actually experiences. (Nonetheless, there is often an uncanny resemblance between the feedback given in the sculpting work and what the actual individuals later report about their own experiences within this particular interpersonal process.)

After debriefing, all participants take on their originally sculpted postures. Ask them to get re-attuned to the feelings they have had.

Now, ask the parent to remember a successful act of resistance they have recently carried out that doesn't 'fit' with this sculpt, and which they have experienced as positive. If they struggle with remembering such an act, you can remind them of one that comes to your mind and ask whether it is good example. This act of resistance should be one that brought about a situation in which the client felt their own parental strength, was in touch with their resources and values and felt connected with other people. It is important to choose an act that occurred in a similar problematic context. Ask the client to put themselves back into the situation in their memory and attune to what they notice around them and inside of themselves. Ask the client to notice their own body sensation as they re-evoke the memory, and give them enough time to familiarise themselves with it. Now tell the client that their position in the current sculpt does not 'fit' with what they are experiencing within themselves in the memory, and ask them to notice their physical impulse to change their position.

Once that physical impulse has grown strong enough, the client should follow that impulse, move to a new position and take up a new posture that fits with their body sensation. However, they should not change the position or posture of anyone else.

You, as the therapist, will notice that the 'gestalt' of the sculpt has become discordant. Go to the sculpt participant, whose position/posture now feels the most 'out of synch', and give a similar instruction, e.g.:

Now that dad has changed his position, you will notice that your own position in this sculpt is out of synch. Notice your body's impulse to move, and when it is strong enough, follow that impulse and move and take up a new position and a different posture, without changing anyone else.

Keep going to each next participant in the sculpt doing the same, until an entirely new 'gestalt' or congruous sculpt has emerged. (The new sculpt doesn't have to represent a 'perfect state of affairs'. We are not looking for a 'healing interpersonal process', but rather for a transforming interpersonal process, one that demonstrates recovery from the setback.)

Debrief every participant again, beginning with the parent.

Then, ask the parent what real-life act of resistance comes up in their mind as a result of this experience, e.g.:

With this feeling of strength that has just come up inside of you, and the realisation of what you are able to do, and what that might mean for everyone involved, how will you wake Jimmy up tomorrow morning when it's time for him to get ready for school? Who will you ask to support you? What will your supporter do, so that you are in touch with your strength and determination tomorrow morning, as you are now?

It can be helpful to ask the parent to show what they will do in role play or pantomime, in order to strengthen the associated embodiment of the future act of resistance.

When discussing the sculpting work in the group, encourage the participants to express their resonance drawn from their own life experience, rather than interpretations or hypothesising.

In resistance sculpting, it is important not to omit planning the next actual step in the parent's constructive resistance before the end of the session. In this way, a connection is made between the memory as a resource and the development of future parent action, which helps the family move towards a transformative interpersonal process. As in the previously described method of the 'solution-oriented question sequence for setbacks in NVR', the temporal frame of reference is expanded to take in the past, present and future, so that the parent can liberate themselves from the psychological imprisonment by 'eternal traumatic here and now'.

Notes

1 See the aforementioned analysis by Frank (2013) about the medical restitution narrative.
2 As mentioned before, O'Hanlon, O'Hanlon and Beadle (1999) have called this way of communicating empathic understanding while countermanding generalising language 'Carl Rogers with a twist'.
3 From a social justice perspective, it is called for to emphasise that the blameworthiness for the setback lies with the perpetrator's domestic abuse.
4 The use of scaling questions is a common technique in solution-focused therapy. One of their advantages is that they help overcome a binary viewpoint such as 'good/bad', 'well/unwell', etc., and enable a progressive narrative to unfold.

Chapter 8

Collaborative psychoeducation in NVR

During a period, in which her son is acting with severe aggression towards her, a mother thinks she is "going mad" because she is having flashbacks of previous violent acts she has suffered from various male partners.

Another woman 'sees his father' in her son when he gets angry. She loses her felt sense that she is the parent of a six-year-old child, not of a dangerous man, and is paralyzed by fear.

A father who was physically and emotionally abused by both of his own parents has a 'corrective script', and always makes sure to act with gentleness towards his children. He experiences complete panic, when his daughter shouts at him or at his wife, even though he desperately tries to maintain harmony in the family. He feels he has failed as a parent.

A caregiver has been recently assaulted by a teenage girl in the residential home. On her way to work, she feels sick and has to throw up. She wonders whether she has gastroenteritis.

The son of a single parent follows his father's instruction, not to "listen to that bitch", when he comes back home to his mother at the end of the weekend. Later that evening, she smokes several joints and drinks several glasses of wine, in order to fall asleep. In the early hours of the morning, she wakes up with heart palpitations. She tells her GP there must be something wrong with her.

What do all these examples have in common? Here, parents or caregivers respond to difficulties relating to having felt helpless while under threat in ways that are seen to be 'symptomatic', and attribute these difficulties to themselves, rather than to the adverse circumstances they are suffering from.

The practitioner – or in the case of the group home, supervisor – can develop new attributions together with the caregiver who has been affected in such a way. These normalise the person's responses and pave the way for using nonviolent principles and methods to develop solutions. They can form a counternarrative to pathologising, victim-blaming professional narratives, which define the parent or caregiver in question as 'chronically disordered', unfit to raise their child or, in the worst case, as responsible for the child's violence on the grounds of their own parental 'mental health disorders'.[1]

DOI: 10.4324/9781032717111-12

Madsen (2013) contrasts deficit-oriented discourses with possibilist discourses in describing 'multi-stressed families'. He sees the former as rooted in mental health and social services' assumptions that as professionals, we identify problems and their causes and then intervene on the basis of this analysis. A possibilist discourse however can generate statements such as: "Here's what I'm learning, here's what I'm excited about, here's who I'm becoming in this program" (p. 327). He posits that graduate students are socialised into talking with clients about problems, a focus on *what isn't and should be,* rather than a focus on how clients envision and strive towards preferred futures. However, while advocating for the introduction of possibilist discourses, Madsen warns against basing all of our work with families that have experienced severe forms of abuse on these ways of constructing their realities alone. From a position of both/and, we can appreciate that clients who have had to survive extreme suffering could feel they have not been heard, that their difficulties are being minimised, when a practitioner exclusively communicates from a resource-oriented, possibilist orientation. It can be necessary to bring an acknowledgement of difficulties which initially feel insurmountable, in harmony with an approach that recognises and appreciates the parents' strengths and resilience, and the way they are moving towards a problem-free future. This both/and of acknowledgement and appreciation can help increase the possibilities parents or caregivers can draw from the methods that NVR offers them.

Madsen further contrasts an expert knowledge discourse with a collaborative discourse. When a professional's attitude towards clients in families facing multiple challenges is based on a deficit discourse, they position themselves as experts towards the person of parent or child. They then apply what they see as 'objective knowledge' about the person to their understanding of the presenting difficulties and their amelioration. While in professional networks their perspectives are seen as valid, the perspectives of family members tend to be valued less, and therefore are not elicited to the same degree. Many social and health services may be involved in interventions and treatment in one and the same case, and there is a tendency in such a treatment system to privilege the expert knowledge of professionals with the highest status, while the knowledge of family members about themselves and each other is generally underprivileged. This can lead to their disempowerment and a weakening of their sense of agency at a point in their lives at which they need an increasing expectation of self-efficacy, in order to generate viable options for action. I am not advocating disregarding the a priori knowledge professionals bring to their practice, but that equal representation of the perspectives of parents, professionals and other members of the larger system around the family can enable a genuinely collaborative way of working towards change. In the process of supporting parents, practitioners can learn alongside their clients, as they absorb family and community members' local knowledge. This will help people whose lives have been adversely impacted by interpersonal control and dominance to develop trust in the professional who is working with them, rather than fearing dominance from this person.

However, the question arises: When parents or caregivers make negative attributions to themselves regarding controlling child behaviour, and information from the professional could help change these negative self-directed attributions by normalising their responses and pointing towards new possibilities for action – is not imparting information anathema to collaborative practice? I believe the answer may lie in 'making sense' of the client's difficulties in conversation, in which abstract practitioner knowledge about trauma and lived experience knowledge of the parent can form a synthesis. The therapist is not only telling, but telling and being told, and the resulting co-authored account becomes richer than each perspective alone.

Positive connotation of parents' drug or alcohol use

Positive connotation of problematic behaviour has already been discussed in regard to critical-prescriptive positioning by people within the larger system around the family.[2] The behaviour of parents who use drugs and alcohol to lower their often chronically high levels of anxious arousal *makes sense*, even if it is ultimately counterproductive. Starting from this premise, we position ourselves in a different way to the parent than if we merely considered the negative effects of such behaviour.

Without approving harmful use of drugs or alcohol, we can explore the parent's positive motivation for doing so. This goes beyond merely stating that the parent is 'self-medicating', which could merely be a form of pathologising their person. Asking about a parent's good reasons for their substance use opens space for exploring their positive motivation for doing so, and thereby enables a positive connotation. Substance use is an option which makes sense within the contexts of their life: an available means of self-regulation for a parent who has been plagued by trauma-induced high arousal baselines that keep getting reactivated in response to controlling child behaviour. Who would not wish to be able to sleep and feel able to bring their children to school the following day or function at work? Who would not wish to feel liberated, even temporarily, from overwhelming anxiety, worry and physical tension and relax? If such motivation is explored in a non-judgemental way, the therapist communicates that they see the parent as a sensible, rational person, who has been acting in a goal-directed and understandable manner. When communicating with each other in such a manner, the parent, not fearing they will be judged, may be open to two new aspects:

1 Evaluating information from the professional that may be useful in their own decision-making regarding use of substances. For example, a practitioner may tell them that drinking alcohol before going to bed will result in falling asleep more easily, but the fact that they wake up in the early hours of the morning and won't fall asleep again is likely to be a result of their alcohol intake the night before. Similarly, their therapist may explain that, while many people use cannabis to alleviate their anxiety when they are high, higher doses of THC such as found in more powerful strains of cannabis are likely to induce greater anxiety over time by raising the arousal baseline and causing heart racing.

2   The synthesis of information from the professional with an account of the client's goal-directed behaviour can then open conversational space for how these goals could be attained in the NVR process in a more effective and healthier way. Constructive alternatives can then often be woven into the process of parental resistance to harmful child behaviour. One example for this is self-exposure to anxiety-provoking child behaviour that utilises sensorimotor resonance.[3]. The NVR practitioner can help parents avail themselves of various grounding techniques and other methods which help bring down arousal levels.[4] Key is finding ways in which such methods can be integrated to support the parent's practice of NVR, e.g. using a grounding technique prior to withholding a service which has been misused by their child.

Jointly planning NVR action using grounding techniques or exploring how certain trauma-focused methods can become part of the parent's life-style – with the purpose of attaining the very same goals that the substance use initially aimed to achieve – is a much more collaborative process than just labelling their substance use as 'self-medication'.

A client had not only experienced trauma-induced stress in the past, but also suffered medial pre-frontal lobe injury as a result of earlier child abuse. Both factors, compounding each other, impeded the parent's emotional self-regulation. Fearing that she could lose self-control when faced with her children's problematic behaviour, this parent learned about the value of using mindfulness techniques for bringing down her overall arousal levels. She reinterpreted an urge to use drugs as an indicator that she needed to practice mindfulness more consistently and attend classes regularly. We subsequently discussed how she could integrate the use of certain mindfulness techniques in preparation of constructive nonviolent action.

Not all self-control and self-regulation methods need to be learned by the parent. In early childhood attachment, we develop our capacity to self-soothe. Rather than premising our understanding of the client's struggle to self-regulate on a binary assumption, that they either 'can' or 'cannot' accomplish this, we can assume that they – and we – may be insufficiently aware of their own self-regulatory abilities. Searching for these and facilitating the parent's re-connection with their self-regulatory abilities can become an important way out of substance use or experiencing chronic high levels of arousal.

Identifying parents' own self-regulation skills

Any conversation that helps us make sense of a caregiver's trauma-induced difficulties can be followed immediately by an examination of the competences with which they seek to counterbalance these specific difficulties which they themselves have often been unaware of.

To make a distinction: avoidance of the child, giving in to coercive behaviour and child demands or acting with submission *are not* forms of self-regulation, even if they result in short-term lowering of arousal. Parents have often learned to reduce threatening behaviour when they experienced domestic violence or child abuse in their own life histories. While also resulting in lower anxious arousal, it is important to help parents who have experienced abuse to make this distinction themselves. Sometimes, professionals mistake submission or appeasement with de-escalation and consider this a viable strategy for the parent to lower the child's escalation. However, the parent's anxiety is merely lowered because of a lowering of immediate risk, while longer-term risk increases when the child's coercive behaviour becomes reinforced by parental acquiescence. This is neither self-regulation nor non-escalatory parental responsiveness; what we see at work here is merely a process of complementary escalation. Apart from reinforcing coercive child behaviour, the parent's avoidance of exposing themselves to anxiety-provoking child behaviour raises their overall propensity for anxiety. Parent and child become entangled in the control trap.

Deferred responsiveness however – 'striking the iron, when it's cold' – is not tantamount to avoidant parent behaviour. Instead, we find here a constructive, pro-active response which can enable the body to lower its trauma-induced propensity for rapid and high psycho-physiological arousal. This tried and tested NVR strategy often creates the opportunity for parents to activate and recognise their own self-regulatory potential. Foregrounding these capacities can significantly increase them, as the parent re-connects with such resources and uses them to greater effect. Ruth's experience exemplifies this process:

Ruth has been diagnosed with so-called 'borderline personality disorder'. Her firstborn child Elias is in kinship care and has little contact with Ruth, as a result of a deep rift within her birth family. She "...breaks up with John" (her second-born 11-year-old child Finn's father), "only to get together with him again and again", in the words of Finn's social worker. Finn's angry aggression elicits Ruth's rage. We discover that her rage compensates for a brief but very intense initial sensation of feeling highly threatened when Finn swears, verbally threatens or squares up to her. Her response flips from flight to fight. She reacts in a similar way to John, when he comes home frustrated and tired from his job as restaurant chef, argues with Ruth and on occasion threatens her, as well: her reactions oscillate back and forth between existential fear, with a powerful impulse to flee, and almost overwhelming rage. She has, on such occasions, hit John, but this is dangerous, and John in the past injured her in an act of violence. Finn is subject to a child protection plan in social services, and Ruth is worried that he may be taken into care, as well. The social worker is pessimistic in regard to the family's prospects, because a psychiatric evaluation has determined that borderline personality disorder[5] is a chronic disorder with little prospect of improvement. Her pessimistic attitude, which the social worker communicates to Ruth, is further confounded by her daily use of cannabis.[6] Ruth says she "can't hack it without (her) spliffs, I can't cope with my life".

Nonetheless, Ruth screams at Finn less often than she used to, because she does not want to lose him. When I ask how she manages to avoid screaming at him, Ruth explains "I've got to get out, I just get out". At first, she has a negative view of her own inability to remain in her son's presence, that she can't "be like any other mum" and remain in the house when Finn "sees red". However, in our conversation, Ruth's 'getting out' begins to take on a different meaning, and we increasingly appreciate this as a competent response: as her propensity to become enraged makes it impossible for her to remain in his presence without screaming at him or even hitting him, she actually prevents a possibly violent, confrontational escalation. How she will be able show a deferred response, 'strike the iron, when it's cold' at a later stage, when their arousal levels have decreased, is not yet clear; we agree to discuss this in a future therapy session. For now, it is important for both of us to learn more about her de-escalatory response, which begins with an important act of self-control – leaving a context that is impossible to manage.

We explore how she begins self-regulating her arousal once she has left the flat. The family's social housing unit[7] is at the edge of a small town. There is a lane at the end of the road that leads out into the fields, where Ruth runs to a horse that grazes in a nearby pasture when she is in emotional turmoil. She holds grass out to the animal, strokes its head and presses her cheek to the horse's. In these moments, she feels a calmness that evades her at other times, and she can cry. Initially feeling embarrassed at telling me about this response, we can share an appreciation of this as a competent response to a situation that yields no other constructive behavioural options. This appreciation opens up new perspectives on further self-regulatory possibilities Ruth may develop.

In a further session, we 'anchor' the 'horse scenario' as a safe place, which Ruth plans to use for a future NVR announcement to Finn, in which she will tell him that she can no longer accept being threatened by him, and which she will deliver together with a friend who acts towards her – and towards Finn – from a safe supportive position.

Further into the work with Ruth, she separates from John. Due to the improved relationship between her and Finn, his social worker becomes more optimistic and refers her to a domestic violence project, in the hope that this will support her not to reconcile with John. Ruth's use of cannabis has reduced to a recreational level.

This example illustrates a kind of psychoeducational work in NVR which synthesises an understanding of trauma-induced reactivity with an exploration of the parent's self-regulation competence. This enables her to envision and eventually enact more options for responding constructively not only to incidents of problematic behaviour by her son, but also to act with greater self-preservation in regard to his father. She attributes her renewed separation from him to her growing ability to act with self-preservation.

Her son's shouting and threatening behaviour had become associated with John's, with her earlier partner's and with her own father's abusive behaviour – an association that would stimulate rapid psycho-physiological arousal, initial fear and subsequent rage. This is the problem-focused story. However, we have seen that Ruth is able to emotionally self-regulate – only she hadn't been aware of this, and nor had we, the professionals who were involved in her and Finn's care. This is the competence-focused story. In our therapeutic conversation, we have been able to foreground this storyline. Both stories, brought together, form a new narrative of a mother who has positive motivation, and who embodies resources that can be actualised in order to form a counterbalance to traumatic reactivity. This new narrative opens new possibilities: we can *build on her pre-existing self-regulation competences* for learning to de-escalate with her son, rather than assuming incompetence. We do not assume that she would need to be taught self-regulation, or that her early life attachment process has left her so fundamentally flawed that she may not have the capacity for such change. Eventually, the mother is able to use the anchoring of the safe place scenario, as we move into planning, carrying out and later debriefing from deferred responses to incidents involving her son's problem behaviour. This process encourages her to accept a referral into a domestic violence project.

This kind of psychoeducational work does not consist of 'teaching' the client about their psychological problems. Instead, the client's local knowledge is seen as having equivalence to the professional's knowledge of trauma; together, these knowledges combine to form a unique and new understanding of the person of the parent.

Thus far, we have examined how collaborative psychoeducational work can support parents in improving their emotional self-regulation. Looking beyond internal resources, we can see how the NVR community of care can be utilised for emotional co-regulation at crucial moments in the NVR process.

Notes

1 See Part I, Chapter 1: Critical/prescriptive positioning.
2 See Chapter 1.
3 See Chapter 9.
4 See e.g. Henden (2017); Dolan (2000).
5 In the UK now more commonly referred to as 'emotionally unstable personality disorder' or 'EUPD'.
6 Cannabis is an illegal substance in the UK, and professional attitudes towards cannabis tend to be less liberal than in countries or states that have legalised it.
7 UK: council house.

NVR as exposure therapy

An erroneous, yet common assumption is that clients need to lose their fear of taking action before they can carry out whatever challenge they face. In supervision, I have often heard colleagues state that a certain client cannot e.g. prepare an NVR announcement, because they are not 'ready' for this. Of course, parents who have experienced abuse may be prone to various different forms of losing control, such as severe dissociative difficulties, panic attacks, hyperventilation or flashbacks to earlier violent attacks. They often become fearful at the thought of taking any kind of action their child may not like and to which said child could react in ways that in their mind are associated with prior violence. They may fear dismissive behaviour or a lack of resonance by the child which could result in a loss of their sense of mattering and a feeling of abandonment. If however parents can reduce their arousal levels, they may feel more able to face situations that stimulate anxiety in them. Importantly, taking nonviolent action can actually help parents who have had traumatic experiences, learn to master situations associated with fear and anxiety and *ameliorate their traumatic load*. Here, NVR becomes trauma therapy.

What is exposure therapy?

It is a natural learned response to avoid situations which we expect will be threatening and leave us feeling we would be unable to protect ourselves or others. Ultimately, habitual avoidance raises levels of anxiety rather than reducing them. One reason for this can be that the person does not become confident they are competent in dealing with what feels threatening. When the impulse to avoid such challenging situations overrides any other impulse and closes down responsive options for parents to raise their presence, a way of overcoming such avoidance can be called for, not only for the benefit of the child, but also for the benefit of the parents themselves.

Exposure therapy is quite simply a form of anxiety treatment in which the person confronts themselves with the stimuli (commonly known as 'triggers') to which they respond with fear and anxiety and which they have learned to avoid. They do this with the help of a competent professional. Often, such a therapeutic effort is spoken about from an outside position – the practitioner 'does this to' a person who is their 'patient'. The 'patient' may either be cooperative, i.e. follow the professional's

DOI: 10.4324/9781032717111-13

instructions, or may not be seen to be 'suitable' for this process. In NVR, the prospect of our clients' self-exposure can raise many different complex questions and concerns. When e.g. parents anticipate negative responses to action such as delivering an announcement, carrying out a sit-in, denying a service which their child is inappropriately demanding, contacting parents of other young people when their teenage child has run away or in some other way carrying out something that amounts to what Omer has called 'breaking a taboo', these are all forms of self-exposure to what parents may previously have avoided. Contemplating such action, they are not only anticipating threat, perhaps even a sense of existential threat, but in some instances very real risk, as well as serious ruptures in the relationship. It is understandable that we, as the NVR practitioners, may wish to mirror our clients' avoidance tendencies by declaring them 'not ready' for action. However, they, and we, become ready to approach the child – by beginning to approach the child, and learning in the process. This requires a realistic appraisal of what is likely to occur, a thorough assessment of risk, and an examination of how that risk will be mitigated not only by the parents' action, but also by that of their supporters. In this way, we come closer to what can be considered 'controlled conditions': the parents cannot control what the child will do, but they can control what they will do, if they plan carefully, with our support.

Joseph Wolpe developed a behaviour therapy method he called 'systematic desensitization' (McGlynn, 2002). In systematic de-sensitisation, a person increasingly exposes themselves to specific, anxiety-inducing situations in controlled conditions. They generally use grounding techniques such as progressive muscle relaxation to enable this. Repetitive self-confrontation with an anxiety-inducing situation is intended to reduce a person's propensity for fear and avoidance by experiencing a sense of mastery.

This particular method is sometimes criticised for its use of relaxation methods as inadvertently promoting a measure of avoidance and thereby drawing out the therapeutic process. However, its promise for parents with severe histories of abuse is that they can approach the child in potentially high anxiety-inducing situations without needing to fear becoming emotionally dysregulated and experiencing a total loss of self-control.

Careful planning of each step in approaching their child enables parents to anticipate these (quasi) – controlled conditions, under which they will expose themselves to the anxiety-provoking responses that are likely to be directed at them. Unlike in classic de-sensitisation scenarios, we can only carefully plan each step the parent will take, but we cannot plan the child's response. Quasi-controlled conditions are created by planning and practising responses which will mitigate risk and make the anticipated situation emotionally bearable. By carrying out constructive action in the real life situation with their child, parents finally expose themselves to what they have hitherto seen as an insurmountable challenge.

Usually, the actual child reaction is less severe and harbours less risk than parents anticipate. There can be a variety of reasons for this:

- Parents with traumatic experiences often anxiously imagine a worst case scenario. This, however, is unlikely to occur due to the preparatory mitigating measures that are carefully planned in therapy sessions. Reality is generally more benign that their unrealistic pessimism would lead parents to believe. I have often experienced trauma cascading out from the parents into my very own embodied response and have found that helping parents come to a more realistic appraisal of what is likely to occur helps me remain emotionally fully regulated as their therapist.

- Some children who have experienced abuse by an adult perpetrator, and whose non-offending parent responded with anxious avoidance in such situations have felt abandoned and unprotected. Their own traumatic response to previous abandonment can be stimulated by a parent's or caregiver's expression of fear, which has become associated with remaining unprotected in highly threatening situations. Having learned that fleeing has previously not been a viable option when feeling at risk, such children may be more prone to respond with an aggressive fight response and feel rage rather than anxiety or fear. If however parents utilise internal resources such as their own idiosyncratic methods of self-regulation or have learned grounding and breathing techniques, or co-regulate with supporters, their body language, proximity, facial expression, prosody of voice, choice of language and other indicators of their state of consciousness communicate inadvertently that they are more emotionally self-regulated. This can actually have a calming effect on the child, who may then be more able to co-regulate along with the parent, rather than reacting to traumatic associations. Simply put, parental fear as a stimulus for child aggression falls away.

- When parents utilise their internal and interpersonal resources to improve their self-regulation, their social perception improves. They become more able to mentalise and respond in prudent and deliberate ways, attune to their child, foster interpersonal resonance, feel and communicate empathy and compassion, and address the child's needs.[1]

- From an attachment point of view, relational- or reconciliation gestures which parents become conversant with[2] are a new kind of experience for a child who in the past has experienced high-level persistent conflict with no resolution. By internalising the process of 'rupture and repair' when their parents use NVR relational gestures to reconnect with a child, by validating their emotion, showing physical affection or addressing the child's needs, interpersonal tension becomes less threatening to the child: the body can learn that things will be alright, the child will not be abandoned. As a result, the child may begin to predict more benign caregiver responses,[3] and their propensity for engaging in intense conflict can diminish. However annoying or even aggravating a parent may be who, instead of avoiding the child, sits with them and asks in a self-contained way how they will exert self-control in the future when they feel angry – this parent is less likely to be perceived as abandoning them, or as the 'enemy'.

- When a parent takes constructive action, the presence of a supporter has a constraining psychological effect on the child; the child is more likely to inhibit their aggressive response and eventually become more emotionally regulated.[4]

- No longer feeling that they need to 'win the argument', a parent who no longer follows the relational logic of control may be more inclined to discontinue constructive action, such as a sit-in, when the situation risks getting out of hand.

Taking all these aspects into consideration, we see that NVR action can enable systematic de-sensitisation. Yet, NVR is not an individual psychological approach, but instead a systemic way of bringing about relational change. The growth of a caring community raises the question: How can important relationships support the parent's de-sensitisation?

Sensorimotor resonance and interpersonal grounding

Until now, we have looked at the parent's grounding and emotional regulation from an intra-psychic point of view: How can extant self-regulation resources be utilised and enhanced? How can simple grounding techniques help parents down-regulate their anxious arousal, so they can take constructive action? We have not yet discussed how the *embodied presence* of an emotionally safe supporter can have a positive effect on the *interpersonal* emotional regulation of a parent, and how this may be therapeutically beneficial.

We can imagine the resonance of a guitar's body when someone plucks its strings. We can *feel* it, when we do it ourselves. This metaphor for neuronal resonance between a parent and their supporter brings to mind the potential for change that is inherent in a relationship in which the parent feels safe. Siegel (2012) explains the neurological interpersonal process at work here, by using the image of a 'neuronal map' that is generated and which animates the brain to reproduce the embodied internal experience of the other person, when both individuals are attuned to one another:

> When we take in nonverbal signals from others – their facial expressions, eye contact, tone of voice or prosody, gestures, posture, and the timing and intensity of their responses – their inner world is being transmitted to our senses. These signals are perceived by our nervous system, assessed by our mirror neuron regions, and relayed downward from these cortical areas through our insula to the limbic, brainstem, and bodily regions below. These areas and these processes are each part of what has been called the social brain. The subcortical shifts that literally resonate with what we see in another are then transmitted back upward, through the insula, to the middle prefrontal area. We call this process resonance, and the circuits that make all of this possible are the resonance circuits.
>
> (19-6; 19-7)

Attention to the other person's nonverbal signals is centrally important to the activation of these 'resonance circuits', as it enables mutual attunement. Attention to each other's signalling becomes the key to flexibility in how we react. Such resonance has a profound effect on the wellbeing of people and on their social cohesion.

The resulting linkage helps form an '*integrated we*' (34-4). Siegel elaborates that this kind of integrative communication evolves, when attunement to the internal state of the other emerges in the context of a congenial attitude. In my view, emotionally safe positioning enables such congenial attitudes. The parent's emotional regulation can thus become the product of interpersonal attunement in an integrative relationship.

As previously discussed, a parent who has had traumatic experiences often becomes unaware of the embodied presence, or even the actual physical presence of an emotionally safe other; implicitly, they feel alone in the world. A parent's attention is drawn away from their supporters' body signals, when hypervigilance to anticipated threat by their child dominates their perceptive processes. In such cases, a therapist can help parents and their supporters generate highly effective sensorimotor resonance. Mira's case exemplifies this:

Mira's children Sameera and Rafi were physically and sexually abused by their now deceased father for many years, and Mira was subjected to domestic violence.

After Mira has learned about the recent sexual abuse of her daughter by a teenage boy who was a friend of Rafi's and reports this to social services, the family members feel threatened in a number of ways: Children's services initiate a child protection investigation, as the social worker learns that a previous incident of sexual abuse against Sameera was left unreported. Rather than understanding this, as Mira explains, as a culturally situated distrust of statutory authority, the questions she and the children are asked in CAMHS[5] and by the social worker seem to communicate a suspicion of neglect and inability to protect on the part of the mother. Further to this, some of this adolescent's associates threaten to kill the family and burn their house down, should Sameena act as a witness in court. The family members, who are of South Asian heritage, are targeted with racist slurs in an overwhelmingly White working class area on social media.

In the wake of these threatening circumstances, Rafi's propensity for aggression against his mother and his sister rises dramatically, while Mira increasingly suffers from nightmares and flashbacks related to the history of physical abuse in the family at a time, when her husband used to beat her and lock the children in their rooms for prolonged periods of time, usually under the influence of alcohol. She no longer feels able to maintain any boundaries for Rafi, is afraid of him and physically avoids him. Sameera no longer leaves the house and refuses to go to school. When Rafi is at home, she spends most of her time in the tiny garden behind the terraced house, even in the rain. This family, which in the recent past made much improvement using NVR, is in crisis, experiencing a very severe setback.

We work with solution-oriented questions for setbacks in the NVR process. Encouraged by this, Mira decides to carry out a sit-in with Rafi; she wants to impress upon him that on the one hand, she believes he is distressed and can understand what may have brought it about,[6] while on the other, she can no longer accept the aggression with which he appears to respond to what is unsettling everyone in the family, as this is harmful to her and Sameera, self-destructive for him, and adds to the distress they are all feeling. The intended purpose of the sit-in is to communicate to him that his mother and the family's supporters expect him to act with self-control and remove himself whenever he feels an aggressive impulse, so that at a later point in time, he can share what has been upsetting him, once everyone is calmer and able to speak to each other in the presence of a supporter. In preparation for the sit-in, Mira brings a supporter along to her therapy session, who has always acted in emotionally safe ways towards all in the family, including Rafi.

As we practise the sit-in in therapy, Mira begins rocking back and forth and humming to herself. She explains that, "In my head, I go off to an island in the sea". Our conversation normalises what would generally be considered a "dissociative response":

Author:	*If someone can't get away, they get away in their mind. That makes perfect sense. Were you calming yourself, when you were rocking back and forth?*
Mira:	*I always do that when I'm upset. I didn't notice it.*
Author:	*Sure. Can I ask you something? (Mira nods). What did you imagine Rafi doing in the sit-in?*
Mira:	*That he's attacking me, hitting me.*
Author:	*Cynthia will be there. Would he still do that with her there?*
Mira:	*No, he wouldn't do it like that, in front of Cynthia.*
Author:	*Cynthia is sitting right there, next to you, because she's going to be there at the sit-in.*
Mira:	*Yeah, I totally forgot.*

We subsequently work with sensorimotor resonance[7] in order to facilitate Mira's attention to Cynthia. Attuning to Cynthia helps Mira to keep from dissociating or becoming emotionally dysregulated in some other way. The following day, she is able to carry out the sit-in in Cynthia's presence and remain sufficiently self-regulated.

This example demonstrates that even parents who have been struggling with a heavy traumatic burden may be able to face serious challenges when they respond to threatening behaviour. Moreover, they can become de-sensitised when they avail themselves of sensorimotor resonance with a supporter who is positioned in an emotionally safe way towards them and towards their child. By doing so, they can rapidly shift from an acute traumatic reaction to a presence state of consciousness. In this case example, by feeling strong and acting in resonance with her supporter, the parent becomes able to raise her presence during the constructive action of a sit-in. From a systemic point of view, we see her re-initiating a transforming interpersonal process; it takes the place of the pathologising interpersonal processes that reemerged more frequently and with great severity in the course of the family's traumatic setback.

The shift from a traumatic state of consciousness, to a state of consciousness in which the parent is reconnected with their resources, their values, has an awareness of their own needs, is mindful of their self-preservation and feels and communicates strength – a presence mindset – can be brought about *swiftly*, when there is focused sensorimotor interpersonal resonance. Of course, a prerequisite for this lies in the relationship with the supporter: a parent must *implicitly* feel that the supporter is disposed towards them in a positive way, in an emotionally safe manner. In the following method section, focusing interpersonal resonance in NVR is illustrated using the example of the sit-in; however, it can be used in any situation, in which parents would like to feel able to carry out constructive nonviolent action, but anticipate a severe traumatic reaction if they did.

Method: Focusing sensorimotor resonance

Ask your client to invite someone into the session with whom they feel emotionally safe and who is likely to remain emotionally regulated in the face of provocation from their child. Generally, supporters who are not close family members will be likely to remain more emotionally regulated. If the witness to the sit-in is to be the other parent, it will be important to assess the likelihood of their emotional self-regulation when receiving threat- or rejection signals from their child.

An empty chair can represent the child. The parent arranges chairs in such a way that the proximity to their supporter has a calming effect.

Ask the client to sit in the child chair so she can gain a sense of whether the seating arrangement feels non-confrontational and inclusive for the child, rather than threatening or rejecting. If necessary, the parent can change the chair arrangement and keep changing it until they have a sense that it feels engaging of the child while at the same time emotionally supportive for them.

Ask the supporter whether they will feel comfortable with the parent observing their body language.

Ask the client to observe their supporter's body language closely: *What do you notice, when you look at …?* Many parents will respond by naming qualities, e.g. *She looks calm, she seems to rest in herself.* Ask the parent to localise what gives them that impression: *What exactly can you see in her body that tells you she's calm?*

Once a parent localises and specifies their perception, e.g. *Her shoulders, they look relaxed; she's upright; her breathing, she's breathing calmly...* Ask them to look at this specific aspect of the supporter's body language for a while and begin noticing where in their own body they feel a corresponding sensation:

Ok, keep looking at her upright posture, the way she's breathing calmly, until you notice in your own body that you're responding to (resonating with) that. Tell me where in your own body you feel a response...? You can then ask the parent to describe and qualify the response: *What is the body sensation like? What emotion comes up? What thoughts or images come to your mind?*

In the next step, ask the parent to imagine their child is sitting on the child chair:

What is the worst thing you imagine your child doing in the presence of (supporter)? What impact does imagining that have on you? Where in your body do you feel that? What is the body sensation like? What emotion comes up when you feel that? What thoughts?

Ask your client to expose themselves to both stimuli at the same time, until they feel an integrated response:

Please look back and forth between (supporter) and (child). Keep looking back and forth, taking your time, until you notice a shift inside of yourself, in your body, in how you feel. Let me know when you notice the shift inside of yourself. (As with all imaginary techniques, it is important to use unconditional language, so *until you notice* rather than *if you notice*.)

Ask the parent, how the internal shift manifests itself:

Where in your body do you notice that shift? What are you feeling in your body? What emotion comes up? What thought? How are you experiencing yourself as a person right now, in this moment? How are you experiencing (child)? What other image of your child comes up inside that is different from that of the (aggressive/hostile/rejecting/dismissive) child?

Next, ask the client: *How will you know when you need to look at (supporter) in the real life situation?* Repeat the client's answer, and follow up with the question: *If you don't notice you need to look at (supporter), would you like (supporter) to get you to look at them, when you have this undesirable reaction? What would you like (supporter) to do?* (e.g. touch the parent's arm and make eye contact).

Ask the supporter to carry out the act the parent has requested. The parent should feel free to keep correcting the supporter, until it *feels just right.*

Ask supporter: *How will you know when (parent) needs you to do this?*

Ask the client again whether they are comfortable for the supporter to perform this act without having been asked to do so, especially if physical contact is involved.

To assess the effect of this preparation, you can ask the parent to rate on a scale, how well they feel prepared for the real life situation.

Schedule the next session for a date after the planned sit-in.

In the following session, you can debrief the client using solution-oriented questions, to draw their attention to their own internal resources, their interpersonal resources and their sense of strength as experienced during the actual sit-in.[8]

So far, an approach has been developed which integrates a trauma-informed perspective with resource-oriented principles and methods in work with NVR. This integration has a twofold significance:

1 Parents with traumatic experience, as any other therapy client, have a right to receive support in ameliorating or overcoming the deleterious effects of abuse, and
2 A presence state of consciousness is necessary for parents to be more able to develop a child focus, so that children who have experienced abuse or neglect will become beneficiaries of their parents' NVR action.

When parents no longer feel threatened in the way they have done, are no longer hypervigilant in the direction of the child, they can direct their attention to the entire person of the child, can attune to them, and become more able to respond compassionately to their emotional needs. The medial pre-frontal cortex will become re-activated in the parent-child relationship.

Not all responses of parents, foster carers or residential carers in families and other social systems facing multiple challenges fit neatly into the textbook framework of 'trauma'. Returning to Weingarten's (2003) conceptualisation of 'common shock', we can identify emotional injuries that emanate from helplessness in the parent's struggle to establish emotional connection with their child. Parents who lose their sense of mattering to their child often suffer an existential crisis of meaning in life, a crisis of social connectedness and of identity. Parents who have experienced emotional abuse, whose confidence has been systematically undermined in their own childhood or in intimate partner relationships, or whose sense of being a person of value has been undermined by societal racism, misogyny, classism, ableism, LGBTQ-hostile attitudes or other forms of social marginalisation and oppression, may have developed a greater vulnerability for having their self-confidence as a parent in particular, and as a person in general, undermined, when they experience rejection or dismissive responses from their child. Not only can deleterious societal discourses indirectly exacerbate the vulnerability of parents to these kinds of injuries of connection, but they may also directly impact on parents in the form of parent-blaming or other adverse responses by professionals. Not only birth parents, but also adoptive parents, foster carers or residential carers will often find their vulnerability increase when they are 'done to' in a hierarchical way by professionals who, intentionally or inadvertently, act as agents of control, and whose communication can undermine their confidence and sense of value as a caregiver and as a human being.

The next chapter will begin to conceptualise what Dulberger has termed (a sense of) 'parental erasure' (Dulberger, Fried and Jakob, 2016; Beckers, Jakob and Schreiter, 2022) and examine its workings. This will be followed by a chapter describing ways of 'unhinging' this state of mind and becoming more able to shift to a state of consciousness, in which the parent feels greater *internal* connection, as well as *external social connection*, reasserts their 'mattering' as a caregiver and regains meaning as a person. This process is important in laying the groundwork for the parent's own healing, and for the development of a focus on the needs of the child. This, in turn, will then generate possibilities for the child who has had adverse experiences to feel more anchored by their caregivers' support and guidance.

Notes

1 See Chapter 13.
2 See Chapter 13.
3 In cognitive neuroscience, predictive coding theory examines the way in which we respond to encoded predictions of the future which are based on past experience, rather than to the actual behaviour of the other person at a given moment in time (De Lange, Heilbron and Kok, 2018). An 'expectation violation' is required to change the encoded prediction. We can see re-coding of expectation as an important cognitive mechanism of change in transforming interpersonal processes brought about in NVR (Beckers, Jakob and Schreiter, 2022).
4 This observation in NVR practice contradicts a mechanistic understanding of threat responsiveness, according to which an automatic unrestrained fight response inevitably underlies any aggressive act by a child. While threat responsiveness is likely to be a *component* of many kinds of aggressive behaviour, it often does not explain its full complexity. Moreover, a child's self-restraint in the presence of a supporter, in particular if it is someone who is not very well known to the child, suggests that many factors can be involved in aggressive behaviour, and that even in its most extreme forms there are remaining vestiges of self-control.
5 Child- and adolescent mental health services.
6 Here, the mentalisation work in preparation of the sit-in introduces an element of child-focused practice (see Part III). While in my view we should not automatically assume that every act of aggression by an adolescent is immediately induced by some form of distress, there was much to suggest that this was the case here.
7 See below.
8 See Chapter 6.

Chapter 10

Mattering and the experience of erasure

The existential crisis of meaning in the life of a parent

In its original conceptualisation, NVR postulates that parents can overcome their sense of helplessness and raise their presence with their child by persisting with action that is methodical, goal-directed and carefully planned and executed, instead of reacting impulsively. However, this assumption leaves out a crucial dimension of the parent's sense of self: the *emotional need* to feel relevant and able to care for their child in a reciprocal relational process.

Relevance as a cornerstone of parental identity

When adults feel that they are no longer of relevance for the child's safety, well-being and development, this is often linked to an absence of responsiveness: a child will not react synchronously to their parents' communication, or persistently reject the caregiver's offers of care. As mentioned before, Reis (2014) describes responsiveness as a fundamental characteristic of all human interaction which helps maintain a relationship and ensures its further development. Marshall and Lambert (2006) found in a large-scale qualitative study that having a perception of *mattering* to their child constituted a significant aspect of participants' sense of agency and self-assuredness as parents. However, a parent's sense of agency should not be seen as a fixed trait, but rather as being dependent on current forms of child behaviour (De Mol et al., 2018). We can infer from the above perspectives that *parents need to perceive and feel, on an ongoing basis, that their child needs them.*

In clinical work, we have seen that the parent's perception and feeling of being needed becomes diminished when, over a prolonged period of time, a child responds to their care attempts with aggression and violence or, importantly, rejection, dismissiveness or humiliating and degrading behaviour. In therapy, we often learn that parents find their entire self-concept undermined (Beckers, Jakob and Schreiter, 2022).

An adoptive mother tells me: My meaning in life, who I am, is to be his mother, and he keeps telling me that I'm not a mother. What's left of me?

DOI: 10.4324/9781032717111-14

Figure 10.1 Rejecting care.

This client expresses an identity crisis – her identity, her sense and understanding of who she is as a person, has been called into question; her son is no longer validating her (Figure 10.1).

When a caregiver is exposed to critical-prescriptive communication by professionals, deleterious dominant discourses in society that seep into the professionals' responses to the parent are likely to compound the effect of the child's communication. Institutional, structural injustice in this way becomes a detrimental exacerbating factor. I would now like to address the question of how such a parental identity problem manifests itself – what parents tell us happens to them when they experience this existential psychological crisis.

The parent's experience of erasure

Hughes and Baylin (2012) discuss the effects of adverse child behaviour on birth- and adoptive parents and other caregivers under the aspect of an internal difficulty or inability to feel and act caringly towards the child. According to their concept of 'blocked care', aversive child behaviour affects caregivers in ways that reflect their personal vulnerabilities, which, in turn, are seen to be rooted in their own attachment histories. They therefore need to become aware of and reflect upon their own attachment histories, in order to protect the child from their own detrimental emotional response. This perspective, while addressing very similar difficulties, differs significantly from the systemic perspective which is developed here.

In my view, pathologising interpersonal processes are sufficient to explain the difficulties parents' experience: *anyone* is likely to respond in such ways when they are exposed to a high degree and intensity of persistent rejection. I do not see investigating vulnerabilities based on parents' earlier life attachment experiences as a generally useful way of ameliorating the difficulties parents' experience.

Understanding erasure as an existential crisis of identity, my understanding of the effects of pathologising interpersonal processes around care for the child far exceeds that of merely postulating a difficulty or inability to act in caring ways:

- In our description of parental erasure, we can recognise that the voice of the parent often seems to have become silenced, and the problematic voices of the child have become foregrounded. In practice, this means that the parents may feel totally immersed in the child's objections to many or all of the ways in which they could be inclined to interact with them. They can be much more aware of such objections, than of their own desired forms of action and motivation to take such action. The child is not physically in the therapy room – but to the therapist, it can feel like the child speaks with the parent's mouth, while the person of the parent seems absent.
- As part of this existential crisis of identity, many parents describe a kind of numbness or inattention to their own needs, wishes and aspirations. Someone who hardly feels they exist in their own right may no longer feel their inclination to *want* for themselves.
- If the parent's sense of self is examined only in the context of the parent-child relationship and the parent's own attachment history, we miss out on an appreciation of socio-cultural interpersonal processes. A parent's sense of mattering can be severely diminished, when they feel blamed for their child's violence, the indifference they may be shown, or the rejection they experience. Mothers in particular can be the subject of messages about them from within the larger system around the family that have been informed by misogynistic parent-blaming discourses. The individualisation of the problem itself, and its location within the mother-child dyad alone, can have this effect.

Interpersonal rejection and marginalisation per se are experienced as threatening. Leary (2015) explains this from an evolutionary perspective: the very physical survival of our ancestors in the African savannah and their opportunity to reproduce depended on securing one's membership to the group, which provided resources, protection from predators and child care. It was vital to possess a highly developed perception of social signals, which could indicate whether one found acceptance by the others in the group, or whether they, in turn, perceived their relationship with a person as of little value. This social-perceptive ability has been called the 'sociometer'. Such highly developed perception in regard to one's degree of social acceptance gave humans the ability to adjust their behaviour in a manner that was desirable, to ensure that they were not excluded from the group. Neuropsychologically, when a person feels excluded, we see increased activity in many areas of the brain that also become activated when the individual is experiencing physical pain: rejection *hurts*. These same areas of the brain also become activated, when a person receives *dismissive* social messages. It is exactly this combination of rejecting and dismissive social signals that many biological parents, adoptive parents, foster carers or other caregivers of children who have had adverse experiences speak of and suffer from. Persistent rejection by the child will generally stimulate a sense of feeling threatened, and it is especially the rejection of the adult's offer of care that raises the threat level that is indicated to the sociometer.

Some parents feel relief, when a professional indicates they are suffering from 'blocked care', because this quasi-diagnostic attribution can help reduce feelings of guilt. However, this attribution can be understood as a fixed trait *within* the parent, which would require intensive therapeutic effort to ameliorate and therefore require a considerable length of time to change. By contrast, the construct of a sense of parental erasure describes merely a state of mind. This state of mind can be explained from within the parent-child interaction and by socio-cultural interpersonal processes that result from pathologising societal discourses, which have been communicated to and inculcated in the minds of parents (and children) from within the larger system around the family.

If however we understand parental erasure as a mindset rather than as an intrinsic trait, we can safely assume that it may be transient. Given a change in context, a parent may be able to move swiftly to an alternative, more desirable mindset. Before we move on to the kind of therapeutic interaction that may help create such a context, it seems pertinent to further describe the erasure state of mind. The construct is based on parents' descriptions of their own felt sense. Here, the example of a mother who is cognisant of the effects of her adoptive son's dismissiveness as well as the critical attitudes of the professionals who are engaged with the family:

Karen, who feels both rejected and dismissed as a caregiver by her nine-year-old adoptive son Mark, describes her sense of erasure in the following way: "So, it's like, he looks right past me when he looks at me, like I'm not there. When I ask him a question, he usually doesn't answer, he ignores me, or he says {shut the f.... up, you're not my mother anyway}. It's like I'm not there any more. Yesterday, I cooked spagbol for him, it always used to be his favourite dish, and when the electrician walked through the kitchen he made a sound like he was going to throw up and said {what's this crap?}. I don't know why he hates me so much, what's wrong with me, what have I done?

And then I think, what have I done to deserve this? I end up feeling bad about myself, I feel guilty, maybe I'm really a bad mother, 'cause, don't get me wrong, I love my son, but a lot of the time, I just don't like him, I don't want to do anything for him any more. Just go to school without your homework, I don't care! And when it's too much, I say things I regret. I've become the mother I never wanted to be. Sometimes I think: Why don't they just send him back to his birth parents? That's awful, isn't it? But I'm really scared he might just do that one day, I'm really afraid that could happen. Will this never end?"

Karen asks whether I will report her "diatribe" to social services. I seek to reassure her that many parents in her situation would often feel this way and thank her for having been so honest.

It is important to let oneself resonate with such a parent's distress, act as a compassionate witness and create the opportunity for her to express herself. This should include their experience of the current relationship with the child, *as well as* their concerns about how they are perceived from within their wider social environment. We can thus normalise their experience and localise their sense of erasure both in the interpersonal processes between them and their child, and at the same time contextualise it in pathologising societal discourses, help them become liberated from the misogynistic verdict of being a 'bad mother'.

Child-centred attitudes, which therapists have often been socialised into and which have been inculcated in our thinking about children and adolescents, can mitigate against a non-judgemental, emotionally safe positioning towards the parent, especially when we fall into a binary victim/perpetrator way of thinking and follow a belief that we need to 'take sides with the child', whom we may identify as the victim of earlier life abuse or neglect and current 'inadequate parenting'. It can be very important to make oneself aware of the fact that a diminution of the caregiver by a professional, however inadvertent, is not in the child's best interest. The child needs to experience parental strength: *a parent I perceive as feeling inadequate will not be able to protect me or support me to face the challenges in my current life.*

It is not only unnecessary to take a critical professional attitude towards a parent who struggles to feel caring; it is also counterproductive. The practitioner's critical response would become braided into the negative descriptions of self the parent has absorbed and, at least in part, internalised. The weave of a backward-looking meta-narrative of the parent(s) and the family, which undermines their sense of efficacy and intrinsic self-value, would be further tightened. If therefore compassionate witnessing can be a first step towards change, what does a professional need to witness without becoming judgemental towards the parent? In the above case example, the mother's own description illustrates some of the painful aspects of a parental sense of erasure:

- The feeling, no longer to 'exist' in the social sphere;
- The perceived impossibility to care for the child, resulting in an absence of 'caring energy';
- Incomprehension and confusion in regard to the child's motivation;
- Shame and guilt in regard to negative feelings towards the child;
- Fragmentation of the parent's sense of self – the parent no longer feels they conform to their own values and the person they feel they have been;
- Fear of loss of the child;
- A narrowed time frame and a sense of endless or infinite suffering;
- A reduced sense of self-efficacy which manifests itself in an inability, when asked, to imagine either resistance to ill-treatment or delivering *emotional, relational* care (as opposed to mere physical care) of the child.

Noticeably, when parents experience a sense of erasure, they many either feel inert, having little energy and being unmotivated, or they may have a low level of tolerance before they become highly aroused. The narrowed time frame and the hyper- or hypo-aroused states parents may experience demonstrate a degree of commonality between erasure and a traumatic state of mind.

But, as with a traumatic state of mind, a parent experiencing erasure can become able to shift rapidly from an erasure state to a presence state of mind. The last-named aspect of erasure, the inability to resist or deliver emotional-relational care, can serve as the key that opens the door to new experiential possibilities. All the practitioner needs to do is help parents imagine resistance, imagine care, and imagine resistance against the child's rejection of care.

Chapter 11

Unhinging erasure, re-establishing a sense of mattering

If we think of a parent's sense of erasure waxing and waning in response to rejection, dismissive responsiveness or open aggression from the child, and with the degree of critical and prescriptive communication they face in the ecological and professional systems around them, we conceptualise that they enter different states of mind dependent on these socio-cultural interpersonal processes – an opening and shutting of a door between different spaces of interaction and internal experience. Some parents feel locked in the 'room' of erasure more than others. Enabling a fluidity of psychological movement from one state of mind to another can become an answer to their distress and, importantly, to the diminution of their parental confidence and agency. The question of how we remove barriers between states of mind becomes salient.

Social constructionist perspectives do not assume that, as professionals, we 'repair damage' that has been done to the person. This does not mean to deny the fact that people are harmed by abuse, but to apply a completely different paradigm to our attempts at understanding their personhood. Instead of seeing a person as damaged or pathological, we can understand them as having developed optimal adaptations for their psychological survival of devaluing, injurious and humiliating social conditions. We can support parents by communicating appreciation of parents' re-adaptation to changing conditions however – conditions they themselves have begun to bring about by virtue of their resistance to ill treatment, be it by their own child, or by dangerous and coercive communication from within the wider system. We are looking at a both/and of adjustment to changing conditions and persistence of resistance against remaining pathologising and problematic socio-cultural interpersonal processes. Persistence of resistance, where professionals in the larger system fail to recognise the emergence of transforming processes, can be important to maintain and promote further therapeutic improvement, as Gabrielle and Adrian's example demonstrates:

Gabrielle, the mother of 14-year-old Adrian, who has been diagnosed with ADHD and an attachment disorder, lives in an English coastal town with high levels of socio-economic disadvantage. Mother and son live largely on benefits, while Gabrielle earns some money as a cleaner. Adrian has just spent several weeks on an inpatient child psychiatric ward and has now returned back home. In a referral

DOI: 10.4324/9781032717111-15

consultation, Adrian's social worker expresses his doubts in regard to the prospects for change, and cites both Adrian's conditions, and his mother's diagnosis of PTSD as well as her history of having had a series of violent partners. He indicates that, in light of her difficulties at emotional self-regulation, her "inability to set bound-aries" and her propensity for screaming at Adrian – which only results in him responding with physical aggression, running away and using drugs – social ser-vices have taken care proceedings, in spite of Adrian's age. He further elaborates that Gabrielle uses too much cannabis and neglects her son. When I ask about the purpose of an NVR intervention, he indicates that legally, it would support social services case in care proceedings, if they can evidence that the family have been offered all available treatment options. It transpires that a further organisation which provides family assessments has already become involved.

In the wake of her initial sessions in NVR, Gabrielle begins leaving the fam-ily home when aggressive confrontations begin to occur. This becomes a matter of concern to the service providing the family assessment, and to Adrian's social worker and the social worker's manager. While our service sees Gabrielle's action as de-escalatory and we believe it may show the possible emergence of a trans-forming process, it is the other professionals' unequivocal conviction that this is a problematic parental response: Gabrielle should be able to control her son, and leaving the home, even temporarily, re-evokes memories of neglect in Adrian. She must, therefore, remain in the home. Gabrielle is caught between competing psy-chological assumptions that are held by different agencies within the professional network – and that are expressed by high status professionals. She finds the injunc-tive expectation to remain in the home but not engage in an aggressive altercation impossible to achieve.

In our service, we reflect on the contexts within which Gabrielle feels put in this bind. We consider the conditions that our service needs, in order to practise in a way that does not put us in an unethical position, and what we need to require from CAMHS and social services in order to establish such conditions. While Gabrielle has been described as incapable of emotional self-regulation, her attempts at de-escalation raise a number of questions:

What motivated Gabrielle to withdraw from situations she feared would get out of hand? How did the idea to do this form in her mind? What were her intentions in doing so? Was it easy, or was it difficult to carry this out? If it was easy: what made it easy? If it was difficult: what constraints did she overcome, in order to walk away from confrontation? What did she notice about her son that may have been different to other occasions in the past, when she had engaged in confrontation? Did anyone support her practically or morally, to walk away? If so, who supported her, and in what way? How was Gabrielle able to make good use of this person's contribution to her efforts at de-escalation?

How and by whom were the concerns about her leaving the house expressed? What has been her emotional response to this? How has it influenced what she actually does? Of the people she knows today, or the people she has known in the past, who would see her new way of responding in a positive light? What has she been learning about herself, about her son, by walking away? What has she been learning about her own ability to deal with conflict? What has she been learning about self-control and self-regulation? What does she feel emotionally when she withdraws from conflict? When she regulates her arousal after walking away? What did she feel in the past when she engaged in the confrontation with Adrian?

Gabrielle decides to continue walking away and to tell her son's social worker that she will continue to do so. I communicate our questions and her answers to these questions to social services and ask for my report to be put on file as evidence in the court. Two aspects of our course of action are dictated by the need to maintain an ethical, social justice informed position: asking questions about the impact of larger system interaction, i.e. expressed professional opinion on Gabrielle, and taking direct action in regard to a positioning by other agencies which we have experienced as intransigent, and thereby potentially harmful to mother and son.

In further work with Gabrielle, I am especially interested in her response to the idea of 'bridge-building de-escalation'. I explain that, in bridge building, she would signal her commitment to her son and imply her realisation that he needs her, while she walks away. Gabrielle expresses interest in this idea and we practise this in role play: She walks away at a measured pace that is neither slow and hesitant, which could be interpreted as submissive, nor unnecessarily fast, which could be perceived by Adrian as expressing anger or fear. While walking away, she turns back to him; tilting her head slightly so as to signal that she is not threatening him, she says in a quiet but clearly audible voice:

"Right now, it's not working between you and me and I want us to get along. I'm going for a walk in the park and we can talk again when we're calm".

Gabrielle notes that this conversation has made her more aware that Adrian needs her. This defines her de-escalation as an act of care, of his need for her to reach out to him even when she is resisting his problematic behaviour.

A further, and we feel hitherto untold story lies in the fact that, having grown up in foster- and residential care, Gabrielle has been able to maintain her son in her own care throughout his life so far, in spite of all difficulties. The questions that arise from our focus on this story paint a picture of persistent care for her son, maternal resilience against all odds, and Gabrielle's propensity for relational learning.

This case vignette does not aim to give an objectively true or 'realistic' rendition of 'fact' about the family. It does not concern itself with 'psychological assessment', nor does it aim to generate a 'positive' image of mother and son or their relationship with one another in competition with what we experience as a pathologising professional narrative. Instead, we wish to add additional perspectives to the pathologising narrative which emerged in the context of child protection procedures and family assessment for court – one that can illuminate competence, the initiation of transformative processes, re-adaptation, and the ability to show a caring parental response while interrupting an established problematic form of interaction. The story that begins to emerge is one in which the mother becomes more aware of her son's need for connection with her. Importantly the mother can begin to co-author the new narrative of their relationship, by virtue of incorporating this story.

In the case example above, the son has also been seen in a one-dimensional way as troubled or deficient: due to a high level of adverse childhood experience, he has been understood to be incapable of self-regulation, as has been his mother, and, as an adolescent male, dangerous. Associated with the perception of the adolescent's dangerousness is the racist trope of the dangerousness of young Black men. It seems quite likely that this trope has been amalgamated in his own mind, his mother's, and possibly in the minds of professionals around the family. Woven into the problem-saturated narrative of the mother and the dangerousness narrative of the son, we find the injunction for the mother to control her son by acts of counter-control. The meta-narrative of impossibility – impossibility of change in the eyes of professionals, impossibility of carrying out the injunctive demands by these very professionals in any way other than escalation – could create a dangerous impasse for the family and cement a perception of *so-being,* rather than opening perspectives on *possibility* and *becoming.* A counterbalance, not a contradiction, to the stories told of individual and family pathology is necessary, if we are to enrich the meta-narrative with previously untold stories and facilitate movement.

A very simple act, yet, difficult to accomplish – to walk away – can become the terminus for a previously untold story. New meaning can emerge in the conjunction of de-escalation and bridge-building: that of parental relevance to the child, the parent's *mattering.* This synergy can come about by virtue of two nonviolent principles: the principle of one-sided action where dialogue is not or not yet possible, and the principle of inner detachment from the need for immediate substantial success in the child's response as an outcome of one's action. Cultivating what has been introduced as the principle of 'anasakti' in Hindu philosophy and psychology as the detachment from the desired outcome of one's action, can promote the parents' ability to take one-sided action. One-sided *caring* action, that is not dependent on immediate external success, can thus become an avenue for reconnection between parent and child.

Unilateral acts of care and their significance

Nonviolent resistance is entirely based on one-sided action. The more that serious dialogue and mutual understanding become possible, the less caregivers need to resist. In relationships in which everyone is open to the needs of others and takes these seriously, we see less conflict and more interpersonal support. However, where dialogue is not yet possible, we cannot expect mutuality. It is not possible to resist harmful behaviour together with the person who is causing harm, regardless of their age or developmental level.

Mutuality here is seen as a congruent, authentic opening of the self for the needs of the other in dialogue; it is not to be mistaken for 'pseudo-mutuality' (Wynne 1984), whereby family members give an outward impression of harmony and mutual understanding which, however, is superficial and inauthentic. Parents may mistake appeasement of their child or submission to their demands with responding to the young person's needs. However, this is an illusory enactment of harmony in the absence of genuine dialogue, an example of pseudo-mutuality. When parents engage in this illusion of harmony, it results in incongruent, self-contradictory relational signalling. Often emerging from a mix of resentment, anxiety, shame and a sense of guilt, yet taking the outward shape of caring interaction, such communication is likely to confuse the child, create relational uncertainty and embodied or emotional unease – even if the child has an initial sense of triumph over the parent. In such instances of inauthenticity, parents become less credible to the child, and the young person's trust in the parent is further undermined. Where we cannot yet expect mutuality, one-sided action is of the order. When parents have become traumatised or experience erasure, persistent, one-sided *caring* action can restore their perception of being of import to the child, provided they continue to recognise the young person's *need of them* in the absence of affirmation or validation, and do not mistake submission for care.

One-sided *caring* action starts by resisting in a manner which is in and of itself connective. The therapeutic system can begin to *move towards* dialogue and cooperation, rather than assuming or constructing a pretence that dialogue already exists. Forms of resistance to harm that incorporate one-sided caring action can initiate transforming interpersonal processes, which, in turn, may pave the way for later healing interpersonal processes.

Yet, how do adults provide one-sided caring action and feel validated, in the absence of the child's acceptance of their care? This does occur naturally as a matter of course in family life (Beckers, Jakob and Schreiter, 2022): a baby may scream and protest against having their nappies changed. Nonetheless, parents will continue to change their nappies even when their child protests, because their nose tells them that this is what the child needs. No one would question the necessity of this act which is carried out without any validation of the parent; the parent is not validated by any resonance with the adult, even if this is what they may wish for. Of course, harmony will be a goal for the parent in their interaction with the child; of course they would wish for their child to feel and express well-being while interacting with the parent – but the parent would not let these wishes dictate that they abandon necessary acts of care to which the child does not show a positive resonance. This is a practical, simple example of anasakti in action, the parent's detachment from at least a part of the goal of their caregiving. Their own knowledge that this act is necessary for the child's well-being, and the realisation that the child cannot care for themselves in this instance, enable the parent to have an awareness of the necessity of their action and that they, the parent, matter, even their act of care does not meet with the child's acceptance. This perspective can enable a parent or caregiver to persist in caring in the absence of reciprocity, and to distinguish, in an ongoing process, between needs and wants of the child.

By persisting with caring action, parents resist the self-destructive tendencies of a young person who rejects their care. They can nurture their own resilience in the face of such rejection by remembering one-sided caring action, and by imagining future one-sided caring action. The realisation that such caring resistance, or one-sided caring action, countermands the child's self-destructive impulses and is of quintessential significance for their developmental trajectory and their emotional well-being, can become a step away from parental erasure.

Remembering unilateral care – Imagining unilateral care

Parents can escape an erasure state by creating associations between memories of different key experiences of unilateral care. These constitute:

1 The perception of rejection of care by the child;
2 Memories of their own positive influence on the child that feel meaningful;
3 Future imagery, in which they can experience themselves as providing positive care in the face of rejection.

Associating these elements can generate a relational story in which the parents feel they matter. The method of remembering unilateral care, which was inspired by Denborough's 'riverbank position' (2018) and developed by Willem Beckers (Beckers, Jakob and Schreiter, 2022), encapsulates these elements.

Method: Remembering unilateral care

Ask the parent:

Please give me an example of when it felt important to care for or support your child – even though your child didn't express feeling cared for or supported at the time... Even if it's just a small memory... Even if it's from a time when your child was little...

And after the parent has told you about their memory, continue with specific questions relating to it:

What was the situation? Tell me more about it.

What did doing this mean to you?

What felt important when you did this, even though your child didn't exactly react in a positive way at the time?

What values that you appreciate about yourself as a parent did that express?

Are there similar memories that represent those values?

How do you feel that those values of yours and your act influence your child's life? How did it contribute to their development? How, over the years, has it contributed to how they've thrived, to their wellbeing?

How did it strengthen your relationship with one another?

Relate the subsequent questions to your client's current identity as a parent:

How do these memories effect your idea of what it means to be a parent?

Relate your final questions to future one-sided action:

How would you like these convictions, these values of yours to guide you over the next few weeks?

What images of the future come up in your mind when you think about these values?

What can you see in your mind's eye that you will do? What small act will you carry out? What conversation will you have with your child? What will be the outcome of that?

It is important to use unconditional language when asking questions about the future. Questions using conditional language such as *"What conversation could you have...?"* can be understood as expressing doubt and uncertainty on the part of the therapist that the parent can carry out the envisioned act. Unconditional language expresses hope and assurance about the future, the practitioner's confidence in the parent, and facilitates the client's imagination.

In the following session, discuss the unilateral caring acts the parent has carried out.

This method creates associative connections between rejection of care by the child and unilateral acts of care which are experienced as meaningful. When an imaginary arc towards future one-sided acts of care is created in the parent's mind, they often feel encouraged to persist with carrying out further acts of care in spite of rejection, dismissive behaviour, aggression and humiliation. In doing so, their growing sense of strength, the reconnection with their parenting values and the increasing conviction that their caring acts matter help restore their injured identity as a parent or caregiver.

Part III

Child-focused NVR

"I admired virtue and good feelings and loved the gentle manners and amiable qualities of my cottagers, but I was shut out from intercourse with them, except through means which I obtained by stealth, when I was unseen and unknown, and which rather increased than satisfied the desire I had of becoming one among my fellows. The gentle words of Agatha and the animated smiles of the charming Arabian were not for me. The mild exhortations of the old man and the lively conversation of the loved Felix were not for me. Miserable, unhappy wretch!"

"I am malicious because I am miserable. Am I not shunned and hated by all mankind?"

"… he cried with sad and solemn enthusiasm: I shall die, and what I now feel be no longer felt."

From Mary Wollstonecraft Shelley's 'Frankenstein'

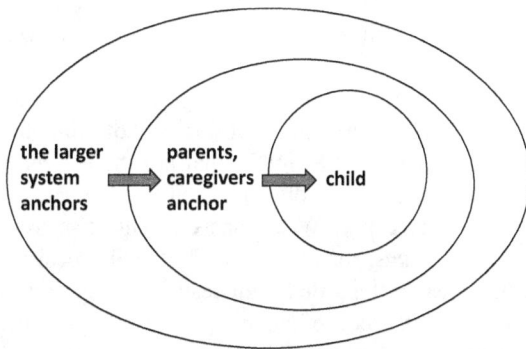

Figure III.1 Anchoring achieved at all system levels.

DOI: 10.4324/9781032717111-16

Chapter 12

Child and trauma

A theoretical integration

There is a widespread assumption that young people who have had adverse childhood experiences have no choice in the matter when they act aggressively, and that each of their acts of aggression is an involuntary threat response. The word 'trigger' lends itself to raising a mechanistic metaphor, the spectre of which becomes alarming: pulling the trigger of a gun brings about an immediate, automatic and irreversible discharge, which can be deadly. In the application of the trigger metaphor to the young person who has experienced trauma, the trigger lies outside of the actant, the child becomes the gun. There are no mediating factors, no self-control, no social influence: the actant has no agency. I remember with discomfort the words of an adoptive mother: 'I know I am my son's trigger'. The total convergence of the person of the mother with the trigger, and the notion of the invariable discharge of the son's aggression – the imposition of the mechanistic metaphor on their relationship – filled me with a sense of helplessness: if this were the case, how would she, how would he ever be able to escape from this predicament, as long as his amygdala inevitably interprets her very being as a trigger, and he is unable to forestall his reaction? What are the effects of this way of thinking on the mother's ability to protect herself from aggression? What are the effects on the ability of people in the social network around mother and son to intervene in a protective way and make their own presence felt? What consequences arise from the attribution of inevitability for his siblings, for his father? Any child receives guidance from their parents that involves teaching them self-restraint of aggressive or destructive impulses; this is an elemental aspect of parenting. Will such guidance be given in his case, or is it considered futile, or even unjust to expect him to refrain from what he is seen to be unable to control in himself, if he is at the mercy of a trigger, or many?

What I see here as a reductive understanding of trauma easily comes about, when we posit that one theory alone can explain all the phenomena we are observing. Any theory operates within a conceptual framework. Any conceptual framework by nature restricts the information that is taken in, and the perspectives that can be gained. When grand theory becomes the single or strongly favoured mode of understanding within a particular social environment, such as an agency of social care or a mental health team, we run the risk of developing understandings that can cloud our vision for possibilities which would lend themselves to the process of

DOI: 10.4324/9781032717111-17

change. In psycho-social practice, the theoretical understandings that are favoured within a team or agency, and upon which individual professionals base their perceptions of the families they work with, invite them to take up certain positions towards their clients. Grand theory invites us to take a position which is based on a fixed mindset. Attitudes, beliefs, responses, feelings about clients that emanate from such a position, this kind of 'theory countertransference', can become more rigid, when the assumptions we hold as psycho-social practitioners constitute a large part of our professional sense of competence. The adoption of singular theory as the privileged viewpoint of the entire team or agency, at the expense of other orientations, will exacerbate this risk: when I believe to *know*, and *I am what I know*, it is easy to feel threatened by alternative viewpoints that are not based on the theoretical model that has become part of *me* or *us*. The theory has become an integral part of my self-concept as a professional.

Theory as a part of the professional's self-concept can be unproblematic if we avail ourselves of a multitude of *different* theoretical perspectives and at the same time remain open to the actual lived experience of our clients by practising deep listening. However, it can be seductive to see everything through the lens of only one theory, which is assumed to explain all the complexities of what we are confronted with – and which leaves *us,* and the ways in which we respond to what we are confronted with, out of the equation. Aggressive, controlling child behaviour can be deeply unsettling, stimulate discomfort and anxiety in parents, the larger family and wider network, and in professionals alike, and the presumptive certainty of a linear, often monocausal explanatory model can be seductive, in that it brings the illusion of order to the chaos of the social field we find ourselves thrown into. This seduction can result in one-sided, rigid narratives of our clients that will not be adapted to different and changing contexts.

Trauma- and attachment theory and cognitive-behavioural theory constitute the dominant discourses in the field of child to parent aggression and other externalising problems. Often, the proponents of each model consider them to be incompatible with each other. NVR offers a further dominant discourse. However, we must avail ourselves of multiple lenses, if we are to develop the kind of three-dimensional depth of understanding that Gregory Bateson (1972/2000) conceptualised at the outset of systemic theorising. Such a three-dimensional viewing can flexibly adapt itself to different contexts. Attempts to find solutions to the complexities of self-destructive or harmful child behaviour on the basis of one viewpoint alone will not fulfil this requirement.

Why is he so aggressive? Or am I even allowed to use that word?

Following an introductory online seminar, some of the participants express concerns to the host organisation. Their contention is my and my co-presenter's use of the phrase *aggressive child behaviour*. We should, in their view, avoid any use of the word *aggressive* in the future, but also not use the word *behaviour*, as this would imply that traumatised children have choice, when they e.g. hit someone. From the vantage point of an inability to self-control, using the word *behaviour* would be blaming. We should therefore only use the phrase *trauma response*.

These professionals express a binary opposition between a discourse of *the trau-matised child* and a discourse of moral judgement or condemnation. This binary distinction constructs *the child per se* – rather than individual children – as a person who is to a significant extent defined by the abuse they have been subjected to. I am not questioning the reality of embodied traumatic threat responsiveness – that is the subject matter of much of this book. I am questioning the construct of *the trau-matised child*, and I am questioning whether the use of a binary victim/perpetra-tor framework is helpful for children who have experienced abuse or neglect, and who have been prone to showing harmful or self-destructive behaviour. The person of the child is more than 'their trauma', and their actual behavioural manifesta-tions are a composite of many factors and influences, including, but not exclusively determined by, their embodied threat responsiveness and its cognitive and emo-tional correlates. If, based on a reductive discourse that constructs *the traumatised child*, we create narratives about individual children that deny them agency. They are, in essence, disablist narratives.

Let us return to the trigger metaphor. As opposed to 'trigger', 'stimulus' is understood as a perception that increases the likelihood of responding in a certain way. This does not need to determine the actual trajectory and outcome of action. There are many kinds of aggressive behaviour, and it seems safe to say that in a number of these, threat responsiveness becomes an ingredient. However, these only rarely follow the trigger metaphor. If e.g. a young person's demands are rou-tinely accommodated by their caregivers, because these fear retaliatory physical aggression directed at them or siblings, verbal abuse or blame, public shaming or humiliation, it stands to reason that this young person will not develop a high level of frustration tolerance. When feeling frustrated, they will be likely to express their feelings in a way that is perceived as threatening by those around them. A poten-tially confrontational setting has emerged, and it is within this setting that threat responsiveness is likely to be generated in the child, who in this instance may perceive the adult, whom they are prepared to attack, as a threat to them. Such a kind of instrumental aggression, in which threat responsiveness plays a role but is not the sole determining factor, is only one of many possible scenarios. Though I have only given a rough and simplified description of this problematic process, it throws a light on the complexity of the matter. Other kinds of aggressive behav-iour, such as seeking confrontation for pleasure, experiencing power over others as rewarding, aggression sanctioned and encouraged by peer group influence, honour code – related aggression, aggression stimulated by the experience or perception of injustice that is displaced onto people who are not causing injustice, intimate part-ner violence in adolescent relationships that arise from misogynistic attitudes and harmful gender-based assumptions, and many more, complicate the issue further.

Let us investigate some of the *implications* of the trigger metaphor. For one, the notion of an inability of self-control would question whether a young person who has experienced trauma can even be held responsible for their future action. This implies that a child requires trauma-informed psychotherapy and/or trauma-informed parenting for change to be possible. Following this notion, until such time, as this kind of therapy or parenting can bring about processing and resolution of trauma, the child's harmful behaviour would either need to be tolerated, they would need to be accommodated further, or the child would need to be removed from the normal social sphere they belong to, in order to protect their caregivers, siblings, other children and members of the public. We indeed see processes of social exclusion of these young people taking place all the time, whether it is temporary or permanent exclusion from mainstream education, foster- or residential care, in-patient child psychiatric care, secure accommodation or prison. Social exclusion of this nature and scale amounts to social injustice for young people who display harmful behaviour.

On a very practical level, if we continued to perpetuate and act upon a disablist narrative, we would need to accept the practice of physical restraint at high levels of frequency, and this is indeed a widespread occurrence. From clinical experience of working in therapy with young people who have been in care, I have become aware that physical restraint re-issues traumatic experience in young people who have experienced physical abuse or have witnessed intimate partner violence.

A further implication of a disablist narrative lies in the reduced availability of a sufficient level of educational attainment due to exclusion from mainstream education. Reduced educational attainment impacts on a young person's proficiency and their sense of accomplishment, thus undermining their autonomy and self-determination and their future life chances.

I would also like to raise the question: What are the relational ruptures that can ensue and are never repaired, when we consider the young person to be unable to self-control – by disrupting the trajectory of an aggressive act – and self-regulate following an act of self-control? One mother spoke about feeling like nothing more than her daughter's punching bag – that this is what, in her experience, the entire relationship amounts to. While attachment-theory informed conversations tend to privilege the need for caregivers to repair relational ruptures they have caused, in order to help the child build more trust and feel more secure in their 'inner world', we see here relational ruptures on an ongoing basis, which become exacerbated by the diktat to accept aggression due to its presumed inevitability. The parent who feels like her daughter's 'punching bag' will struggle to respond to her in a way that is well-meaning and self-assured instead of anxious, driven by shame and humiliation and passively rejecting; she will find it hard to be attentive, attuned and empathic. We can see the emergence of reciprocal relational rupture. In such circumstances, the needs of young people who have experienced abuse or neglect, and who act with self-destructive or harmful behaviour, will be very difficult to address. We need an understanding of the needs of children with traumatic experiences that lie outside of the trigger metaphor. It is in this context important to note that previous experience of abuse is neither a sufficient nor a necessary condition for child to parent violence to emerge (Holt and Shon, 2018).

Understanding trauma without a disablist narrative

Even though traumatic experience is neither a necessary nor a sufficient condition for the development of harmful or self-destructive behaviour habits in a young person, high levels of adverse childhood experience *predict* high levels of these problems.

If we decide not to engage in disablist narration of children who have had adverse experiences, not to accept a mechanistic, monocausal model of aggression, can we work in NVR in a manner that is trauma-informed, and that takes the insufficiently met needs of children who have been abused, neglected, have witnessed violence *or who have been socially and economically disadvantaged,* into consideration? Can we discover a *contribution* by traumatic experience to intentional aggressive behaviour, even where we do not see it as a determinant? Can we, conceptually, move out of this binary of traumatic determinism versus disregard of traumatic influence? Can therefore a trauma-informed view of the child be compatible with NVR?

In supervision, a colleague speaks about Andrew, the adoptive father's perception of his daughter Layla. He has complained about her increasing aggression. I am confused, because a moment earlier, my colleague reported that Layla's adoptive mother now does things that seemed impossible only a month ago, such as going shopping with her or taking her to a playground in the park, where she even plays with other children without there being severe temper tantrums. Upon further questioning, it transpires that there has only been one single incident over the past month, in which the child tried to hit someone, whereas aggressive incidents had in the past been a daily occurrence.

Preceding this reduction in aggression, the parents had carried out sit-ins and used other NVR-based methods. We assume that the child's level of aggression may not have increased very recently – on the contrary – but that perhaps her aggressive behaviour feels in some way worse to her father? Perhaps the father felt in the past that his daughter had no choice but to hit others due to her earlier life experience, but that now, something may have changed in his interpretation of her aggressive behaviour, even if its frequency is lower than it used to be?

In a later therapy session, it indeed transpires that, having witnessed her affect control on several occasions, Andrew now assumes that Layla acts intentionally, while in the past he had interpreted her behaviour as involuntary.

In this case example, we can recognise a narrative theme that arises from a disablist narrative, which stands in binary opposition to a moral accountability narrative. Having assumed that his daughter's responses had been inevitable, the father must now assume that his daughter is in some way 'bad', if that is the only alternative discourse that informs his interpretation. While I feel that the father's perception seems to have been perturbed in a constructive way, it would not be helpful to respond in a way that is primarily informed by this moral accountability discourse.

In a further supervision session, my colleague shares an account of an exceptional occurrence. Having taken Layla to a toyshop, she insisted on getting an additional toy to the doll she had been promised. While she glared at him when her father told the cashier not to run up the other toy, Layla did not act out aggressively. Afterwards, she burst into tears. Her father comforted her and Layla eventually stopped crying.

The outcome *feels good* to us. What has happened here? In solution-focused terms, we see an exception to the problem; in terms of narrative therapy, it is a story with a unique outcome. Instead of avoiding exposure to the social sphere due to a belief in the inevitability of a severe aggressive outburst, we see the father more assured that he will be able to manage a difficult situation and go to a toy shop. Importantly, we see a *different emotional response* emerge as the daughter shows vulnerability, followed by an acceptance of the father's comforting response.

This unique outcome offers us several new narrative threads:

- If the child can act intentionally, one can also expect them to act with greater self-control, even if this is effortful for the child. By no longer avoiding social situations in which the child has in the past exerted control over them or others, and at the same time refusing calmly to give in to her demands, parents can find themselves able to promote her self-control, self-regulation and ultimately her tolerance for frustration. The child's propensity for aggressive responsiveness decreases.
- Decreased aggressive responsiveness enables the child's greater social integration and more freedom of movement for her and the entire family.
- The reduced aggressive responsiveness enables an emotional shift within the child. When difficult emotions that left her vulnerable were previously compensated by angry-aggressive behaviour, they now become more apparent, enabling the parents to respond compassionately: her loss of power over the parents enables her tears to flow; the tears enable the parent to comfort the child. Instead of understanding the past traumatic experience as the root cause of the aggressive behaviour, we can understand the aggression as a constraint to an emotionally constructive, trust-building interaction. The family have not yet achieved all therapeutic goals, but it is the combination of resistance and compassionate care that has overcome the constraint, and to which we can attribute the emergence of an important transforming interpersonal process.

The understanding of such a unique outcome can allow space for 'safe uncertainty' (Mason, 2015). Neither parents nor practitioners *know* or can explain in any definitive way, what internal movement is occurring in the child's mind; she cannot yet articulate or even understand it, as she is being held in her father's arms. Nonetheless, we feel that we are seeing a significant change event, one in which a child is signalling emotional distress rather than showing angry aggression, and a parent is able to provide caring comfort. Dialogue is not only mutual explicit expression or 'talking about' – here, we see the beginning of *dialogue in action* between a parent and a child.

From an attribution theory point of view, psychological assumptions lead to the attribution of certain traits in clients. Such attributions can be harmful (Furman and Ahola, 1989), and I have attempted to show how a binary view of a reductive trauma-based discourse versus a judgemental moral accountability discourse can become counterproductive. However, we need to assume that disposition can have a role in the emergence of problematic externalising behaviour. For example, children with 4 or more adverse childhood experiences are 32 times more likely to be diagnosed with a serious learning difficulty or a behavioural problem (Kelleher, 2021; Ward et al., 2021). Mainstream education is generally not well equipped to meet the needs of these children, which can lead to punitive and exclusionary responses and can be seen as a factor in mental health problems and/or criminal trajectories in adult life (Mallet, 2016).

A dispositional understanding does not contradict the possibility of short-term change, but it does call for the need to support a child that has shown a propensity for harmful behaviour that is borne out of adverse experiences. This must be support that goes beyond the ordinary intervention or therapy, support that helps maintain this child's social inclusion. Borne out of a possibilist position, adults entrusted with care of this child can integrate a growth mindset – a belief that the child can learn to effect self-control in the short term and that non-escalatory resistance to their aggressive behaviour is a key ingredient in such change – with a tragic view rather than a demonising or pathologising one (Alon and Omer, 2006) and orient themselves towards the future.

Eco-systemic narrative intervention

A new narrative of child and family requires an evidentiary action base, if it is to be credible to people in the social environment around the young person. The NVR-based resistance methods which caregivers use enable new and different forms of action that provide the terminus for transforming interpersonal processes. New, credible storylines can then be woven into the ecological social environment's narrative of the child and their family.

On the way to the airport, a taxi driver asks my wife what she does for a living. Answering that she works for social services, he responds: "Yeah yeah, the apple doesn't fall far from the tree...".

We can see how narratives that are informed by such a prejudicial discourse on children in care or in families facing multiple challenges are formed on the basis of highly selective information. Ultimately, we see what these children are up against, if this is a widespread discourse. Intersectionality often comes into play here, as well: economically disadvantaged children, children with disabilities, children of colour or belonging to ethnic minorities, trans-youth, young people whose parents have been affected by severe mental difficulties or serious drug – or alcohol habits – will find that the prejudices that flow into observations, perceptions and interpretations of their behaviour will confound the prejudice towards being in care or living in a family facing multiple challenges.

If we wish to develop an intervention that can bring about a change to the meta-narrative of a child and family that has had traumatic experience, we need to apprehend the complexity of the systems the child moves through (Käser, 1998). We can begin by drawing a social-ecological map. Some guiding questions for this map are:

- *Which people who are part of the social-ecological system are relevant to the child and their significant others?*
- *What kinds of stories do these people tell about the child and their significant others?*
- *How do these stories weave into a meta-narrative around the child and their significant others?*
- *How do the meanings that are attached to this meta-narrative in its different storylines influence the specific, concrete and observable interactions, the socio-cultural interpersonal processes between the child and their significant others, and between these and members of the wider system?*
- *How do these socio-cultural interpersonal processes relate to insufficiently met psychological needs of the child?*

Having mapped out the child's eco-systemic environment by answering these questions, we can search for what may become pivotal points for unhinging the entire meta-narrative. Stories of exception – unique outcomes – can be pivotal in such a way. In order to weave them into the overarching master-narrative, we need to find or establish a suitable communication platform that can act as a multiplier for story-telling. New storylines can be disseminated from such a platform. Freddie's case (Jakob, 2021) exemplifies this approach:

Freddie experienced extreme forms of abuse in his biological family, and later came into care. Following the serious injury of another child, he was permanently excluded from mainstream education. While our work aims at re-integrating him into mainstream education, a professional in a statutory agency comments that:

"He is on his best way to Broadmoor".[1]

His teacher and the Headteacher of his school have been informed that, according to a psychological assessment, Freddie suffers from a disorganised attachment disorder which seriously impedes his ability to interact with other children. A respite foster carer says to him:

"Freddie, you just can't manage to be with other children, it's too much for you".

Freddie himself seems to have internalised these attributions, and it appears that they provide a rationalisation for aggressive behaviour. On one occasion, after he has hurt another child, Freddie says that he couldn't help it that he isn't a normal child, because his mother's boyfriend used to hit him and her, – an internalisation that I believe hampers his social integration and sets him on a disadvantageous developmental trajectory.

Freddie would like to play basketball, but he is not allowed to; he is perceived as too much of a risk to other children. While he is told that he can't handle this situation, comments such as

"Do you want to know what he's done today?"

abound in the staff room. Recounting problematic incidents elicits powerful emotions, which are communicated in teachers' postures, facial expressions, prosody of voice, and in the decisions they make about Freddie. However, the fact that on a certain occasion he may have paid attention and worked hard during an English lesson, or on another occasion has helped another child, is unlikely to inform a story about him.

Outside of the school gates, "that boy in care" is often spoken about. His foster carer is ashamed and avoids eye contact with parents who have come to pick up their children from school. Freddie's comments indicate he has noticed she doesn't speak to the other parents.

Many storylines come into a narrative fabric that has a different or similar weave in different social spaces. This narrative fabric shapes the ways in which others perceive Freddie: his foster carer, his mother, his classmates and other children in school, their parents, his teachers. They also shape perceptions of his foster carer, and the ways in which Freddie perceives himself and understands his own persona. Perceptions of Freddie shape decisions about what he is allowed to participate in, or what he can choose to abstain from, in his everyday life at school; they shape how he is communicated with by different people in school, and the ways in which he is socially integrated or marginalised and excluded.

We work on the basis of the NVR principle of vigilant care. Freddie has a physically fit teaching assistant, who initially runs alongside him during basketball practice. Whenever Freddie appears to start becoming aggressive, he takes him to the side early on this behavioural pathway, but takes him back into game after only a short while, running alongside again. Eventually, Freddie's behaviour shows some improvement, and his teaching assistant runs in parallel to Freddie down the side of the gym, but no longer right alongside him. Eventually, the teaching assistant takes a standing position at the side of the gym, only to intervene when required. After a visit home with his mother, Freddie is 'unsettled' for several days, and his teaching assistant resumes running alongside him, but takes up his standing position again once his self-regulation appears to have returned back to the pre-visit level.

On one occasion, when he struggles with a maths assignment in class, Freddie kicks his teaching assistant. The next day, his foster carer and his teaching assistant enter the class together, and the teacher halts the lesson. Freddie's foster carer distributes chocolate brownies which she and Freddie baked together, as a reparative gesture for his violent act the previous day. This reparative act – unlike a punitive response, supported directly by the foster carer and in part carried out on his behalf to help prevent him being overwhelmed by a degree of shame he would not have been able to regulate – becomes a transitional ritual which marks Freddie's re-entry into the community of the classroom.

A number of teachers and parents of other children follow our invitation to a conversation about Freddie. His teaching assistant, his foster carer and his teacher give accounts of Freddie's successive integration in the basketball team, his participation in the reparational gesture, the foster carer's efforts, and his ongoing improvement. Another teacher conveys how glad it made her to see the joyful expression on Freddie's face after a basketball game, at which she had cheered him on (a need-based relational gesture that had been part of the careful planning of the overall intervention). Following these accounts, there is a general conversation about how these successes have become possible. The observed and recounted positive events, and the meanings attributed to them, substantiate the understanding that Freddie can change and become an integral part of the community of the school. Some of the participants agree to relate the information from this meeting to other parents. His foster carer records well-wishes by the parents on her phone and plays the videos back to Freddie later that day. New storylines have been woven into the narrative fabric around Freddie and his foster family.

Subsequent to this meeting, teaching staff notice that during break time, Freddie and other children play more often with each other than before. Soon, Freddie takes part in the daily school assemblies, and his foster carer and parents of other children speak more with each other at the school gates. Freddie's positions undergo an evolution over time: from 'outsider' to 'changing child' to, at a much later point, 'captain of the basketball team'!

The carefully planned and executed integration measures in this case example are based on a number of NVR principles, including vigilant care (Omer, Satran and Driter, 2016), reparation, presence-raising action such as sit-ins with teaching staff and foster carer, and relational gestures. Importantly, however, they are also utilised in the production of a new narrative around child and foster home, by virtue of underscoring the credibility of the claim that he is involved in a process of change. This storyline, in turn, raises the willingness to perceive and appreciate his ability to change within the wider social-ecological environment. Key in the NVR-based measures and the production of a new narrative, is the alliance between foster carer and teaching staff, which required intensive involvement by myself as the NVR practitioner, and which resulted in a two-pronged approach: non-acceptance of aggressive behaviour by raising presence in a determined way, while at the same time making a concerted effort to promote the child's social integration as a way of addressing his insufficiently met need. The invitation to parents of other children facilitated appreciative witnessing of the change process, including the foster carer's efforts, and thereby helped her own shame regulation. The new narrative that ultimately emerged was progressive, as opposed to the previous regressive narrative that incorporated stories identifying Freddie as pathologically disabled or morally compromised. Every single measure was undertaken with attention to the child's need to belong.

The anchoring function of attachment for young people who have experienced trauma

I have posited that a two-pronged approach to working with young people who show harmful behaviour, and who have experienced adversity is productive: resisting harmful behaviour nonviolently, while attending to a child's needs that often arise from trauma. What rationale underpins this notion? In developing the construct of the anchoring function of attachment (Omer et al, 2013; Omer and Dulberger, 2015), Omer made a significant contribution to an aspect of attachment that has been widely overlooked: in addition to a safe base provided by parents that a child internalises and can return to when the challenges they face threaten to overwhelm them, the child also requires a strong experience of parental *strength*. In this regard, Omer refers to Baumrind's (1981) understanding of two key parenting factors: responsivity on the one hand; guidance, support and an attitude of constructive expectation on the other. Baumrind understands responsivity as attunement, emotional warmth and availability to the child; this is the historic observational framework of attachment theory. We can understand the second aspect, that of guidance, support and constructive expectation, as the foundation of parental strength.

Omer considers both factors essential to the development of attachment security in a child. Caregivers resist harmful behaviour not only for their own sake or for the protection of other young people; they also resist for the benefit of the child who is acting in harmful ways. In other words, an adolescent who acts on their self-destructive impulses, a teenager who harms others – these young people need adults to resist them acting upon their dangerous impulses, so they themselves can feel safer in life. Instead of alienating them, resistance thus targeted can help them feel more connected to their parents, even if they resist the resistance. It is evidentiary to this that many children and adolescents respond very favourably to their parents' or caregivers' announcements, provided they incorporate both determination to resist and an expression of love and care. Clinically, we find that nonescalatory resistance seems to support young people's emotional self-regulation. Omer distinguishes four areas, in which parents *anchor* their children:

- By providing a safe *structure* of family life, in which parents define rules and routine and attend to these being observed, while at the same time supporting the child in acting according to these rules without overwhelming them with rigid firmness;
- By being *present*, in a way that, among others, is expressed in vigilance[2];
- By accessing social support as a transparent basis for parental authority[3] and
- By exerting *self-control* that is manifested when parents or caregivers neither escalate symmetrically with the child in an aggressive manner in order to exert power over the child, nor give in to intimidation.[4]

To ensure the structure of family life, when children or adolescents harm others in their social environment and strive to exert control over them, it is necessary for parents to be able to *predictably* resist in a nonviolent manner. In my view, children who have experienced their parents in the past as dependent on drugs or alcohol, or as severely depressed, or who have had to witness the disruption of family life by domestic abuse, child sexual abuse or physical violence, and/or who have experienced disruption by having to live in the care system, may strive to maintain the predictability of their social environment by aiming to exert control over it. Bureau,

Ann Easlerbrooks and Lyons-Ruth (2009) established a significantly higher rate of earlier childhood involvement with child protection agencies in children who in mid-childhood show hostile-controlling behaviours than in others. Depressive symptoms in mothers were associated with a higher rate of controlling child behaviour (Marchand, Hock and Widaman, 2002).

Of course, the research referenced above does not evidence a motivation in children with controlling behaviour to render their social environment more predictable. However, in clinical practice, we often see signs of distress in young people who are beginning to reduce or abandon their aggressive behaviour in the wake of their caregivers' nonviolent resistance. Behavioural change can go hand in hand with more communicated vulnerability:

Anthony witnessed domestic abuse and experienced physical child abuse in his biological family. He was threatened with physical chastisement, should he report any of this at school.

At the age of 7, Anthony is taken into foster care. After several months of NVR-based responses to his extremely violent behaviour and the reduction in his foster carers' fear of his angry-aggressive outbursts, the frequency and severity of violent incidents is dramatically lower than before. Soon, Anthony and his foster carers can all laugh about some of his occasionally recurring controlling verbalisations, such as threatening to tell his social worker that his foster carer has hit him, if she doesn't buy him an ice cream.

His foster carers observe what appears to be an inverse correlation in Anthony's behaviours: The more his aggressive behaviour diminishes, the more readily he discloses anxious associations and memories from his biological family, and the more he shares his anxiety about anticipated challenges at school. His foster carers support him by diligently observing family rituals which make his life more predictable, and eventually Anthony is referred for trauma-informed child psychotherapy by his social worker.

Four factors have been identified as being involved in the anchoring function of attachment: providing structure, presence, support of the child and emotional self-regulation of the parent (Kahn et al., 2019). It would stand to reason that, where these factors are present to a high enough degree in the parents' attitudes and responses to the child, the future could feel predictable. However, the anchoring must be perceived as such by the child. We can ask: does the parental anchoring function need to differ for young people who have had previous adverse childhood experiences from those who also engage in harmful or self-destructive behaviour, yet have not been exposed to such adversity? And if so, how? Starting from a recognition that children with traumatic experience often perceive their social environment as more threatening, and show a propensity to be aroused anxiously or angrily more readily, it becomes apparent that their caregiver's nonviolent attitude *in the widest sense* is of the utmost importance. We can understand this as an embodied attitude that is free from punitive or retaliatory responses, hostile or rejecting explicit or implicit communication, blame, rejection, shame-inducing criticism or affection that is conditional upon the child fulfilling the adult's expectations – an attitude that goes hand in hand with perseverance of resistance to harm by the young person, and with the provision of structure and guidance. The difference in emotionally anchoring children with traumatic experience to anchoring children who have not had high levels of adverse life experiences is not a qualitative one: children with traumatic experience simply need more strongly developed nonviolent attitudes in the adults who care for them. Statutory services such as CAMHS or social services, and other psycho-social providers need to support caregivers to cultivate their own nonviolent attitudes. Ultimately, these agencies require adequate funding to structure their service provision accordingly. Where they do not receive adequate funding to do so, the needs of children and young people with high levels of adverse experiences are neglected. It then becomes an issue of structural, systemic injustice, and NVR practitioners may find it important to identify certain vectors of resistance that lie outside of the family, such as resisting inadequate service provision by their own or partner agencies.

Figure 12.1 illustrates the necessity for even more diligent reflective planning and execution of nonviolent action, greater persistence and even more determined effort at nonviolence in the widest possible sense, without practitioners becoming critical of caregivers who are not yet meeting their expectations. In other words, as NVR practitioners, we are held to embody those very nonviolent attitudes *towards* caregivers as best possible that we would like them to embody towards the young people in their care.

We have developed the quadrant in the figure below to highlight two dimensions of resistance: its degree of violence/nonviolence, and the degree to which someone practising resistance is doing so in a manner that is more immediate, spontaneous, localised in one moment in time, unplanned, and marked by individual action (primary resistance), or to a greater extent long-term, planned, alliance-forming,

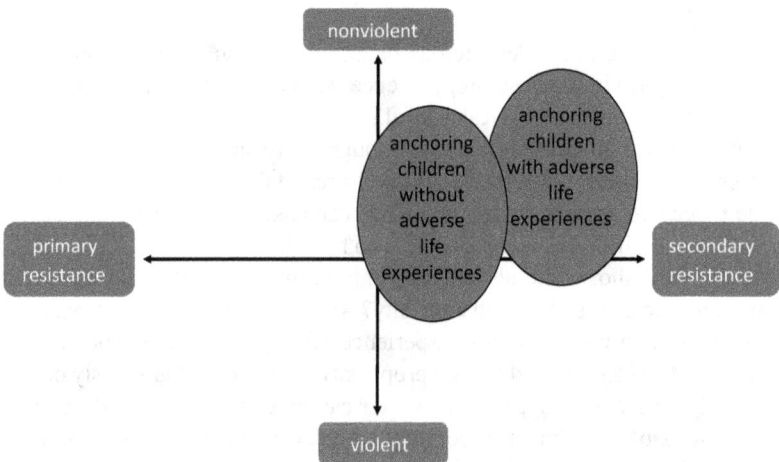

Figure 12.1 Anchoring function of attachment for children with adverse life experiences.

goal-oriented and imbued with meaning (secondary resistance). The vertical axis represents the violent/nonviolent dimension, while the horizontal axis represents the primary/secondary resistance axis. Using a definition of nonviolence that goes beyond mere apparent aggression or physical violence, we see that no-one who resists can maintain a consistently nonviolent stance; one can only act in ways that are more or less nonviolent. Even caregivers who embrace NVR will find that they have not always been able to act in a way that is both goal-oriented and free of harm:

A voice is raised in irritation of anger, a spontaneous, not a goal-oriented response. An adult wants to assert themselves here and now, perhaps feels the wish that the child or adolescent should "see what it's like" to feel humiliated, rejected or disempowered or hurt in some other way. The adult makes a cynical remark which targets a child whose behaviour has caused them much emotional pain.

From an attachment perspective, even a brief, spontaneous response of that nature represents a relational rupture, and where a young person has experienced so much relational rupture with hardly any repair in their life history, they are likely to be more susceptible to injury than others who have had more trusting relationships. The caregiver who just made that cynical remark has just moved a little vertically towards 'violent', and a little horizontally towards 'primary' – or, in the case of a child who has had disruptive and traumatic experience, probably more than just a little.

The more parents or other caregivers become able to move towards the upper right field of this quadrant, the better they can provide the anchoring function. Many children with adverse experiences show neurobiological and neuroendo-crinological adaptations to threat, or better, *perceived threat* (Teicher and Samson, 2016). They perceive threat more readily than others, and their body responds more readily to perceived threat. While some children show remarkable resilience, others can be exceedingly vulnerable in regard to further injury (Ohashi et al., 2019). Many show embodied threat responses to a social environment that others might experience as neutral or benign. As expounded earlier, it has been demonstrated that male adolescents with aggressive behaviour as well as male adolescents with anxious-avoidant behaviour interpret neutral facial expressions as more hostile than male adolescents with neither behaviour pattern.

Relational rupture occurs in daily life in all relationships. Often, small subtle responses cause relational rupture. Where there is a good foundation of trust in parent-child relationships, these frequent micro-ruptures do not affect attachment security, because often enough, rupture is repaired. Relational repair can be facilitated in family therapy, and family therapy has been demonstrated to increase attachment security (Diamond, Russon and Levy, 2016). While in systemic work with NVR conjoint family therapy is not yet possible, caregivers can nonetheless support the development of more secure attachment, by carefully planning and frequently using relational/reconciliation gestures to help repair relational rupture – as a venue towards building trust.

Mentalising messages can represent one form of delivering relational gestures. Mentalising is the ability to interpret, name and communicate about thoughts, beliefs, attitudes and emotions in oneself and in others, while remaining cognisant of the fact that one person can never be certain to have identified these internal processes in the other, and also communicating that understanding. There is a substantial body of evidence for the beneficial effect of improving mentalisation capacity on attachment security (Allen, 2018). Adults can counterbalance elevated threat perception and responsiveness in children, by combining their acts of resistance with carefully delivered messages about what they believe the child may be experiencing. In this way, they can bring a connective act in convergence with an act of resistance to harm. I believe it is a quintessential human need to feel the other is showing sincere effort to understand, even if they cannot fathom the depth of one's emotion.

However, mentalisation research has been criticised for not extending its observation to embodied responsiveness and the narrative construction of meaning (Køster, 2017). As traumatic threat responsiveness is powerfully embodied, and narrative that generates or reproduces meaning is generally fragmented where there has been trauma, I consider it necessary to incorporate these areas of experience into mentalising messages that are incorporated in relational gestures. While the occurrences in Ahmed's example predate the current (2023) war in Gaza, the more recent terrible events have given it special salience:

Ahmed[5] is 15 years of age. His cousin was injured by a gunshot in his leg during protests at the border fence between Gaza and Israel. He went to the hospital with his cousin, who died there from his injury. Ahmed has said that he feels he failed by not having been able to save his cousin's life.

Ahmed has suffered from insomnia since this event. He has frequent intrusive memories of his cousin's death and dying. The previously popular and affable teenager has developed aggressive behaviour patterns. He assaults other students and destroys chairs, desks and other furniture in his school. When asked why he behaves in this way, Ahmed retorts that he needs to defend himself. The other students, his siblings, parents, teachers and the school bus driver have all been severely affected by this violence.

In supervision, we develop an announcement, which will be delivered to him in person:

"Ahmed, you are an upright, honourable and loyal young man. We can see how engaged you are for justice, for your family and for your community. We love you, and we are proud of you.

Soldiers shot at you and your cousin. What you had to witness was terrible. You had to witness your cousin dying, and you stayed with him until the end. We are glad that he had you with him in his last moments.

You may often feel that you are being attacked, but your classmates, your friends and your family are not soldiers. When you attack them, you harm them, your family, your teachers and everyone who witnesses it. You also harm yourself, because you damage your relationships. We can no longer accept this violence, and we will do everything in our power, so you and the people who are close to you can live in peace with each other.

Your classmates, your teachers and your family do not want you to act with vio-
lence. Allah does not want you to act with violence. We do this, so that we can all
live together in peace. You belong to us".

In subsequent supervision sessions, our colleagues in Gaza report back a sig-
nificant improvement in Ahmed's behaviour, even before further NVR action has
been taken.

This case exemplifies the way in which an act of resistance can be modified to
support the anchoring function of attachment with a young person who has experienced serious trauma:

- The announcement begins with a positive description of the young person, which
  is in step with shared cultural values. A close, inclusive and loving attitude towards
  him is expressed. Several mentalising messages are incorporated that address
  Ahmed's possible internal processes, especially an embodied sense of threat. However, a direct empathic message, which could inadvertently have a shaming effect,
  is avoided. Instead of saying: 'You feel threatened', the announcement states:
  'You may often feel you are being attacked...' so he does not feel characterised
  as 'weak' and can save face yet feel understood. Initially, the announcement uses
  his own words. Importantly, the words 'you *may* often feel...' indicate that the
  adults do not assume to *know* with certainty what Ahmed is feeling and thinking.
  This aims to prevent a power imbalance between Ahmed and the adults who are
  delivering the announcement, so that Ahmed does not feel humiliated or shamed.
- Everyone, including Ahmed himself, is characterised as affected by violence.
  In a subtle way, violence is externalised, while Ahmed himself is held responsible for his future action. By including Ahmed in the group of people who
  are affected by violence, the adults take a position of multi-directional partiality: the way in which each individual is affected is considered and addressed.
  Multi-directional partiality here has an inclusive quality: it constructs a *we*,
  rather than a *you versus us*.
- While the problem externalisation of violence and the expressed multi-
  directional partiality has an implicitly inclusive quality, his inclusion in the
  community is also articulated explicitly. All inclusive messages are intended to
  counterbalance the sense of isolation that is generally an effect of trauma, and
  which in Ahmed's case was exacerbated by the avoidance of him by his friends
  and classmates in response to the aggressive behaviour he was demonstrating.
- Inclusion and appreciation of his person buffer the relational rupture the adults
  necessarily effect by demanding behaviour change.

Many practices in NVR may prove valuable in anchoring a young person, and
can be braided into acts of resistance. While Omer emphasises the importance
of structure and boundaries for the anchoring function, many children who have
been abused will find boundary setting by adults threatening if they associate this
with their earlier life experience of this having been done in violent, threatening

ways. For this reason, it can be important to routinely bring boundary setting into convergence with relational gestures. I often speak with clients about the notion of *being the boundary*, which alludes to embodied presence. This opens space for questions such as:

What kind of a boundary would you like to be? How will you be a boundary that reassures (child in question)? What, as that boundary, would you like to do that will reassure (child in question) that you love them/can be affectionate/care about them/won't abandon them/can protect them/can support them when they need you?

These questions can give rise to conversations in which relational gestures, that will be delivered around acts of resistance, can be carefully planned, in order to reassure a child with traumatic experience, that *this* boundary is a benign one.

Offering attention as a relational gesture can be reassuring to children who have experienced neglect. Unlike attention such children command when they act out aggressively or in other ways, a relational gesture of attention is not reactive; it is given proactively, as a one-sided act of care. In this way, it is not *taken from* the adult in the course of controlling behaviour, but *freely given* without antecedent demand. Rather than breeding resentment in the adult, when they feel coerced into paying attention, or the child experiencing the attention as devalued because *they had to demand it*, such gestures begin to restore interpersonal processes around caregiving.

Whatever the nature of the child's need that the adult's relational gesture aims to address, it is vital that a therapist supports the caregiver to make the gesture without any expectation of responsivity from the child. This is a true emotional trial given our dependence on responsivity. There is an implicit relational logic in the child rejecting a relational gesture, and the adult continuing to make relational gestures even though previous ones have been rejected: *If I reject your offer, am not nice to you, but you offer again, and again, and again – you really have to mean it!* This underscores unconditionality of the offer of care, which is delivered in conjunction with the setting of a boundary. Many parents or caregivers balk intuitively at this notion: *What, I'm supposed to be nice to her, when she has treated me so badly?* Therapists who work from an almost exclusively child-centred position run danger of becoming insensitive to the parents' need for affirmation by the child – which would be a given, were the child to graciously or happily accept their offer of care. Instead of giving the parent the message that they *should* interact in this way, and thereby taking up a critical and prescriptive position, a practitioner can face the parent empathically and show compassion for the parent's distress over missing responsivity from their child. In the next step, they can ask the parent to imagine future responsivity that they believe may ensue once the process of change is more advanced.[6]

An important aspect of the parental anchoring function lies in an often poorly understood relational logic. Children or adolescents who feel overly threatened in their social environments often do not implicitly feel that their parents will protect them. Not to be or to feel protected is a fundamental early life experience for many children in families where there is violence, abuse or neglect. In ordinary developmental trajectories, infants seek comfort and protection, when they reach out to parents, make eye contact, cry, etc. This kind of appeal for protection is a fundamental survival mechanism by a child who can neither show a flight nor a fight response, and where even an immobilising response would be insufficient. Very young children act with agency when they signal their need for protection in threatening situations in such ways. Both the embodiment of protection as a kind of 'physiological imprint', and the representation of the parent in the child's mind, play an important role in attachment processes, and Bowlby's notion of the parent as the 'safe base' is built on the assumption that the parent is available emotionally, can comfort the child and provide a sense of security (Cassidy, Ehrlich and Sherman, 2014). If we consider the circumstances of children growing up in highly dangerous conditions, a safe base would mean to assure mere survival in the face of overwhelming threat. If a non-offending or less threatening parent has been unable to respond effectively to the child's protection-seeking signalling, e.g. due to their own survival reactivity, showing fright, flag or submission to the assailing other adult, or because they have become severely depressed, dissociative or are using mind-altering substances in response to the psychological effects of the abuse they are suffering, the child has lost that particular form of agency. Seeking protection becomes a waste of energy.

A child with traumatic experience faces the developmental challenge to learn to trust that the caregiver is not only willing, but importantly, *predictably able* to protect. If they feel that they can intimidate and control the adult, they will not have an adequate perception of parental *strength*. Only a strong parent can protect. Mirroring a child's affect will be insufficient to reassure a child and help them trust the adult; they need to experience the adult resisting their controlling behaviour, in order to feel that this adult is strong enough to be able to protect; at the same time, they need to be reassured by the adult's emotional self-regulation and by the adult's relational gestures towards them. When parents' reactions are based on responsiveness alone, yet neglect resistance to acting out and controlling behaviour, there is a risk that the child continues to feel overly threatened in the world and compensates with aggression, which is a form of agency the child has developed. In the both/and of responsivity and resistance lies the formula for building trust and helping the young person feel more secure.

Child and shame

A psychologist once called the sit-in the *NVR shaming ritual*. It was her belief that in NVR, the child is intentionally shamed as a deterrent to acting with aggression. The notion that shaming is an element or at least an unintended byproduct of constructive resistance is not uncommon among some professionals who work in a trauma-informed way. It is their contention and concern that children who are already suffering from victim shame, are then subjected to an increased burden of shame. Weinblatt (2018) however made the very opposite observation: instead of creating a sheer unbearable burden of shame, NVR seemed to actually help children *regulate* shame better. This was also the case when members of the caring community/support network communicated to the young person that they knew about their problematic behaviour. How can this be explained?

A key function of shaming is to warn an individual or group about the possibility of social exclusion. It aims to ensure adherence to social norms by giving the message: *The way you now are, we don't want anything to do with you. If you continue to be like this, we won't have anything to do with you any longer.* By threatening exclusion, shaming aims to ensure conformity and coherence within a group or community. However, threatening exclusion can also become an instrument of ensuring power of others:

My granddaughter attends the first year of primary school. She is very proud of being a "big girl" now. At lunch, three girls sit together. As a fourth girl makes an attempt to sit with them, one of the girls makes a face and tells her:

"You can't sit with us!"

My granddaughter moves to sit down with the girl who has just been rejected. She intuitively knows that social exclusion is hurtful and acts with caring compassion, in order to buffer the other child's emotional injury. Later, she tells her parents about this incident, indicating that she continues to be emotionally and cognitively engaged with what happened earlier.

In discussing critical-prescriptive communication, I drew attention to the way in which rejecting communication, or communication that indicates one is seen to be of reduced relational value, activates brain circuits in a similar way to when a person experiences physical pain (Reis, 2014). This can render active shaming, which communicates reduced relational value and thereby threatens social exclusion, a harmful aversive behaviour. Such shaming is likely to have a negative impact on young people who have experienced social exclusion or who struggle with victim shame. If however there is transparency about harmful or self-destructive behaviour, while at the same time caregivers and supporters clearly communicate that they highly value the relationship with the young person by constructing a positive narrative of them, it will be much easier for the child to *regulate* shame.

Unlike shaming and being overwhelmed by shame, shame regulation is a constructive interpersonal and internal psychological process. Shame regulation is also fundamentally different from shame avoidance, which can have a very detrimental effect on a child's self-concept and confidence. Weinblatt (2018, p. 7) emphasises in reference to Potter-Efron (2007) that *"Shame likes to hide behind anger"*. Acknowledging, experiencing or even communicating shame causes a person to feel vulnerable, while anger creates a feeling of strength, if only temporarily. If however shame is not regulated, the potential for experiencing a high level of shame remains, as does the potential for anger.

Shame avoidance is an obstacle to shame regulation. Most of us are familiar with processes involving shame regulation. Who has not had the experience of feeling relief, when something they were ashamed about came to light, and they still felt accepted and valued by others? We can see that shame regulation is an important interpersonal process, while in shame avoidance, the burden of shame actually remains untouched. Shame is not only avoided by the young person themselves; its avoidance is also a systemic process. When parents wish to avoid their child feeling the discomfort of shame, or fear negative repercussions were their child to feel shame and therefore keep harmful, injurious behaviour secret, they inadvertently enable shame avoidance. In such an instance, unregulated shame increases the propensity for their child to avoid feeling shame by getting angry. If however a child with traumatic experiences becomes more able to accept their feelings of shame without becoming overwhelmed, shame regulation is given a chance. As with any emotion that is regulated, shame becomes bearable and passes with time. Strong messages of inclusion in the family, group and community support this process. Adults can promote shame regulation in a number of ways:

- Parents and supporters make intentional, targeted and persistent efforts to keep re-connecting with the child, even when the child appears to reject their efforts. They use *unconditional, socially inclusive relational gestures* in doing so.
- Caregivers *support* the child in making acts of reparation (rather than pressurising the child to carry these out as punishment), which improves the representation of the child in the eyes of people who have been upset or harmed by the child, or those who have witnessed what the child has done. This improved representation has a socially inclusive effect and facilitates re-integration. At the same time, the child learns to perform repair of relational rupture and experiences this as a positive interpersonal process. By learning that they can have a positive impact on relationships with others by repairing ruptures they have instigated, the child develops greater *relational agency* and can become less reliant on controlling agency.
- Based on the principle of unilateral action in nonviolent resistance, the adults can decide to undertake reparation on behalf of the young person, if their child is unwilling to do so. In doing this, they implicitly give the message: *We can't make you do this, but we can do the right thing on your behalf!* Acting on behalf of someone signifies their membership to the group – and at the same time promotes the inclusion of the group or family the child belongs to in the wider community.

The possibility of supporting a child to make reparation, and the possibility of making reparation on a child's behalf, are systemically significant. It is not uncommon for adults to avoid social contact with others due to the shame they feel in regard to a child's behaviour. This then has an isolating effect on the adults, but acts of reparation can reverse this isolating effect by helping the adults to regulate their own shame:

A foster carer has often felt controlled by the nine-year-old boy in her care, who will scream out loud that she is hurting him, even though she has not touched him at all, when she is setting a boundary, e.g. telling him he cannot go out to play wearing just a T-shirt in midwinter. Even though she diligently submits an incident report whenever this occurs, she is aware that the neighbour will have heard the child screaming, and no longer makes eye contact or greets the neighbour. It is only in the course of going next door to apologise for the disturbance, together with the fostering support social worker, and bringing a box of chocolates, that she and the neighbour can enter a conversation about the difficulties everyone in the foster family is experiencing. The neighbour agrees to pay the child a visit and brings him a magazine about fishing as a relational gesture, having learned about his budding interest in it. After telling him that his screaming has been upsetting to her, she tells him that her husband – who happens to enjoy fishing himself – is inviting him to join them on a fishing trip together with the foster dad.

Not for the first time, in a residential home, a teenage boy shouts obscenities from the flat roof of the garage in the middle of the night. Neighbours have been circulating a petition for removal of the home due to anti-social behaviour. A carer, whose attempts to stop him shouting obscenities that night are futile, rushes out to the car the next morning to avoid having any contact with any of the neighbours. In a carefully planned act of reparation, a next door neighbour agrees to ask the adolescent into her house in the company of one of his carers. Surprisingly, he agrees to go next door to make an apology, bringing biscuits he has bought from his own money. He makes an apology to the neighbour, who invites them for tea with the biscuits he has brought her, and they stay for about ½ hour. The carer feels proud of him, but feels it is better to show her pride in him nonverbally. For days afterwards, he expresses his surprise at "how nice" the neighbour is. The neighbour also agrees to tell other people in the street about this act of reparation.

In both cases, socially inclusive relational gestures were made to the young person to support them in regulating their shame. Importantly, the acts of reparation supported the shame regulation in the caregivers as well as in the young people themselves, thereby facilitating social integration not only of the individual young person, but of the entire group/family.

A particularly effective way of supporting shame regulation can be the positive campaign of concern. While derived from Omer's (2021c) original *public opinion intervention,* in which supporters communicate with the young person about problematic incidents to express their non-acceptance of such behaviour, in the positive campaign of concern,[7] supporters also communicate with the young person, but in a manner that can help construct a more positive narrative of the child.

How can communication by supporters be carried out in a manner that helps a young person to feel included rather than gaining the impression that *everybody is against me* or feel threatened by social exclusion in some other way? How can communication by supporters avoid reinforcing negative, self-directed beliefs? How can supporters show acceptance, and that they value the person of the child and their relationship with them, while at the same time communicate clearly that they cannot accept harmful behaviour? Changing the name of the method itself from 'public opinion intervention' to 'positive campaign of concern' already signifies an attitude that makes such an outcome more likely: supporters feel and express *multidirectional concern* – concern for parents, teachers, siblings, other children in school – and concern for the child themselves that has acted harmfully, while emphasising that this child belongs to 'us'. I cannot feel concern for a person and at the same time reject them.

I adopted Frank van Holen's (personal communication) idea that supporters can respond to positive events in foster homes. Van Holen uses a ratio of 3 to 1, i.e. messages about three 'positive events' for every time there are messages pertaining to a matter of concern. I believe that this kind of supporter communication contributes significantly to the success of NVR work in foster care in Belgium (Van Holen, Vanderfaeillie and Omer, 2016). From a solution-oriented point of view, it makes sense to direct attention to constructive child behaviours – and to interpersonal processes around such behaviours. The magnification of these exceptions can help increase such transforming interpersonal processes in the family, children's home, in the foster family or in school.

We can infer from neuropsychological research into social resonance (Wheatley and Sievers, 2016) that it may be useful not only to draw attention to exceptions to the problem, but also to any indication of thriving in a young person. When there is synchronicity of brain function, two people concurrently process information in the same way. They are, so to speak, on the same wavelength. Their synchronicity manifests itself on different 'channels' at the same time, such as prosody of voice, posture, movement and facial expression. The greater the attention to one another, the more brain synchronisation takes place. The more attention the adult pays to the child when communicating about positive events, the more synchronisation will likely take place. We can use the campaign of concern to establish mutual attention and brain function synchronicity in communication about exceptions and thrive signals, and in doing so create feedback loops in and around the family. When constructive behavioural options are chosen by the child, mutual attention in communication about them can, by virtue of brain synchronisation, reinforce these and attenuate problematic options. We create a different 'atmosphere' by 'coming onto the same wavelength'.

Both/and communication in the campaign of concern can promote an integration of apparently contradictory messages about the child: 'This needs to change' *and* 'You are important to us'; 'I am concerned about what you did there' *and* 'I appreciate that about you'. This both/and expresses itself more implicitly, 'atmospherically', than explicitly.

Method: The positive campaign of concern Part I: From initiating the campaign to messages of concern

You can initiate the campaign of concern towards the end of a supporters meeting, by describing the procedure, its rationale and its 'spirit'.

After the meeting, the parents or caregivers set up a WhatsApp group with supporters who have agreed to take part in the campaign. One parent takes over the moderation of the group and reports positive events and problematic incidents at a ratio of at least 3 to 1 (rule of 3).

When there have been especially serious incidents, it is advisable to avoid and discourage any speculation about why it occurred (e.g. 'trauma-speculation'). The moderator simply reports factually what the child did and how the parents responded. If the parent or parents acted in an escalatory way themselves, they should also report this and let the child know they are reporting their own problematic behaviour as well, for the sake of transparency and fairness, and to raise the parents' moral authority.

The moderator nominates certain supporters to respond to the child, preferably in person or failing that by video call, in regard to a specific problematic incident or a positive event. Again, the rule of 3 applies: there should be 3× as many positive events to which supporters respond, as problematic incidents.

Where a young person refuses to speak to a supporter in person, messages can still be transmitted in other ways, e.g. by text, videorecording or in form of a traditional, hand-written letter! I have seen many creative forms of messages, using cartoons, video-clips, music, poetry, etc. It is helpful to make messages interesting for the young person.

It is important not to express any expectation as to how the young person should react to the message, e.g. ask them to promise not to do this again or to show remorse. This can also be escalatory.

Multi-directional partiality should be adhered to. Concern should be expressed for every one affected by the problem behaviour, *including the child who has instigated it.* It would, however, be counterproductive if, from a child-centred position, the supporter *only* expressed concern for the child who instigated the harmful or self-destructive act: this would be an invitation to self-centredness without attention to the wellbeing of others.

Any message concerning a problematic incident should include a connective, bridge-building signal, to give it an inclusive quality. Implicit bridge-building signals are better that explicit ones:

Hi Frank, I'm calling round because I wanted to see how everyone is today after the argument that broke out yesterday... (pause, to give child a chance to respond). I was concerned when I heard that you pushed your mum against the wall and threatened her with your first, because she got really frightened, and I know you've been really upset when you've done something like this. It's normal to feel angry sometimes, but the aggression has got to stop, for your and your mum's sake. Listen, when things get too much, you can always come over, you're always a welcome guest in our house. By the way, we're having a barbeque on Saturday, and Leon would really like you to come. He wants to show you his new video game. You free?

Problem incident messages should be brief and concise; long-winded messages can have a shaming or escalating effect, and the young person will simply stop listening.

The bridge-building signal emphasises that the supporter takes on a position of concern for the young person, rather than being judgemental, and reassures them by showing a benevolent attitude – thereby supporting their shame regulation. Without any expectation that they should respond in a certain way, the young person can absorb the message and process it in their own time, without losing face.

Messages in response to events that show signs of thriving in the young person, or messages about exceptions to problematic interaction, balance messages of concern. Influenced by positive psychology (Brown et al., 2017), I consider thrive events to be of great value in a positive campaign of concern. They differ from exceptions, in that they are not specifically related to the absence of the problem and processes which occur instead of it. Three specific areas of thriving seem to be especially important to highlight and useful to focus on in the campaign of concern:

1   Prosociality (Zaki and Mitchell, 2016),
2   Showing effort to increase endurance and frustration tolerance, and
3   Showing resilience in the face of challenges.

Young people often express their appreciation for such positive messages. However, positive messaging should be revised and adapted to reflect the learning of parents and the caring community:

A young woman, Ruth, was adopted as a one-year-old. She has often communicated that she feels out of place among peers, feels in some undefined not normal, and has an undesirable appearance. At the outset of her mother's work with NVR, Ruth shows adult entrenched dependency (Dulberger and Omer, 2021): She has withdrawn socially, has reversed her night/day rhythm and no longer attends college or work, threatens suicide and has at times responded with physical aggression to her adoptive mother.

Ruth tells her mother that she feels humiliated when she receives appreciative messages about things that 'anyone could be expected to do'. Her mother subsequently only requests messages to her daughter for extraordinary events, such as when Ruth goes back to college for the first time. Ruth appreciates these extraordinary event messages and finds them encouraging – especially the bottle of prosecco a supporter gives her after she has taken her first exam![8]

Method: The positive campaign of concern Part II: Positive event messages

Supporters can relate messages – best in person, on video call or as a video message – that highlight two kinds of positive events: exceptions to the problem and 'thrive events'.

Exceptions are occasions on which, in a similar context, problematic behaviour could have been expected, but an alternative response was shown by the young person instead. The messages should be brief. First person messages are advisable. Instead of referring to the absence of problem behaviour, the message should merely highlight the alternative behaviour, e.g.:

Good to hear you guys had a nice weekend camping in the Lakes. We went there last year. Here are some pics, or

So you went to the British Museum to see the Roman Legion exhibition. Here's a link I thought you might find interesting.

Implicit in both messages is the absence of an aggressive incident which ordinarily would have been expected during an outing, yet they subtly highlight alternative behaviour by the young person.

First person messages can give a subtle impression of the positive effect the young person's behaviour has on the supporter, thereby drawing attention to their relational agency: *I really enjoyed looking at the nature photos you took; they brought up some nice memories of when we all went on that camping trip.*

Unlike exceptions, thrive signals do not seem to be immediately linked to the absence of the problem, yet they often emerge at times when the problem does not manifest itself frequently. Thrive signals can be an early indication of future *healing interpersonal processes*. Examples are: a child shows effort in class, rather than giving up easily; a teenager has been enjoying skateboarding more than they used to; an adolescent befriends and supports another girl who is new to the school; a young person is trying to secure an apprenticeship; a young adult has gone to college every day for a prolonged period of time and is making new friends.

Adults should be very careful in their use of praise, or even avoid praise altogether. Often, difficult behaviours emerge with greater severity a few hours or days after a young person has received praise. Praise can be perceived as dominant communication, in that the adult is judging the young person, or they may feel the praise is not credible and it can therefore reinforce a negative self-directed belief or self-concept. Praise can also set a standard that is perceived as too high and the young person feels they cannot attain that standard, resulting in performance pressure and fear of unregulated shame: *She's taking the piss again!*. Instead, *indirect* messages which communicate that the supporter has become aware of the exception to the problem or early signs of thriving can act as appreciative responses in a powerful way. For example, a young person's previous social worker was now volunteering as a supporter. When he learned that the teenager had signed up for a GCSE astronomy course and was developing a keen interest in the subject, he brought up an old telescope that had been in his basement, cleaned it and gifted it to the young person.

Supporters should feed back to the moderator – a parent or caregiver – the message they are giving and any response they may have had from the young person, especially if there has been a personal conversation.

As the practitioner, you may wish to monitor the communication in the WhatsApp group. Caring communities develop a culture of their own, and many elements of these cultures can be very beneficial to the change process, e.g. when parents receive moral support for difficult steps they are taking. I do not tend to involve myself directly in the group's communication, but find it useful to direct-message parents to support their moderation of the group and help ensure that productive communication is maintained. Often, parents quickly grow accustomed to improved interaction in the family, such as an absence of physical aggression and severe escalation and overlook the supporters' needs to learn about this improvement. Moderators can feed back improvement to the WhatsApp group, including the contributions they themselves have been making. Informing supporters about improvement can help ensure that they feel their efforts are important and meaningful. As well as feeling the need for information about improvement, supporters also find it helpful to receive instructions and advice on how to communicate with the young person (Hicks, Jakob and Kustner, 2020).

It is important to help supporters appreciate that it would be counter-productive to expect responsivity. I often speak about the relational logic, whereby continued messaging against the background of the child's rejection or ignoring of their efforts communicates to the young person that the supporters must *really mean it*.

I am increasingly using positive campaigns of concern with positive event messages only, finding this especially helpful where the nature of the child problem behaviour is more internalising rather than directly harmful to others, such as school refusal and social self-isolation and withdrawal or adult entrenched dependency (Dulberger and Omer, 2021), physical self-harm or suicidal thinking and behaviour.

The positive campaign of concern can support the construction of a coherent and sufficiently positive narrative of the child and family.[9] Supporters around the family communicate to the young person that they value the relationship with them. These carefully planned yet simple messages can help the young person integrate different attributions of their person. The implicit message is: *We like/love/care about/ appreciate you. You belong to us! You are able to be nonviolent – now!* This both/ and of seemingly contradictory attributions can support the young person's shame regulation. The bridge-building, connective character of communicating with them promotes social integration and the young person's sense of belonging. The perception of the child can improve among supporters who participate in a positive campaign of concern. The young person, in turn, can look at themselves through the eyes of supporters and feel they are being perceived in a benign, friendly and appreciative way. This can help them integrate the adults' non-acceptance of harmful behaviour.

Connective resistance: Creative methods for effective anchoring

I illustrated that *especially* emotionally safe communication can help children with aversive experiences feel anchored and develop more secure attachment. Whenever steps are taken to resist harmful or self-destructive behaviour, it is advisable to also undertake something that can nurture the relationship between parent and child.

One way of bringing a child focus and constructive resistance together is to resist specifically such behaviours, which prevent the young person's own emotional and social needs from being met. One way of doing so is to construct creative acts of resistance that are in and of themselves relational gestures (Shoesmith and Castle, 2019). Sadie's example, which needs to be understood in the context of comprehensive therapeutic work in a residential service for young people, illustrates this principle:

14-year old Sadie is taken into the residential service after spending several months on an inpatient child psychiatric ward following an earlier attempt to take her own life while she was living in foster care. Due to the attempts on her own life, her foster carers did not accept her back into the family. There are three adolescents in the group home. Against the backdrop of serious child abuse, gender violence by her father and her mother's and her mother's later partners' heroin dependency, Sadie remembers imagining again and again over the years that she is looking into her classroom from the outside and seeing that her own chair is empty. She often feels remote from everyone and from ordinary life, has a sense that she does not belong on Earth, and that she will die young. At other times however, Sadie can also be good-humoured and engage on a deep emotional level with other young people. She is popular with her carers and with many other young people. Together with her carers and the managers of her home, she resists the inertia by social services' in failing to facilitate regular and more frequent contact with her brothers, who are in care elsewhere.

An adolescent in the group instigates emotional abuse against Sadie for a significant length of time. One way in which he does this is to ridicule her for the kind of childhood abuse she has had to suffer. He systematically alienates the other teenager from her and forms an alliance in which they deprecate her.

The caregiver team resist the adolescent's emotional abuse of Sadie by calling in a campaign of concern and carrying out several house occupations.[10] These measures have some effect, and the emotional abuse of Sadie is reduced. Eventually, he is moved to another group home. Nonetheless, Sadie has been re-traumatised, and her carers are concerned that her suicide risk may have risen. My risk assessment confirms this. Her social cognition has become skewed: Sadie has very little awareness of the attention significant others pay her, and she feels estranged from them. When asked about other people who are close to her, such as her brothers, her mother, friends and caregivers who all care about her, Sadie expresses her belief that they would all be relieved from a burden if she weren't around. Everyone around her might be sad for a week or two.

Our resistance is directed at Sadie's social perception, at her negative self-concept and the sense of estrangement that developed over many years of experiencing and witnessing abuse, and that has been actualised by the recent emotional abuse.

To begin with, her acute risk needs to be reduced. Sadie had experienced the supervision on the previous psychiatric ward as observation, low in emotional warmth, distant and protocol-driven. While these responses may have prevented serious self-harm at that point in time, they appear to have done very little to counterbalance Sadie's sense of social alienation. Therefore, a great effort is made by her caregivers to practise vigilant care in the group home while creating an atmosphere of warmth. Young female supporters intensify their contact with Sadie, watch rom-coms together; the caregivers adjust the level of their vigilance according to indicators of relative risk or relative safety. This helps to support her during the first, acute phase of risk.

In a campaign of concern, Sadie's skewed social cognition and her restricted social perception are resisted. For a prolonged period of time, a number of supporters send Sadie messages, in which they implicitly indicate that they are bearing her in mind. This campaign is moderated by a manager in the service, who receives all messages and passes them on to Sadie in a manner in which she feels they can have the best effect. In particular, we use messages that show people are thinking of her, including carers from other group homes. We will not let her "forget" that we are there, and that she exists in her relationships with us! We persevere in giving her the message that we "carry Sadie in us". My own contribution to the campaign of concern, as the residential service's psychologist and a supporter, is to send pictures of landscapes I hike through on vacation.

Omer (2017); Omer, Satran and Driter (2016) distinguish between 'supervision' and 'vigilant care'. In vigilant care, we aim to not only prevent self-harm in the moment, but also create a warm interpersonal atmosphere and reduce physical as well as emotional distance by raising presence (Omer and Dulberger, 2015). This kind of unilateral resistance is intended to have a relationally connective effect. The resistance method here becomes an important relational gesture which implicitly communicates: *We are here. We won't remain invisible. You can't shake us off or forget about us. We are here for you. You matter to us!* The young person will only experience such gestures as meaningful and connective, if the adults are attuned to them to a high degree and their action is infused with a deeply felt, real interest in their wellbeing. This, in turn, requires a high level of professional support and mutual support among caregivers.

The supporters' ability to persist in their presence-raising acts – the face of very little resonance by the young person – needs to be cultivated, especially when crises erupt every so often over a prolonged period of time. They need to feel enabled to come together, plan and carry out such action repeatedly, because young people with traumatic experience can have a significant propensity for setbacks, when traumatic states of consciousness reestablish themselves and gain traction over more functional states in response to occurrences in the social environments. From an attachment-oriented perspective, we can see a particular relational logic at work here: if a young person, who periodically experiences setbacks, finds that the adults around them 'stay the course' whenever they fall into the pattern of acting with harm or in self-destructive ways, they can develop a felt sense that "they'll be there for me in the future, too. They won't abandon me". This can be a corrective experience which is of a radically different nature to the earlier childhood experience of neglect, abandonment and lack of protection.

When young people perceive that the adults' action which combines resistance with relational gestures requires much effort or even personal sacrifice, this can powerfully appeal to them. Mahatma Gandhi's hunger strike inspired the idea to act in ways that require some degree of personal sacrifice. However, unlike Gandhi's hunger strike, these kinds of action should not result in self-harm, but have a constructive effect on the life of the adult, as well. A further episode in Sadie's life illustrates this:

Sadie is very intelligent. Even though she has missed school for two years due to neglect and frequently changing care arrangements, she is capable of catching up and achieving passable grades. This is in part due to her ability to concentrate and apply herself to her learning. At such times, she can even see a future for herself in life, and thinks about becoming a psychologist. The last suicidal crisis occurred over a year ago, and her GCSE exams[11] are imminent. Suddenly, Sadie refuses to go to school and stays in bed until the afternoon. In keeping with the narrative which has reasserted itself in her thinking, according to which she does not belong in the world, is different from everyone else and cannot face challenges like others do, Sadie is certain that she will fail her exams. All efforts by her carers to encourage her to get up and attend her classes fail.

In order to demonstrate to Sadie that performance anxiety can be bearable and that we believe in anyone's innate capacity to face difficult challenges, her carers and other supporters decide to undergo certain ordeals, which will stimulate emotional discomfort or even anxiety in us, but at the same time will have a positive effect on our lives. For example, a manager who has not played her instrument for many years takes lessons, practices and gives a concert, even though this is fraught with stage fright. Some of the supporters go and work out at the gym or undertake other effortful activities. All action is recorded, and the videos are sent to her. Sometimes, Sadie and her carers have to laugh at what they see.

Some teachers agree to invigilate[12] certain exams at home. Sadie agrees to take some other exams at school, where this is not possible. She succeeds in attaining GCSEs.

Here, we see an approach that operates on several levels: the ordeals which carers and supporters undergo are unconditional gestures of care. At the same time, they stand against the young person's self-destructive anxious avoidance. The sacrificial nature of the ordeals – going further than the 'extra mile' – generates a powerful demand characteristic. At the same time, they are connective and inclusive. Any kind of communication that could be understood to be threatening, punitive or devaluing is scrupulously avoided so that no message risks becoming associated in the young person's mind with traumatic experiences in her family, on the psychiatric ward or in other care contexts.

Nurturing constructive parental attitudes

We have examined the parental anchoring function in light of adverse experiences in early life. I suggested ways in which adults can adjust their action in ways that can build the young person's trust, in order to fulfil the anchoring function against a backdrop of trauma and attachment insecurity. I further emphasised the importance of the experience of parental strength as a necessary quality of interaction that can help the young person feel that the adult can potentially act in protective ways. This strength can help the young person feel more secure, as long as the adult's attitude is *perceived* to be completely non-threatening. Of course, in spite of their best efforts, caregivers will at times feel ambivalently towards the young person, and the adult cannot be realistically expected to consistently provide the kind of mindful care the young person needs in this respect. A young person with adverse experiences may be more likely to selectively direct their attention to subtle incongruences in their caregivers' communication, even if, overall, the adult embodies a positive attitude.

It would be unhelpful for a therapist to evaluate parents on the basis of how well they communicate warmth and a positive attitude towards the young person, or fail to do so. This would engender critical-prescriptive communication towards the caregiver, undermine their confidence and weigh heavily on the relationship with the practitioner. Instead, a practitioner can aim to form an *alliance* with the caregiver and support them in acquiring more of the kind of parental attitude they themselves wish to embody. It is therefore helpful to think of acquiring a more congruent, benign embodied attitude towards the child as an ongoing change process, rather than expecting it to be prevalent in a normative way. Mindfulness practices have been demonstrated to reduce parental stress (Burgdorf, Szabó and Abbott, 2019). The mindfulness exercise below is an example of how a parent can be supported to cultivate their desired attitude.

Method: Mindfulness exercise for cultivating parental presence

You can use this exercise when working with parents to prepare for positive action such as an *announcement* or a *sit-in*. It is also suitable for working with groups or in clinical supervision. It is important to stress that this exercise aims to help parents cultivate the attitude they wish to embody – it is a preparation for their internal process, not what they will actually do when they take action. It can be useful to practise the actual parental behaviour in role play immediately after this exercise.

I would recommend experiencing this exercise oneself in peer-supervision, before offering it to clients.

When using this exercise with parents, one parent can represent themselves while the other assumes the role of the child. If you are working with one caregiver only, they should represent themselves, while the child is represented by an empty chair.

The client just listens, while you introduce them to the exercise and subsequently read the text. Deliver the introduction and the mindfulness text slowly, giving them the opportunity to assume a mindful state.

Introduction:

One of you will imagine that you are (son/daughter/child), who, not for the first time, has acted with aggression or caused harm in some other way. The other one will be the parent/caregiver, who has been hurt/harmed/hit/attacked. In the course of the next few minutes, you will sit together in silence. Of course, this exercise doesn't mirror your reality – in reality, (child) would be unlikely to sit there quietly in a sit-in. The purpose of this exercise is merely to experience the kind of thoughts, feelings and body sensations that are likely to arise in you when you take nonviolent constructive action or, in the role of the child, to learn how it may feel towards them when the parent/caregiver undertakes such action. Please do not discuss anything, just determine who will be the child and which of you will be yourself, and sit with one another quietly for a while.

To the parent/caregiver:

As the adult, I would like to ask you to imagine you are sitting out of protest against what the young person has done. You have allowed enough time to pass before taking this action. This is your response, using yourself as a person. Your aim is not to punish (child) – it is to raise your presence, to make yourself felt as best you can, as the whole person you are.

Please notice the focus of your attention. Are you looking at (child)? Are you looking away? Take some time to realise the quality of your gaze. Notice how your awareness changes over time.

Notice your breathing. Start on the outbreath. Out, in. Do not try to alter your breathing. Is your breathing deep or shallow? Slow or fast? Is it easy to breath, or hard? Just notice how you are breathing.

Allow yourself to notice how your body feels. What part of your body do you notice the most? Allow yourself to become aware of tension in any part of your body; to become aware of any part of your body that feels relaxed and comfortable. Do you feel energised? Does your body feel tired or heavy? Do you feel an impulse to move? Where do you feel that impulse?

Please notice your emotion, as you sit in silence with (child). Do not censor yourself; it is ok to feel whatever you are feeling, just notice what you feel emotionally. As you pay attention to it long enough, you will notice your emotion changing; it may become more or less intense; it may pass and give way to another feeling. Just notice your emotion; notice it changing.

How do you want to see your child? How do you want to feel about your child? What is the parent like that you wish to be, at this moment in time? What parent do you want your child to see, to hear, to be aware of? What of this parent do you find in yourself right now? How does it feel to be this parent? Find in yourself your resistance against what (child) has done; find in yourself what you wish for your child.

To the adult in the child's role:

As (child), please notice mother/father/carer) who is sitting with you. What do you see in their face, in their body? What does that say to you about how they are relating to you, here and now, in this moment? Do you sense peacefulness? Do you sense hostility? Does (parent/carergiver) look determined? Do they seem strong? Tense? Calm?

Notice your thoughts about (parent/caregiver). Do you just hold one thought in mind, or are there several? Notice how your thinking changes, as they sit quietly with you.

Allow yourself to be aware of your body sensation, as you sit with the adult. Do parts of your body feel comfortable? Do you feel discomfort in your body? Where do you feel this in your body? Please notice any impulse to move in your body.

Notice your emotion. You do not need to label it; just feel what you feel. Notice as your emotion changes over time, while you observe it. It may become more or less intense; it may pass and give way to another feeling. Just notice.

Please notice your feelings about what you have done. Notice how they change, as (parent/caregiver) sits with you now.

Who, to you, is this parent you are sitting with at this moment? What is the young person like that she/he/they is looking for in you? What of this person that she/he/they is looking for do you find in yourself?

Thank you for remaining silent. If you would like to, you can share your experience now.

The exercise above aims to help parents and other caregivers notice their emotional and physiological responses to the child. This can help them attune to their child in real life situations, in a manner that is congruent with their preferred parent self. The adult who is in the role of the child can notice the way in which the parent's body language is free from aversive responsiveness, or they will be able to give feedback when this is not the case. Finally, the exercise can elucidate that there needs to be no binary opposition between resistance and care for the child.

Overcoming constraints to adult care for the child is the terminus for child-focused work in NVR. We can attempt to resolve conflict, distrust and estrangement in dialogue, but where dialogue is not yet possible, resistance is necessary. However, resistance can be organised and carried out in a way that *moves adult-child communication towards dialogue*. The future dialogue should be of a kind that will enable parents to feel caring and act with care towards their child, and will address the younger person's existential and psychological needs. This will be a dialogue, in which the child recognises the caring quality of the adult's mindset towards them and, beyond that, validates the adult in that capacity. The following chapter will investigate some avenues which can move interpersonal processes in the direction of such dialogue.

Notes

1 High security psychiatric hospital in England. In British English, 'Broadmoor' is associated with dangerous, sociopathic or mentally ill patients prone to high levels of criminality.
2 I feel that, from a trauma-informed point of view, a key aspect of parental presence is that of its embodiment, which enables co-regulation with this child. (See Chapter 5.) This is especially important when it comes to children who show high threat reactivity.
3 See Chapter 2.
4 I would like to distinguish between self-control and self-regulation: Self-control entails the parent resisting their own angry-aggressive or anxious-submissive/anxious-avoidant impulses and leaving the behavioural pathways they would be on if they gave in to such impulses, while self-regulation, which is essentially the down-regulation of heightened psycho-physiological arousal, occurs in the wake of acts of self-control. Persisting in self-control helps improve caregivers' capacity for self-regulation, which, in turn, supports children's co-regulation with them.
5 This case was discussed in supervision with practitioners who have been trained and supervised by the NGO "Bridges for Hope and Peace" (B4HP) in Gaza, to carry out interventions based on NVR (there, known as "New Family Authority").
6 See Chapter 13.
7 See Chapter 2.
8 It is important to note that the celebratory gift is given for *attending* an exam, not for exam success.
9 See Chapter 13.
10 A house occupation is an NVR method in which a number of supporters spend hours or days in the home of a person who has been targeted with aggression, to communicate their firm will to protect this person and express their solidarity with them.
11 Intermediate secondary school exams which are usually taken at the age of 16 in the UK.
12 American English: proctor.

Chapter 13

Caring dialogue

I have previously begun to formulate a critique of the concept of 'blocked care' (Hughes and Baylin, 2012), according to which certain child behaviours actualise emotional injuries in their parents' own attachment histories, thus incapacitating the adult's ability to attune to the child and show emotional resonance. My contention is not with the actual occurrence of earlier emotional injuries becoming actualised in the wake of certain child behaviours, of course that can be the case; it is with what I see as the reductive framing of difficult interpersonal processes by this explanatory model. I consider it problematic for a number of reasons.

- 'Blocked care' sits within an attachment understanding that pathologises parents. To this day, child care largely remains a female occupation. Implicitly and explicitly, more responsibility for child wellbeing is attributed to women than to men. Attachment theory continues to focus largely on mother-child interaction. This creates mono-causal attributions of insecure attachment to what is identified as maternal failure that, in turn, is seen as deeply rooted in the female parent's psychology. In other words: insecure attachment becomes maternal failure. When therefore a mother or other female caregiver is identified as someone who 'has blocked care', and attributions of failure are internalised, parents – and disproportionately mothers – are at risk of developing deep feelings of guilt.
- Feminist critique in systemic thinking has identified a significant gender difference, which is not addressed in the blocked care concept. For many women, child care contributes far more to their identity formation, their sense of accomplishment in life and their self-affirmation than for men. To feel charged, implicitly or explicitly, and internalising the charge of parental failure, can effect serious loss of identity in women (Walters et al., 1991).
- The focus on the parent's own attachment history and the immediate parent-child interaction localises problematic interpersonal processes within this dyad and in the parent's internal world alone, thereby de-contextualising these difficulties. At the intersection of different discriminating societal discourses, internalisations of the above nature can have a particularly devastating effect on parents' confidence, such as when they are single mothers or belong to a disadvantaged ethnic or racial group in society (Phoenix, 2013). Economic disadvantage and

DOI: 10.4324/9781032717111-18

devaluing attitudes towards single parents can further exacerbate such processes (Funcke and Menne, 2020). What meanings are e.g. attributed to the difficulties in the behaviour of e.g. a Black or Brown child of a single Black or Brown mother who is economically disadvantaged? How do these meanings impact upon her self-concept and identity as a person, and her confidence and ability to attune to her child?

- We can highlight constraints that are associated with economic disadvantage or structural injustice: What is the quality of affordable housing or of affordable day-care for the child in the family's particular socio-economic environment?
- Fathers often feel irrelevant or marginalised, when conversations that are shaped by traditional attachment understandings focus on the mother-child dyad. It is rarely made a topic of conversation, when fathers indicate they have no time to attend therapeutic or family support sessions or other meetings that are relevant to their child. Patriarchally shaped expectations of heterosexual cisgender masculinity may lead fathers or step-fathers to experience explicit or implicit criticism, or feeling cast as 'unmanly', when they do not respond to difficult child behaviour in ways that conform to such expectations: *Why did he just stand there, when his son hit her?*
- Stereotypical, prejudicial images of fathers who belong to ethnic or cultural minorities, particularly Black men, can have very negative effects on their sense of self value (Banks-Rogers, 2020), especially when they feel under pressure to demonstrate competence as a responsible father, and thereby undermine their capacity to attune to their child.
- As noted earlier in reference to parental erasure, the blocked care concept does not encompass the notion that *any* parent will have a need to feel validated by their child, and that their own disposition, rooted in their attachment history, is neither a sufficient nor a necessary condition for often experiencing what in this book is called an erased state of consciousness. It is in my experience frequently the case that this reductive framing of the parent's difficulty in showing resonance with their child results in a deficit orientation among professionals, which can then manifest itself in critical-prescriptive positioning.

The following example illustrates some of the contexts which may be central to a non-stigmatising, non-discriminatory understanding of a parent's difficulty in being attentive to their child, attuning to them, showing resonance and acting with care and compassion:

Celia is a single mother of Black Caribbean heritage. Of low income, she holds two cleaning jobs and struggles to spend as much time with her children as she would like to and feels she needs to. Her son Deandre, who has been diagnosed with ADHD and has often been the subject of 'consequences' in accordance with his secondary school's behaviour policy, truants much of the time. Eventually, he is drawn into the periphery of a street gang, where he experiences acceptance and feels competent at bottom-level drug dealing. The grooming in this environment reduces his mother's influence on him further, so that escalating conflicts emerge between them. He also becomes successively alienated from his previous friends and from his teachers, resulting in a further decrease in school attendance. Celia feels increasingly powerless and resigned, and focuses more of her attention on the younger children.

This parent's difficulty in resonating with her son could easily be construed as a manifestation of internal psychological disposition. This de-contextualising of what I would see as largely socio-cultural interpersonal processes, and the localisation of what I would consider to be the parent's sense of erasure within her individual psyche as 'blocked care' could become a distraction from the possibility of initiating processes that may bring about change, in what otherwise could feel like a hopeless situation. If we create conversational space for identifying, understanding and appreciating transforming interpersonal processes rather than directing our attention to pathologising interpersonal processes alone, we may be able to help magnify and reinforce change-oriented patterns, thereby increasing their frequency and duration. It is for this reason that erasure or traumatic reactivity have been described as temporary or possibly transient states, from which, under certain circumstances, parents can rapidly shift into more functional presence states of consciousness. If interactional patterns between parent and child, between supporters and parent, between parent and professionals change, then states of consciousness may also change along with these processes. Internal change then concurs with interpersonal change.

I work on the assumption that most parents wish to be able to resonate with their child and address their child's needs, and possess at least a rudimentary, if not greater potential to do so. For this reason, I would like to propose the concept of a *caring dialogue* as an alternative to that of blocked care. While blocked care frames a narrative that is static, fixed in time and formulates inability, caring dialogue frames a progressive narrative of a change process, which formulates varying ability in relation to context, and in which there can be and often is growth of interpersonal resonance. From a systemic perspective, we can be interested in ascertaining how a caring dialogue can be kindled at specific pivotal points with certain simple kinds of NVR-based action. To do so, we need to create an image of such a warmth-generating dialogue. Simply put: rather than focusing on what is going wrong, we focus on what can change in a positive way, and how that may be brought about.

Caring dialogue: A two-way street to more secure attachment and parental mattering

Complex dialogical interactions between caregivers and those who are cared-for enable adults to address children's needs and stimulate reciprocity. Elements of such dialogue are children's signalling of distress or discomfort, parental sensibility to such *signals of need*, their responses to these signals and, importantly, validation of parental care by the child. Validation of parental care is manifested, when the young person accepts their caring acts, at least often enough, and signals emotional or physical need again at later points in time.

When a young person tolerates their own vulnerability and communicates this – openly or in coded form – to the parent, they are showing basic trust in the adult and acting upon certain expectations or core beliefs about their caregiver:

- That the adult can respond with strength. This perception can reassure the young person that they will be protected by their caregiver from external threat to their physical or emotional wellbeing and integrity, *and* that they will be protected from acting out their own harmful or self-destructive impulses;
- That the parent's strength is associated with the adult's ability for self-control and emotional self-regulation and is anchored in a benevolent attitude towards the child, so the young person does not need to be vigilant in respect of possible threat or emotional injury;
- That the parent will respond with sensitivity to the existential and emotional needs of the child.

In the course of such dialogue, parents increasingly and often enough show attention to the child and attune to their need signalling. They distinguish between needs, wants and inappropriate or harmful demands the young person makes, and respond in different ways to these, using different sources of information, (such as conversations with other parents, teachers, media) to revise and adapt these distinctions in an ongoing process. Increasingly or often enough, parents respond in a balanced way by protecting their child on the one hand, and supporting them to meet developmental challenges with growing autonomy, on the other. In this way, they help the child to develop their own agency and expectation of self-efficacy (Lebowitz and Omer, 2013).

Adolescents often feel ambivalent in regard to their need to feel autonomous and self-determined on the one hand, and their need for parental support on the other. Due to this tension, need signalling by adolescents is often ambiguous and encoded, necessitating parental responses that are often indirect and subtle. When their teenage offspring signal their need in an encoded way, parents can feel validated, provided they are able to decode these signals and recognise their nature. In this way, the parent's experience of relational agency can grow.

However, parental validation does not only exist in the intimate dyadic sphere between adult and child; it also relies on emotionally safe, uncritical societal discourses and the valuing of the adult's parenting efforts from within the wider system around the family. This accentuates the need for an emotionally safe caring community as described in Part I.

Of course, there are seldom any ideal-typical communication processes. No relationship is free of the kinds of tensions and ruptures which occur on a daily basis. Trust between adults, and between adults and children does not grow from harmony alone; it grows from the repair of emotional rupture – not always, but often enough and at important junctures in the relationship. Increasing an openness for recognising that one has caused rupture and emotional injury to others and growing willingness to acknowledge this and to take responsibility for rectifying such injury are all part and parcel of caring dialogue.

A dialogical view of the person does not assume a unified self or see their attributes as rooted in a fixed, coherent internal structure. Instead, we can assume a 'polyphonic self' (Shotter, 2008). Depending on the way in which someone positions themselves in relation to another person, their communication creates different demand characteristics on the other. The encounter with that person in a certain position then generates a specific selfhood, which is an idiosyncratic response to these demand characteristics, a specific 'voice' or aspect of self, a kind of 'answer' to their position. In differentiation from classic attachment theory, we would not assume that the child is simply in possession of more or less trust in their parent. Instead, from a dialogical point of view, we can assume that there can be different internal beliefs in regard to one and the same caregiver, different levels of trust, different kinds of embodied responsiveness, different modalities of responding, depending on context. While some of these 'voices' or possibilities of selfhood may remain concealed over prolonged periods of time, we can nonetheless assume their existence; they may become actualised, when caregivers and other adults reposition themselves in certain ways.

As practitioners, we can see ourselves as being in the business of facilitating the repositioning of parent and child, in order to help expand caring dialogue. This begins with the repositioning of the parent by virtue of unilateral action. One route to this that takes the adult's need for validation into account – validation that is not yet forthcoming – is to help parents *imagine* their child signalling their needs, and to *imagine* they are able to respond to these signals of need in a way that the young person *will communicate* is meaningful and important to them. This can generate a different state of mind in the parent and a different positioning vis-a-vis their child, one in which the parent is responding *as if* their child were validating their care, even if this in not yet forthcoming in any considerable measure. These acts of imagination – and parental care that emerges by virtue of such imagination – can become the pivots around which caring dialogue is stimulated. New communicated demand characteristics that emerge with the parent's repositioning can then invite the child to eventually reposition themselves, as well. However, before describing the kinds of parental action that may be helpful in re-kindling caring dialogue later in this chapter, I would like to outline various aspects of insufficiently met need in children with adverse histories. These can guide parents' imaginative processes and later help re-shape parental responses to the child in real life.

Insufficiently met psychological needs of young people with adverse childhood experiences

From a dialogical point of view, we consider the young person to be an assemblage of self-aspects or possibilities of self, some of which are more apparent, while others may remain obscured. Using the 'voice' metaphor, Wilson asks:

> If it should be that a child's aggressive and violent behaviour is more than a familial habit that has become exaggerated to the point of near destruction,

then what other feathrues contribute to aggressive and violent acts? If a child's behaviour has meaning beyond habit formation, what is also being expressed when the fist hits the face? Domestic violence is multi-faceted and has no single origin. Violence expressed in families can have origins beyond immediate family relational patterns. Political violence enacted on refugees, cultural deprivation, early trauma and disrupted relationships, may also be present when the fist hits the face.

(Jakob, Wilson and Newman, 2014, p. 37)

He sees the child as having multiple identities, yet expresses concern that the 'voice of the child' is all too often used by mental health professionals in a superficial way, while their practice of formulation individualises their difficulties. With Holzman (2009), Wilson goes on to state that the child is multi-dimensional and that they shift within an emotional, cognitive and behavioural context to become other than they have been.

When young people begin to demonstrate less aggression, withdrawal, rejection, deprecating or self-destructive behaviour, we can often see them signalling need more strongly, even if in codified form. In my clinical experience, we often see such need signalling in the following areas:

- Safety;
- Autonomy and self-determination;
- Sense of belonging and actual social integration;
- A coherent and sufficiently positive narrative of family and self (attachment narrative);
- Justice.

Safety encompasses both attachment security and safety from threat to the child's physical or emotional integrity: *Certain adults will show emotional resonance to me. I feel that some of my important ways of thinking and feeling will be understood – or at least, I will perceive that the adults will make a sincere effort to understand me (what does not mean that they will always do what I want them to!). They will not abandon me, but consistently be available to me when I need them. I will be able to return to their care and attention, when I will feel distressed because I have not or not yet been able to meet certain challenges in the wider world outside of our relationship, and I will be comforted and receive support and acceptance of my person in such instances. I also implicitly expect that my parents will possess the strength they need to raise their presence in a way that dissuades me from acting upon my impulses to harm others or myself (notwithstanding how such impulses may have originated), yet they will do so in a way that is not threatening, deprecating, rejecting, shaming or injurious in some other way, but instead accepting of my person. Even when I am in conflict with the adults, they will not respond with fear, anxiety, submission or withdrawal, and I know implicitly that their strength means they will be able to act protectively on my behalf should I need this. My sense of safety also means that I know I will feel supported or protected from exposure to danger from dangerous-controlling other adults, even if these are significant others.*

A child has *autonomy* if their life conditions enable them to make their own decisions in accordance with their developmental stage. Their *self-determination* is the competence or ability to do so. As the many case examples in this book illustrate, parental resistance against harmful behaviour often enables a young person to have greater autonomy. As their autonomy increases, they can grow more self-determined: when they no longer compensate for their difficulties in meeting life challenges by becoming angry and aggressive or avoiding these challenges by virtue of controlling behaviour, young people are more likely to develop the skills required to what may have felt like insurmountable hurdles to the satisfaction or their needs. A key component of self-determination is *relational agency*. De Mol et al. (2018) consider agency to always have a relational aspect, differentiating this notion from Bandura's (2001) understanding of self-efficacy expectation, which sees agency as lying in the ability to assert oneself within one's social environment. The concept of relational agency points to the person's expectation that they will be able to act in a socially competent manner; their responsivity to the other and ability for affective mutuality will influence their social environment, rather than exerting control within it. If therefore caregivers wish to support a child to increase their relational agency, they can aim to reinforce the child's ability to attune to others, but also reinforce the child's ability to cope in such instances, when their socially competent communication does not lead to the desired response in the other person. I see such *social frustration tolerance* as an important component of relational agency.

Alongside the growth in relational agency, the acquisition of cognitive, intellectual and physical competencies also enable greater self-determination. When children or adolescents with traumatic experiences begin to behave in nonviolent ways in situations where they have not done so before, their psycho-physiological arousal levels are likely to decrease to a more functional level. Less hypervigilant or prone to exaggerated motor activity, they persevere more, can concentrate more easily and show greater willingness to face and tackle academic or work life challenges. Their task-related frustration tolerance is likely to increase. Caregivers can support the expansion of a skill base which hitherto has been insufficiently developed, by showing attention to a child's constructive behaviour and communicating their appreciation as the child becomes more accomplished. Communicating such appreciation by showing attention to a child's growing effortful development of their skills will generally be more productive than praise and attention to outcomes.

The need for a *sense of belonging* and actual *social integration* has been highlighted extensively. This is one of the most common insufficiently met needs in the life of a child who has experienced trauma: internal fragmentation is mirrored by social fragmentation. I have discussed the evolutionary development of the sociometer in humans, which enables us to be highly sensitive for signals which could indicate marginalisation or exclusion from the group. Efforts at increasing social integration, as well as resistance to the child's own behaviours that have resulted in increasing social exclusion and isolation, can address this existential psychological need. Many children and adolescents who have previously not felt they belong due to a traumatically induced sense of alienation, frequent life disruption in the care system, and social rejection in response to controlling behaviour, experience more social integration and a better sense of belonging, leading to greater emotional wellbeing and performance in school, when this need is addressed.

Children who have lived in chaotic, unpredictable and dangerous environments, or have had to suffer frequent life disruption from coming into care, often struggle with constructing a *coherent* and *sufficiently positive narrative of family and self* or *attachment narrative*. Their stories of 'family' are often structurally incoherent and can have content in which people are being frightened or harmed. These stories represent a meta-narrative that mirrors an inner representation of their relationships with significant others. These significant others, namely their mostly adult caregivers, are often represented as threatening, neglectful and emotionally labile. Research using the MacArthur Story Stem Battery has shown that when mothers experienced gender-based partner violence and trauma prior to the child's age of four, children after the age of four produced stories with higher levels of uncontrolled aggression and danger-focused vigilance as content. Their stories also showed greater structural incoherence (Schechter et al., 2007). A further study using this methodology involving children in foster care demonstrated more positive representation of adults, when their foster carers expressed positive perceptions of the child's sense of belonging to the foster family (Mögel, 2019). These children's narrative self-representations were also more positive. The children's stories indicated a higher level of perceived commitment by their foster carers, and there were more themes relating to cooperation, affiliation and positive self-imagery. Structurally, their narratives were more coherent than the ones of children, whose sense of belonging was not evaluated as positively by their foster carers.

When representations of adults become more benign, the child will perceive their social environment as less threatening. Children who feel they belong will be more likely to approach others in a connective way and respond positively to relational offers by others. Dallos and Dallos (2013) have worked on re-authoring the attachment narratives of children who have been adopted or taken into care under the assumption that an internal working model of their relationships, which promises greater security, will result in an expectation that their caregivers will be physically and psychologically available to them when they come to feel under threat.

Justice can be seen as a fundamental human need (Desai, personal communication). A perception of justice having been done is often missing in the lives of children who have been abused or who have had other kinds of adverse life experiences. Past abuse by a parent, a failure or inability to protect, or neglect of a child that may e.g. have been due to the non-offending parent's domestic violence-related depression or self-calming with drugs or alcohol is rarely spoken about, even when e.g. the parent has become free of violence or is recovering from a drug habit or mental health problems. Overburdening feelings of shame and guilt, and the fear of re-traumatisation, can mitigate against a necessary dialogue between parent and child. When however in the process of NVR-based work with a parent such dialogue becomes possible, and a parent is perceived by the child to have been making reparation, the parent is likely to gain in moral *authority*: the child will feel that the parent has the right to provide guidance and care and, where necessary, act as a boundary to harmful or self-destructive behaviour.

This overview of often not sufficiently met psychological needs in children who have been abused or otherwise experienced ill treatment is intended for the orientation of practitioners who support parents or other caregivers in their work with NVR. I am *not* concerned with any formulation of 'mental health conditions', but with sensitising our perceptive capacities for ways in which adults, who are significant others to children, can communicate with them meaningfully in addressing their – often disguised – psychological needs.

Martin Buber, the founder of modern dialogical theory, has discussed the repositioning of oneself towards the other in dialogue in a manner that has been seen as significant for social psychology (Meindl, 2021). In his concise formulation, the word-pairs 'I/you' and 'I/thou' mark two completely different positions. In I/it, I relate to the other as if they were an object; I turn the other into an object in my perception of them and in the way I respond to them. In I/thou, I open myself for the experience of the world by the other, including their experience of myself. Thereby, I assume a completely different attitudinal, perceptive and interactional position. Importantly, in each of these two word-pairs, the 'I' is a qualitatively different expression or enactment of self. The two Is represent two different kinds of person. For the I to become actualised, it is necessary for the person to find a way of opening themselves for the experience of the world in the other. Caregivers involved in the NVR process, even when they have experienced trauma or erasure, can begin to accomplish this with increasing acuity by crafting and delivering relational/reconciliation gestures which aim to address insufficiently met child needs. The unilateralism of adult action in NVR enables parents to persevere in making such gestures, even when they are not met with any acceptance or validation of the adult's efforts by the child. When the child's trust in the adult yet needs to grow to a sufficient degree, the unconditional nature of parents' relational gestures can become the match that lights the kindling to caring dialogue.

Wilson (2018) highlights the importance of cooperation between parent and child in child-focused systemic practice. In most instances of harmful behaviour, we cannot assume that such cooperation will be immediately possible. However, the use of relational gestures can initiate transforming interpersonal processes that move the family system towards cooperative interaction, what I have formulated as caring dialogue. In doing so, we can follow Wilson's recommendation to use play, symbolism and therapeutic rituals. I consider relational gestures to be valuable therapeutic rituals, especially if they become an integral and ubiquitous feature of adult resistance.

As in Noam's example, acts of resistance, which aim to incorporate attention to the young person's psychological needs, can be carried out with ritual character.

They can have a demand characteristic that invites the young person to cooperate when all words fail:

14-year old Noam has assaulted one of the caregivers in his residential home. She has been physically and psychologically injured and no longer wants to work in child care. All the adults in the home decide to wear black as an expression of their grief over this situation. They explain to Noam why they are wearing black. It is suggested that he may wish to wear black as well, to express his own feelings and because he belongs to the community of the home. Eventually, Noam wears black as well, of his own accord. His carers believe that this helps him regulate his shame, and occasionally he is able to speak about the violent incident. Subsequently, there is a series of restorative justice meetings between Noam and staff members who have been affected by the incident, in which they are able to share some of the feelings the incident has evoked in them. In this way, they raise their presence further and move the dialogue from a mainly symbolic and implicit level to a more explicit level.

Noam's example illustrates how a powerfully symbolic ritual as an act of resistance, that also incorporates attention to the young person's needs by emphasising that he belongs to the community of the home, can invite them to cooperate. Much of the dialogue that is initiated here is implicit in the symbolism of the act and the absence of punishment or exclusion of the young person. The structure of resistance distinguishes between the person of the child, and the act against which members of staff are protesting. The ritual offers an open invitation to the adolescent to re-join the community by joining their rejection of violence. By wearing black and expressing his grief over what has happened, he takes on the identity of belonging to the community.

The relational/reconciliation gesture as an unconditional expression of loving care

To consider love, even a parent's love for their child, to be unconditional can be seen as an idealistic, but perhaps unrealistic expectation, one that can be problematic when the parental feeling of love finds expression in unconditional acceptance of the child's behaviour and demands (Dulberger, personal communication). Where this is the case, nonviolent resistance to entrenched dependence of younger adults on their parents, or to the social self-isolation of adolescents, requires parents to de-accommodate their adult or adolescent child and make their provision of material goods and services conditional upon the younger person acting with more self-determination (Dulberger and Omer, 2021). This is even or especially necessary, if the adult or adolescent child considers the provision of goods and services as the only possible acceptable act of loving care from their parents.

A relational gesture is not an act of providing goods or services to a young person who is dependent on them in a manner that is not commensurate with their developmental stage in life. Parents would be acting against the younger person's need for autonomy and self-determination, if they were to provide goods or services that are not in keeping with their child's developmental stage. Needs are not the same as wants, and it is important for an NVR practitioner to help parents distinguish between the two. Relational or reconciliation gestures are also not acts in which parents meet inappropriate demands, or acts which demonstrate an acceptance of violence, aggression or self-destructive behaviour. They are not reactive to the young person, but instead initiated independently by the parent, at a time of their own choosing and in a manner that, while responsive to, is not determined or dictated by the child.

A relational gesture is a caring gesture that is unconditional *per se*. The gesture offers connection without any antecedent demand by the parent, or communicated expectation of reciprocity. It demonstrates how the adult values the child and communicates their love or fondness. In child-focused NVR, it communicates how the parent 'gets it', their perception of what the child needs from them, not what the child wants. The implicit message in such a child-focused relational gesture is:

I am paying you attention. I will attune to you and try to understand what it is that is happening inside you, and what you need, as best I can. I wish to be with you in your distress; I wish to share your joy with you; I want to recognise your strengths and celebrate your successes with you. I will address all of this, even if you turn me away or even want to forbid me to do it.

Children and adolescents who show controlling behaviour often reject their parents' or caregivers' attention and affection or even try to prohibit these parental responses in a controlling way. This can be especially the case where a child has experienced inconsistent and conditional attention and affection, which may have undermined their intrinsic sense that caregivers are trustworthy when they offer care. When in such circumstances caregivers persist in offering relational gestures that embody a caring attitude, in the face of rejection, they communicate the unconditionality of their offering. Raising caring presence with this form of care as resistance requires a similarly determined fortitude, as resistance against externalising behaviour.

If a parent communicates, that they *require* a positive response to their relational gesture, that they are very hurt or very disappointed by the child's lack of responsivity, shows anger or acts with rejection towards the child, then the gesture loses its connective power. Persistence in the face of the child's rejection of caring, need-focused relational gestures implicitly demonstrates the adult's sincerity, and, importantly, their reliability. There may even be a necessity for the child to reject the parent's gestures, in order to feel and become reassured that the gesture is made for the child's and not for the parent's emotional benefit, and that the parent will be consistent in their care. In this way, the child can begin to trust their caregiver.

This relational logic, according to which the parent communicates sincerity, consistency and a responsiveness to the needs of the child by continuing to make relational gestures in the face of their non-acceptance, is a cornerstone of child-focused work in NVR. In this way, the notion of child-focused relational gestures goes beyond the original conceptualisation of the reconciliation gesture in NVR. Omer (2001, 2021c) originally saw the reconciliation gesture as a strategic move: if the parent communicates a congenial attitude in their gestures, the child will feel a greater inhibition of acting with aggression towards them. In the words of someone who had been in prison as a teenager: *It's a lot harder to punch a friendly face.*

This strategic view is very valuable, especially during the early phase of the NVR process, when it is crucial to end dangerous behaviour such as high level physical violence, and the parents do not yet inhabit a presence mindset with its embodied sense of strength often enough. In child-focused NVR, relational gestures which focus on the child's emotional needs can help parent and child move in the direction of caring dialogue. This becomes possible, when the parent's relational – or reconciliation gestures address insufficiently met needs of the child in a specific manner.

Acknowledging guilt, omission or failure as a parental gesture of reconciliation

It is an injustice, when a child is abused. It is a further injustice, when the abuse of this child is denied, minimised or remains unacknowledged. As obvious as these statements may seem, it is not obvious that adults will act upon the child's need to perceive justice being done. When there has been child abuse or another kind of ill treatment, this injustice requires child-focused work in NVR, if we are to help the parent regain moral authority and enable the child to experience the parental anchoring function. Not to address the elephant in the room would mean to prolong and compound injustice further.

Many young people who have been abused or neglected see the adult world as fundamentally unjust and not trustworthy. When children perceive adults to be unjust and untrustworthy – whether the adult is acting unjustly or not, they will not accept their authority. Adults who have not yet made reparation for past shortcomings cannot yet have a claim to authority in the eyes of the child. The child will not feel they have a moral justification, when these adults resist harmful or destructive behaviour. They must first acknowledge their past shortcomings. Acts of reparation, in which parents acknowledge their past shortcomings and make a commitment to change or ensure they maintain the changes they have already brought about, are among the most important relational gestures that can be made to children who have been abused or who have suffered on account of their parent's omissions. Relational gestures that are performed as acts of reparation are truly reconciliation gestures in the original sense of the word.

It would hardly be helpful for professionals to demand or 'strongly advise' a parent to acknowledge shortcomings or guilt. The ethicist and political philosopher Iris Marion Young (2010) has made an important distinction between the temporal punctuation of 'accountability' and 'responsibility', and the different positions we take when operating within their different frameworks. Accountability is backwards looking. When holding another accountable, one sits in judgement over what the other person has done that is deemed to be unethical or immoral. There is a punitive intent. Responsibility is forward-looking. When I hold a person responsible,

I communicate an expectation of what I believe they are morally obligated to do from hereon in. NVR operates largely within the second frame. For example, when parents carry out a sit-in, they are holding their child responsible for their future action. As the position is not one of judgement, but of guidance, it structures the relationship in a very different way and includes important aspects of enabling:

It only makes sense to hold you responsible for what you will do in the future, if I believe that you will be able to do so. I communicate to you that I believe in your capacity to act in a morally just way. I further communicate that I believe in your potential willingness to do so, which encompasses my belief in your willingness to no longer harm another person. While accountability in this distinction has a punitive character, I believe that responsibility has a strong enabling aspect: I am less concerned with you as a person who has done wrong, but more concerned with you as a person in whom the potential to do right by others is inherently given.

Not only would we seek to invite parents into a position of holding responsible in the NVR process, but such an understanding of responsibility can also guide a professional in how they may wish to position themselves towards a parent, who in some way has harmed or failed their child in the past. As the professional, I am not holding the parent accountable. If it is the parent's wish to do right by their child, they can engage in addressing their child's need for justice, and I will support them therapeutically in so doing. Being concerned with acting responsibly towards their child, they may recognise that the child needs them to acknowledge their own past failure to keep them safe, or to acknowledge the harm they have caused, to express feelings such as remorse and regret, and to reassure their child of their future acts. It is then and only then that their moral authority begins to grow, and they can, at some stage, justifiably engage in action that is required to deter the child from causing harm to others or to themself.

Taking a judgemental, critical-prescriptive position of holding the parent to account would not only undermine the NVR practitioner's therapeutic relationship with the parent; it could also have a troubling or unsettling effect on the child. However vehemently a young person may appear to wish for a coalition against their parent at a certain moment in time, their bond of loyalty will also militate against a practitioner taking that they may perceive as an antagonistic attitude towards the parent.

Lizzy's example in Part I illustrated the way in which care staff in a residential service were able to support a parent who *followed their invitation* to acknowledge shortcomings to her daughter. Here, the practitioners first attuned to the mother's needs: her need to matter or be of import for her daughter; her need to feel connected with her, and her need to be a parent in real life caring engagement with her, not just the parent on the daughter's birth certificate. This dialogue with the parent created a trusting, collaborative atmosphere which enabled all adults – mother and carers – to work together in recognising and addressing the girl's insufficiently met needs. One of these was to be in possession of a coherent and sufficiently positive narrative of the family, and of a positive self-concept within this narrative. In the wake of recognising her daughter's need in an empathic way, her mother became motivated to contribute to the forming of such a narrative, by making reparation to her daughter. The efforts by her care staff, and her mother's own motivation, distinguish this process of *inviting* the parent to act responsibly from one, in which professionals would have communicated in a prescriptive manner that the parent *should* take such action – but also from a process in which they would have dismissed her as unable or unwilling to respond in a way that resonated with her daughter's needs.

Lizzy's mother addressed her daughter's need for such an attachment narrative in her NVR announcement to her daughter. She acknowledged where she had fallen short and in this way enabled her daughter to change her inner representation of her mother: *My mother is no longer the person who got me to go shoplifting. The person she is today wants the best for me.*[1] With such a narrative between and around them, mother and daughter no longer require an external enemy to feel close to each other, and their connection is of a different quality from one that was largely based on a coalition of enmity towards a third party. The team's focus on the mother's need seemed to have helped enable her to focus on her daughter's need in a significant way. These were the first steps in the direction of caring dialogue.

It can be more effective, if a parent's acknowledgement of past guilt or shortcoming is carried out in a quasi-ritual or ritual manner. This provides a structure to their communication that helps reduce the uncertainty that can be inherent in unstructured communication, thereby providing emotional safety and preventing counterproductive conflict. The following examples illustrate structured, quasi-ritualistic forms of reparation as parental reconciliation gestures:

Liam makes homophobic, verbally aggressive comments to his adoptive father Matthew's male partner. Matthew, who himself experienced physical and emotional abuse in childhood, hits Liam hard in the face. Matthew and I work together in writing a report to social services. He further writes a self-announcement,[2] in which he takes full responsibility for having hit Liam, makes a commitment not to lay hand on Liam again and sends it to all supporters in the family's caring community. Matthew shows Liam the report to social services and his self-announcement in the presence of a supporter, reads the self-announcement out loud and lets him know that it has been sent to all supporters. Part of the announcement indicates that Matthew will now break the "chain of violence" that has been passed from the grandparents through him to Liam.[3] Over the next few days, supporters inform Liam that they have read his father's self-announcement, and that they will support his father to remain nonviolent buy calling Matthew frequently and enabling him to share when he feels frustrated or upset with Liam. Matthew addresses his son's homophobic behaviour after a month in which he himself has abstained from any form of violence, even in the face of provocation by Liam. This interim period is necessary for Matthew to demonstrate that he is living up to his commitment and in this way become credible and trustworthy in his son's eyes. He has in this way regained moral authority and can express in a sit-in that he feels Liam owes his partner an act of reparation for his previous homophobic abuse, and that he will support Liam in carrying this out. In the same sit-in, he also offers Liam to take part in a joint family therapy session, in which he would have the opportunity to speak about the emotional difficulties that may have arisen for Liam from his father's relationship with another man. In this way, Mattew starts creating the conditions for dialogue.

Angie had several relationships with violent men in the past. Using alcohol to cope, she became dependent. Angie is now abstinent regularly attends AA meetings and frequently avails herself of support from her mentor. She has however not felt able to speak about the past constructively with her daughter. As part of her 12-step work[4] and the NVR process, Angie gives her daughter a hand-written letter in which she acknowledges shortcomings of the past and tentatively expresses how she believes her daughter may still feel burdened by her mother's history of alcohol dependency. In her letter, Angie also explains where things stand in her own recovery and, importantly, in her resistance to any form of domestic abuse, how she knows that she has become stronger, and that this strength is enabling her to be there for Ines. She further writes about aspects of Ines' personality that deeply move her, strengths she has detected in Ines, and her wishes for her daughter's future.

Rita is a carer for young people with emotional and behavioural difficulties in a residential children's home. On one occasion, she loses her temper and shouts at Monica. Rita takes part in a restorative meeting, in which Monica can express what she felt being shouted at and how this reminds her of verbal and physical aggression in her family. Rita also shares the difficult feelings that Monica provoked in her, but only after Monica has finished speaking and Rita has shown an empathic response to Rita.

In each of these examples, an adult makes an antecedent gesture without expecting any reciprocity from the child. Only when acts of reparation become disaggregated from any expectation of behaviour change do they become genuine reconciliation gestures. Even a deeply held desire for resonance and reciprocity cannot shape the adult's communication, if their gesture is to be fully unconditional. It is therefore necessary to discuss such an – understandable – wish with the adult, and to plan their action in such a way that this wish will not interfere with the unconditionality of their gesture and turn it into a demand upon the child. This tension between the parent's wish for resonance and reciprocity, and the need to ensure that any reconciliation gesture is unconditional, is an important area for the therapist to address, if caring dialogue is to be stimulated.

Stimulating caring dialogue in the parent's imagination

Some of the potential of methods involving parental imagination have already been explored.[5] We can now ask: "Will imaginary methods support parents to not only cope with the apparently insurmountable tension between their wish for mutuality and its absence in the child, but even integrate this in their behavioural repertoire in a constructive way?"

Imagined interaction theory has investigated a number of everyday functions of imagined interaction (Honeycutt, Vickery and Hatcher, 2015). Two of these functions, which can be important in NVR for helping parents to deal with this tension in a constructive way, are:

1   Practising communication, and
2   Compensation for the absence of real interaction.

By utilising imagined interaction with a view to these two functions, a practitioner can support parents or caregivers to develop a position of 'anasakti', in which they can detach themselves internally from their need for external success of their action, while maintaining such action in a persistent manner.[6] Success is represented internally, in the parent's imagination. In his Mountaintop Speech on the evening before his assassination (King, 1968) Martin Luther King demonstrated this attitude:

> Like anybody, I would like to live a long life. Longevity has its place. But I'm not concerned about that now. I just want to do God's will. And He's allowed me to go up to the mountain. And I've looked over. And I've seen the Promised Land. I may not get there with you. But I want you to know tonight, that we, as a people, will get to the promised land!

With these tragically prophetic words, MLK brought his vision for a more just society, in which there would be racial equality, in harmony with the very real possibility, that he himself was unlikely to see this vision come true. The very tension between vision and the ability to bear that it does not or not yet materialise lies at the heart of nonviolent resistance. King expresses how an act of imagination can compensate for the absence of material change with the words *"And He's allowed me to go up to the mountain. And I've looked over. And I've seen the Promised Land"*.

It would be very difficult to find the motivation for change-oriented action without a vision, and in child-focused NVR, this vision comes about by imagining caring dialogue. When a parent imagines the child's future resonance to their acts of care, it can compensate for the absence of the child's validating response in the here and now. Their vision can compensate for the not yet established caring dialogue. The imagination of caring dialogue not only becomes a precursor to caring dialogue-in-action, but also serves as a practice field on which further options for real life communication can be rehearsed. The following two imaginary methods can be used to bring about this internal process in the parent.

In this method, an important synergy is generated between parent and therapist. Their imaginary resonance can significantly enhance the credibility of this 'future narrative'. They can, metaphorically speaking, wander together in an imaginary landscape of the future, in which the parent has become more empowered. By intuitively affirming the parent's caring competence, the therapist can help reinforce their relational agency.

Method: Imaginary caring dialogue

Prior to developing a child focus, make sure that the parent feels connected with their internal sense of strength. If they struggle to actualise their sense of strength, you can use the 'moment of strength'.[7]

Imagined caring dialogue is a co-creative process: both client and therapist imagine together that caring dialogue is taking place between parent and child. Whenever the therapist articulates their own imagined content, they ask the client whether they can imagine this as well, and the client shares their own imagined content. In this way, therapist and client develop imaginary resonance:

So can we imagine, together, that Ian comes home from school, maybe tomorrow after you've undertaken a sit-in the day before, or some other time, and he's angry, maybe he raises his voice, but he's not as aggressive as he used to be? OK, so you can imagine that... Does it feel real? OK, that's good. So, what is he doing now? OK, so he's going up to his room, OK...

Continue to use unconditional (substantive) language to create a sense of certainty and help the client suspend disbelief, repeating the client's phrases:

So he's gone up to his room... OK. I'm imagining that you're waiting a while and making him a hot chocolate. So you're bringing it up to his room... Where are you now? OK, you're looking into his room... What do you see? OK, so he's lying on his bed, facing the wall. He's got his earphones on his head...

As the practitioner, use your own imagined content to stimulate your client's imagination further:

So, I'm imagining you putting the hot chocolate next to him, on his bedside table. I'm imagining that you sit down on his bed. Can you imagine that? OK, where on his bed are you sitting? OK, at the bottom of the bed. So you're sitting at the bottom of the bed and after a while you say something, what are you saying?

Emphasise any verbalisations of the client that articulate care:

OK, so you've saying: Rough day at school huh? What can you see that he's doing? Is he saying anything? OK, so he's turning even further into the wall. Does he look more angry or more troubled? OK, so he looks more troubled. In what way? Somehow like he's been humiliated, I see. Maybe that's the reason his body is expressing what he feels, maybe he's got no words for it. Maybe it's shame; or maybe it's something else that's hard for him to express.

Ask the parent to imagine a relational gesture that aims to relate to the child's need:[8]

So it's the next day. Imagine you're doing something that shows him you get it. OK, so you're sending a text message... several text messages... So, what do they say? Just "Hope you're having a better day" and such. How is he reacting? OK, so he's reading your WhatsApp messages... I wonder how that feels for him, to know you're thinking about him?

Come out of the imaginary process and begin planning the actual relational gesture:

Can you actually do that tomorrow? How often do you want to send text messages tomorrow and next week? OK, a few over the course of the day tomorrow and one every day next week. Sounds good.

Reaffirm the principle of unilateral action by reminding the parent that their relational gesture may be rejected or ignored. Discuss that they can powerfully demonstrate the unconditional nature of their caring act by persevering in the face of any such rejection.

The second method is an adaptation of 'internalized other interviewing', which was introduced to a wider systemic audience by Karl Tomm, and which aims to improve empathy between significant others (Haydon-Laurelut and Wilson, 2011). In the 'interview of the future child' version of this method, parents are asked to specifically imagine their child communicating their need or vulnerability more openly *at a certain point in the future.* They are guided to imagine need signalling by the child, which may be more or less coded. By speaking in the 'voice of their future child', a parent can fine tune their empathic understanding and imagine the child expressing their need to be cared for. This, in turn, helps develop need-focused relational gestures, which can then be delivered in real life.

Method: Interview of the internalised future child

You and the parent imagine together that you, as the therapist, are interviewing the child.

Ask the parent to act in the role of the child. The parent should *not* represent the child as they often act at the current time, particularly when this is aggressive, hostile, rejecting, indifferent or dismissive. Instead, the parent should represent a preferred future, in which the child is able to articulate their more vulnerable 'voice', the need for support, and their need for connection with the parent. This will help deepen the parent's attunement and empathy and help them suspend disbelief:

I'd like to ask you not to role play (child) in the way you have often experienced them in the more difficult or worst moments; instead, I would like to invite you to look behind the veil of these behaviours; to walk in their shoes and to imagine that they are able to share some of what troubles them, even if it is in an indirect way. Please try to get into what it feels like to be them, maybe uncertain, anxious, scared or hurt, or ashamed, or something else, and to need you, their parent. Please try to speak with that voice of your child, even if you don't often hear much of it in everyday life yet. Do you think you can try and do that? OK...

Ask the parent to use the first person singular and the present tense when they speak in the more vulnerable voice of the child, so not e.g. *"He would say..."* but instead *"I get upset when..."*.

Use the second person singular to address the 'internalised future child', and conduct your conversation as you would in therapy with an actual child. The more you as the practitioner suspend disbelief, the better you become attuned to the parent's empathy for their child.

Once you are satisfied that a high level of empathic understanding of the child has been reached, you can ask the 'internalised child' about what kind of relational gesture their 'parent' could make, in order to reassure them that the parent is making a real effort to understand them and to address what they need, e.g. *So you're worried that your foster dad may not think about you when he's not around. How could your foster dad show you that he thinks about you, even when you're not together in the same place? What could he do?*

After coming out of role play, ask the caregiver for feedback, including how accurate they believe their empathic understanding of the child has been.[9]

You can then move on to planning the actual relational gesture the parent will wish to carry out. As in any conversation planning a relational gesture, discuss the need for unconditionality, and that persisting in delivering such gestures in the face of rejection, hostility or dismissiveness can reassure the child of the unconditionality of the gesture.

As mentioned before, Honeycutt et al.'s second postulated function of imaginary interaction, which I find of relevance for stimulating caring dialogue, is communication rehearsal. With growing attunement to the child and attention to their need signalling, parents are likely to find it easier to imagine need-focused relational gestures. By imagining that they are carrying out such gestures while raising their attention and attunement further, they are rehearsing child-focused communication.

When caregivers actually carry out the relational gestures that have been devised in the imaginary work, they signal their attunement to, empathy and compassion with the child much more clearly than before. By persisting to do so, even or especially in the face of rejection, they enable a child to eventually appreciate the adult's sincerity and the authenticity of their communicated caring attitude. We see this in Martin's example:

Eight year old Martin has been in foster care for three years. The child, who experienced a failure to protect him by his non-offending mother, refuses any contact with her; he believes she did not care about the fact that her partner physically and sexually abused him. It appears that Martin finds it hard to trust most people;, he repeatedly attacks his foster carers and other children and has physical injured his 'foster mum' and other children. After threatening the school's head teacher with scissors from her desk, he is permanently excluded from school.

Several measures are put into place. After any violent incident, sit-ins take place involving supporters in the caring community. There is a long-running positive campaign of concern, in the course of which supporters come to the foster home to express concern about any aggressive incident, but importantly also to acknowledge and show appreciation for any event in which Martin has demonstrated pro-social behaviour, or for any exception to the problematic behaviour pattern. Martin's aggression diminishes significantly in the wake of these measures. His foster carers notice that they allow themselves to be physically closer Martin than before, and explain this with feeling more at ease around him. They realise that in the recent past, they had been staying out of his way a lot when they found him threatening.

For the first time since he has been in the family, his foster 'mum' Bettina trusts herself to go on a day trip with her friends, leaving him in the sole care of his foster 'dad'. She attributes this to the way her confidence that 'things will be alright' has grown, and that she feels less anxious. Bettina reports that, upon her return home: "Of course there was a lot of trouble".

However, on this occasion, Martin does not attack anyone physically and does not destroy things in the living room; instead, he goes up into his room and throws a few toys around. Bettina acknowledges that in the past, he would have attacked someone and 'trashed' the living room. The two foster carers and I discuss this outcome and acknowledge the change that has already taken place, including the sense of strength that has grown in them. Their perception of their agency and strength manifests itself in their body language and facial expressions – they simply look really pleased.

We then work with the imaginary caring dialogue: Bettina and I imagine that she will go on another day trip with friends in a few weeks' time. In her imagination, Martin again shows anger upon her return, though this time, it's more muted; he storms up to his room, throws a book at the wall and calms down more quickly than in the past. In this imaginary scenario, Bettina waits a while before bringing a hot chocolate up to his room. She sits in his room for a while and then says: It's been a long day. In this way, she alludes to her absence that day. Bettina immediately feels she knows his response: "You didn't even think about me!" Even though she still imagines that he is expressing his feelings angrily and in a blaming way, Bettina envisions a response in which his previous naked rage has given way to a coded expression of his need: the need to feel that she bears him in mind and cares about his wellbeing when she is not physically present with him. "His" voice and the content of his message give away his vulnerability, in a way that did not occur before.

We end the imaginary caring dialogue and plan a real life relational gesture to address what has emerged in Bettina's mind as a likely need of Martin's. The gesture will aim to help Martin feel that his foster carers and other supporters in the caring community bear him in mind, when they are not physically present. It is November, and Bettina crafts an advent calendar from Christmas crackers; she replaces their content with carefully chosen objects that will draw his attention to moments when others have thought about Martin; e.g. Betty's adult son, who is a biker and has taken Martin on rides before, writes on the back of a postcard which bears an illustration of a motocross bike: I saw this and it reminded me of when we watched the motocross race on TV together last week. Contrary to expectation, Martin does not tear up the advent calendar, but opens up one Christmas cracker at a time, each day until Christmas.

A new transforming interpersonal process is beginning to be established: More and more often, Martin expresses anger in a more moderate way and only for a short while, and sometimes later, when asked what has been 'bugging him', expresses what he has found difficult – while his carers are shifting their attention more often from anxious vigilance to perception of his vulnerabilities. We can see these as positive events which are acknowledged and commented on by supporters in the positive campaign of concern in carefully formulated, subtle ways.

There are more indicators for improvement. Martin, who previously was isolated because he had been unable to sustain any play time for longer than about ten minutes without becoming aggressive, and who had come to be avoided by other children, begins to play with the neighbour's son more often. He shows more pro-social behaviour, such as compromising on what they will play or the rules they will follow. His foster dad notices that Martin is beginning to accept his guidance on how to make friends. Having been permanently excluded from school, including special education, he can enter a school for children with special educational needs when he comes of secondary school age. Two years later, Martin is admitted to a mainstream secondary school.

He is not yet ready or prepared to have any form of contact with his mother, but he has begun speaking about wanting to meet her at some point in the future. A social worker works with her on a self-announcement to Martin, in which she will acknowledge his difficult experiences of the past.

The imaginary work that was undertaken in preparation of a child-focused relational gesture supported his foster carers in becoming more attentive and attuned to his need signalling. It also helped the foster 'mum' become more aware of the empathic reservoir she already held, enabling her to gain a felt sense of this empathic reservoir and to actualise it. Of course, the carers first needed to liberate themselves from their anxiety-driven responses, such as avoiding his physical presence for fear aggressive escalation. In doing so, they moved out of a victim position, gaining personal and parental strength. They felt supported by a caring community, members of which went on a day trip with the foster 'mum' and supported the family by participating in an elaborate, well thought out and carefully planned relational gesture. It would be safe to assume that the increased attention to the child's signalling of need in his everyday life will have encouraged him to allow himself to be vulnerable in their presence, rather than converting his vulnerability immediately into angry aggression.

Neuroscientific research has demonstrated that the likelihood with which we perceive certain kinds of social information increases, when previously an expectation of such information has been established (Otten, Seth and Pinto, 2017; De Lange, Heilbron and Kok, 2018). We can infer from this that parents are more likely to perceive and recognise coded messages expressing a child's need, if they have formed an expectation that such signalling will be forthcoming. Sensorimotor imagination of a future caring dialogue can, in my view, bring about such an expectation – not only of the child's future resonance with the adult, but also of the caregiver's own response to such resonance. The caregiver will be more likely to implicitly communicate such an expectation to the child and thereby promote and reinforce the child's propensity to communicate their needs to the adult – thereby moving more strongly towards establishing transforming interpersonal processes that involve caring dialogue. Ultimately, hidden needs become visible, audible, tangible. Further need-focused relational gestures communicate to the child that the parents will persist in their effort to act with care, and that these efforts are not conditional upon the child agreeing to them. Finally, parent and child can find a way out of trauma and erasure, towards a more connected and caring relationship. It is this relationship that will make the birth family, adoptive family, foster home or group home into a social system, in which people can heal.

Notes

1 In terms of predictive coding theory, this may be understood as an 'expectation violation' which can enable new encoding of expectations.
2 See Chapter 2.
3 Writing that he *will* no longer hit Liam is of importance. To articulate that he will *try to do so* would not represent a commitment.
4 Step 9 of the 12-step programme.
5 See Chapter 5.
6 See Chapter 6.
7 See Chapter 5.
8 I have been asked whether such a gesture should be made if parents are uncertain about the nature of the child's need. Adults often engage in caring dialogue without certainty of the nature of the child's need; we can even see not knowing and improving attunement to the child, de-coding signals that are difficult to interpret, etc., as a core part of this process. Often, the 'precision' of the parent's perception is of less importance than the child's perception that the parent is making an effort to understand their thoughts and feelings.
9 Mentalisation requires the person to appreciate that their understanding of another person's internal processes can be more or less accurate, and that they cannot actually *know* what the other is experiencing.

Epilogue

The younger person's resistance

A German study found a significant increase in parental stress, domestic violence and adverse child experiences in a subset of its cohort during COVID lockdown (Calvano et al., 2021). Yet, the data cannot create an image in our minds of what many of these families have had to struggle with. Our empathy and compassion only grow in the actual encounter with people who have experienced such adversity, whether it is in the media or in direct contact with them. At the same time, we can appreciate their sincere efforts, their resilience and their positive intentions at coping with such circumstances. The pandemic, which had a powerful impact on most, affected some people more at the interface of aspects of social and economic disadvantage.

Work with families who have had to struggle with multiple challenges will need to do justice to the intersectionality of the disadvantage they face. Yet, how can the practitioner have agency in the tangle of these criss-crossing and often mutually compounding factors that impede people's lives and their recovery from hardship? This book has investigated the possibilities that are inherent in uncovering, highlighting and actualising resilience, change that is already taking place, discovering exceptions to problematic interaction, utilising the maps that offer methods of resistance, reconciliation, restoration and connection in NVR – and weaving from these threads heroic relational narratives, in which the seemingly mundane becomes extraordinary.

It is likely that multi-dimensional transformative processes will emerge in the course of change. When all family members, including children who have acted in ways which were harmful to themselves or to others, have had to experience abuse, it may at some point become necessary that they themselves feel empowered by resisting what may still impact upon their lives. As a therapist, it can then be important to shift one's position and help take resistance in a new direction. One such direction is becoming the young person's resistance coach (Jakob and Sarah, 2021). The younger person may wish or need to resist still extant elements of abuse that have become elephants in the room. These elements may have grown 'invisible' due to the conceptual framework of diagnoses such as '*post*-traumatic stress disorder' or 'attachment disorder', which individualise the emotional difficulties a person suffers and distract from ongoing, remaining pathologising interpersonal

DOI: 10.4324/9781032717111-19

processes. Where abusive patterns persist, be it that past violence is being denied or minimised, or its effects are disregarded, there is ongoing harm and injustice, and there is a right and at times a necessity to resist. Lamya's situation exemplifies the necessity of finding a new direction for resisting:

16-year old Lamya is of Sudanese heritage. For months she keeps running away from her foster home. Again and again, her foster carers go to places where she might be, and supporters keep sending her messages encouraging her to return. The implicit, and sometimes explicit message is:

We are concerned for your safety. We won't give up on you! You deserve the safety we want to give you!

Whenever she returns, Lamya is welcomed back into the foster home, rather than reprimanded for running away. On one occasion, she is stunned to encounter her foster carer, who has come to look for her, at a major city's train station. It takes about four months for her to feel she can 'give (her foster carer) the time of day'. Lamiya runs away less and less often and eventually gives up running away altogether.[1]

Lamiya's father, who continues to deny his abuse of her, puts her under pressure to have contact with him. He threatens to prevent her from seeing her mother or her siblings – in spite of having separated from her mother – if she refuses contact. Unfortunately, Lamiya also feels under pressure by her social worker to meet with her father. In conjunction with her foster carer and myself as her therapist, she decides to resist her father's pressure to conform to his demand. She agrees to only one meeting, which her foster carer will attend with her. They prepare the room, by putting a table between their chairs and his, to pre-empt any attempt of his to embrace his daughter. When they finally meet, Lamiya pushes a written announcement over the table for her father to read:

"We both know what you have done. I will do everything I can to keep seeing Umiy, Nafisa and Sabrina, but I can't let myself be forced to see you. If we see each other in the future, it will only be because I decide to meet you".

After he has read the text, Lamya and her foster carer end the meeting. They send a copy of the announcement to her social worker.

Lamya's trauma symptoms reduce significantly over the course of the following weeks and months.

It has not been an easy process of recovery for Lamya, and however necessary it was to resist the pressure she was put under, this act of resistance, carried out in solidarity, has not been a panacea for all ills that she had to endure from abuse and various failings of the care – and child mental health systems. However, we now see her, years later, as a young adult, leading a constructive life as an advocate for others and a social activist, who is beginning to thrive.

This case exemplifies the possibilities that are inherent in expanding the framework of NVR beyond the adult-child relationship, by identifying residual elements of abusive communication, finding ways to resist these, and facilitating the opportunity for the young person's own sense of agency to grow. It is important to note here that, in divergence from the male gender of both her father and her social worker, it was her female foster carer who supported her in her original, difficult act of resistance, thus underscoring female solidarity, strength and care in the face of abusive power. Resistance in this example is directed not only at the gendered oppressive power of a parent, but also at structural injustice and institutional violence, which was manifested in the indifference towards the risk posed to a young person of colour by a professional.

Having previously worked with the young person's foster carers on resisting her self-destructive tendency to run away, and helping them move towards caring dialogue, it was in my view ethically imperative to offer to work with her in person, and to re-direct my efforts at supporting her resistance against several still extant dimensions of abuse, which included the father's efforts at forcing his will on his daughter, her siblings and their mother, and the denial of the harmful re-traumatising effects of this on the young person herself by the social worker and his own implicit legitimisation of the father's oppressive, controlling behaviour. This proved to be therapeutically effective in a way that may have been unlikely to achieve, had adults merely acted on her behalf, but not together with her. The joint act of resistance, its preparation and aftermath brought her in contact with her own ability to form a protective boundary. In this example, Lamiya is not a passive recipient of her foster carers' protective stance. Beyond protection by others, her self-determination grows, ensuring greater emotional – and actual physical – safety. She becomes the protagonist of her own narrative of resistance. While the abusive communication by her father and its enabling by her social worker persist, Lamiya is not a defenceless recipient of their control and dominance, but an autonomous agent acting in self-determination, with the support of a caring community.

Children, adolescents and adults who have been subjected to abuse, neglect or disadvantage have a right to justice. As long as justice is denied, strands of the abuse persist. I concur with Reynolds (2019), who considers supporting people who have been disempowered, to struggle for justice within a community that acts in solidarity with them, to be a cornerstone of critical, socially responsible therapy. NVR can fulfil this requirement, as it moves beyond the frame of the relationship between caregiver and child. Its methods offer a structure of *effective* resistance, skills of which can be honed in the therapy room. Instead of seeing ourselves as professionals who provide 'treatment', we can re-position ourselves as sometimes resistance coach, sometimes witness, sometimes facilitator of the caring community, en route with our client in a quest for greater freedom from oppressive practices and towards a more fulfilled life in which they can flourish. The preamble of the German postwar constitution beautifully articulates its ambition: *Human dignity is inviolable.* When we work with NVR in a way that is oriented towards justice, we can strive to help make this ambition a reality.

Note

1 It should be stressed that running away was a reasonable adaptation by the young person to distressing events in the home and in the mental health and care systems.

References

Agnew, R., & Huguley, S. (1989). Adolescent violence towards parents. *Journal of Marriage and the Family, 51*, 699–711.

Allen, J. G. (2018). *Mentalizing in the development and treatment of attachment trauma*. New York: Routledge.

Alon, N., & Omer, H. (2006). *The psychology of demonization: Promoting acceptance and reducing conflict*. New York: Routledge.

Aylmer, R. Personal communication.

Bandura, A. (1983). Self-efficacy determinants of anticipated fears and calamities. *Journal of Personality and Social Psychology, 45*(2), 464–469.

Bandura, A. (2001). Social cognitive theory: An agentic perspective. *Annual Review of Psychology, 52*, 1–26.

Banks-Rogers, P. S. (2020). The African American father. A survey of recent scholarly research. *The Journal of Negro Education, 89*(1), 82–85.

Barthelmess, M. (2016). *Die systemische Haltung. Was systemisches Arbeiten im Kern ausmacht*. Göttingen: Vandenhoeck & Ruprecht.

Bateson, G. (2000). *Steps to an ecology of mind: Collected essays in anthropology, psychiatry, evolution, and epistemology*. Chicago: University of Chicago Press. (originally published 1972).

Baumrind, D. (1981). Kindererziehung zwischen Biologie und Emanzipation. Neue Trends der Entwicklungspsychologie. *Psychologie Heute, 8*(2), 66–74.

Beckers, W., Jakob, P., & Schreiter, M. L. (2022). Mattering and parental presence in systemic therapy using nonviolent resistance: The utilization of imaginary methods. *Family Process, 61*(2), 507–519.

Boszormenyi-Nagy, I. (2014). *Invisible loyalties*. New York: Routledge.

Brown, D. J., Arnold, R., Fletcher, D., & Standage, M. (2017). Human thriving. *European Psychologist, 22*(3), 167–179.

Bureau, J. F., Ann Easlerbrooks, M., & Lyons-Ruth, K. (2009). Attachment disorganization and controlling behavior in middle childhood. Maternal and child precursors and correlates. *Attachment and Human Development, 11*(3), 265–284.

Burgdorf, V., Szabó, M., & Abbott, M. J. (2019). The effect of mindfulness interventions for parents on parenting stress and youth psychological outcomes: A systematic review and meta-analysis. *Frontiers in Psychology, 10*, 1336.

Burnes, B., & Cooke, B. (2013). Kurt Lewin's Field Theory: A review and re-evaluation. *International Journal of Management Reviews, 15*(4), 408–425.

Calvano, C., Engelke, L., Di Bella, J., & Kindermann, J. (2021). Families in the COVID-19 pandemic: Parental stress, parent mental health and the occurrence of adverse childhood experiences – Results of a representative survey in Germany. *European Child & Adolescent Psychiatry*. Retrieved January 17, 2022, from https://doi.org/10.1007/s00787-021-01739-0

Cassidy, J., Ehrlich, K. B., & Sherman, L. J. (2013). Child-parent attachment and response to threat: A move from the level of representation. In M. Mikulincer & P. R Shaver (Eds.), *Nature and development of social connections: From brain to group*, 125–144. Washington, DC: American Psychological Association.

Charles, A. V. (1986). Physically abused parents. *Journal of Family Violence, 1*, 343–355.

Cioffi, F. (2013). The case of Freuds sexual etiology of the neuroses. In M. Pigliucci & M. Boudry (Eds.), *Philosophy of Pseudoscience. Reconsidering the demarcation problem*. Chicago: University of Chicago Press, 321.

Cofré, R., Herzog, R., Mediano, P. A., Piccinini, J., Rosas, F. E., Sanz Perl, Y., & Tagliazucchi, E. (2020). Whole-brain models to explore altered states of consciousness from the bottom up. *Brain Sciences, 10*(9), 626.

Cottrell, B. (2001). *Parent abuse: The abuse of parents by their teenage children*. Family Violence Prevention Unit, Health Canada.

Cottrell, B., & Monk, P. (2004). Adolescent-to-parent abuse: A qualitative overview of common themes. *Journal of Family Issues, 25*(8), 1072–1095.

Dallos, R., & Dallos, A. (2013). Using an attachment narrative approach with families where the children are looked after or adopted. In M. Tarren-Sweeny & A. Vetere (Eds.), *Mental Health Services for vulnerable children and young people*, 133–152. New York: Routledge.

Dallos, R., & Vetere, A. (2021). *Systemic therapy and attachment narratives: Applications in a range of clinical settings*. Abingdon: Routledge.

De Brun, A., McCarthy, K., McKenzie, K., & McGloin, A. (2013). "Fat is your fault". Gatekeepers to health, attributions of responsibility and the portrayal of gender in the Irish media representation of obesity. *Appetite, 62*, 17–26.

DeCou, C. R., Lynch, S. M., Weber, S., Richner, D., Mozafari, A., Huggins, H., & Perschon, B. (2023). On the association between trauma-related shame and symptoms of psychopathology: A meta-analysis. *Trauma, Violence, & Abuse, 24*(3), 1193–1201.

De Jong, P., & Berg, I. K. (2012). *Interviewing for solutions*. Boston, MA: Cengage Learning

De Lange, F. P., Heilbron, M., & Kok, P. (2018). How do expectations shape perception? *Trends in Cognitive Sciences, 22*(9), 764–779.

De Mol, J., Reimers, E., Verhofstadt, L., & Kuczynski, L. (2018). Reconstructing a sense of relational agency in family therapy. *Australian and New Zealand Journal of Family Therapy, 39*(1), 54–66.

Denborough, D. (2018). *Do you want to hear a story?: Adventures in collective narrative practice*. Adelaide: Dulwich Centre Publications.

Department for Education (2020). *Permanent and fixed-period exclusions in England 2019*. Retrieved May 14, 2021, from https://explore-education-statistics.service.gov.uk/find-statistics/permanent-and-fixed-period-exclusions-in-england

Desai, S. Personal communication.

Diamond, G., Russon, J., & Levy, S. (2016). Attachment-based family therapy: A review of the empirical support. *Family Process, 55*(3), 595–610.

Doidge, J. C., Higgins, D. J., Delfabbro, P., Edwards, B., Vassallo, S., Toumbourou, J. W., & Segal, L. (2017). Economic predictors of child maltreatment in an Australian population-based birth cohort. *Children and Youth Services Review, 72*, 14–25.

Dolan, Y. M. (2000). *One small step: Moving beyond trauma and therapy to a life of joy.* Lincoln, NE: Authors Choice Press.

Douglass, F. (1845/2003). *Narrative of the life of Frederick Douglass, an American slave.* New York: Barnes and Noble.

Dulberger, D. (2021). *Actually, what is NVR?* Presentation at the 6th International Conference on Nonviolent Resistance (NVR), Linz, Austria.

Dulberger, D. Personal communication.

Dulberger, D., Fried, M., & Jakob, P. (2016). *The presence mind: Functional states of consciousness and responsiveness.* Presentation at the 4th International Conference on Non-violent Resistance, Malmö, Sweden.

Dulberger, D., & Omer, H. (2021). *Non-emerging adulthood: Helping parents of adult children with entrenched dependence.* Cambridge: Cambridge University Press.

Dweck, C. S. (2000). *Self-theories: Their role in motivation, personality, and development.* London: Psychology Press.

Dweck, C. S., & Yeager, D. S. (2019). Mindset: A view from two eras. *Perspectives on Psychological Science, 14*(3), 481–496.

Eddy, J. M., Leve, L. D., & Fagot, B. I. (2001). Coercive family processes: A replication and extension of Patterson's coercion model. *Aggressive Behavior: Official Journal of the International Society for Research on Aggression, 27*(1), 14–25.

Eisenberger, N. I., Lieberman, M. D., & Williams, K. D. (2003). Does rejection hurt? An fMRI study of social exclusion. *Science, 302*(5643), 290–292.

Frank, A. (2013). *The wounded storyteller. Body, illness & ethics* (2nd edition). Chicago: University of Chicago Press.

Franklin, D.L. (2010). *The effects of solution-oriented intake questions on the perception of hope.* West Lafayette, IN: Purdue University ProQuest Dissertations Publishing.

Freeman, A., Lavercombe, A., Chikwariro, B., Combs, C., Alvispalma, D., Jenkins, M., Buttress, N., Singh, R., Ferris, S., Desai, S., & Samuda, S. (2013). *Report on the first phase of implementation of NVR (Non Violent Resistance) in Birmingham CAMHS (Tier 3 and YOS).* Unpublished manuskript: Birmingham Children's Hospital.

Funcke, A., & Menne, S. (2020). *Armutsrisiko „alleinerziehend" – wieso, weshalb, warum?* Gütersloh: Bertelsmann.

Furman, B., & Ahola, T. (1989). Adverse effects of psychotherapeutic beliefs: An application of attribution theory to the critical study of psychotherapy. *Family Systems Medicine, 7*(2), 183–195.

Giddens, R. (2018). *I'm on my way* (songtext). LyricsMode. Retrieved January 5, 2023, from https://www.lyricsmode.com/rhiannon_giddens-im_on_my_way-1697251.html

Grabbe, M. (2012). Bündnisrhetorik und Resilienz im gewaltlosen Widerstand. In A. v. Schlippe & M. Grabbe (Eds.), *Werkstattbuch Elterncoaching. Elterliche Präsenz und gewaltloser Widerstand in der Praxis* (3rd edition), 26–46. Göttingen: Vandenhoeck & Ruprecht.

Grabbe, M. (2013). Wo fahren wir hin und wo ankern wir? Vom Navigieren in der Eltern-Kind-Beziehung. In M. Grabbe, J. Borke, C. Tsirigotis (Eds.), *Autorität, Autonomie und Bindung. Die Ankerfunktion bei elterlicher und professioneller Präsenz*, 61–85. Göttingen: Vandenhoeck & Ruprecht.

Harbin, H. T., & Madden, D. J. (1979). Battered parents: A new syndrome. *American Journal of Psychiatry, 136*, 1288–1291.

Harré, R. (2015). Positioning theory. In J. Martin, J. Sugarman, & K. L. Slaney (Eds.), *The Wiley handbook of theoretical and philosophical psychology: Methods, approaches, and new directions for social sciences*, 263–276. Hoboken: Wiley.

Havel, W. (1991). *Disturbing the peace*. New York: Vintage.

Haw, A. (2010). Parenting over violence. In *Understanding and empowering mothers affected by adolescent violence in the home*. Perth: Patricia Giles Centre.

Haydon-Laurelut, M., & Wilson, J. C. (2011). Interviewing the internalized other: Attending to voices of the »other«. *Journal of Systemic Therapies, 30*(1), 24–37.

Heismann, E., Jude, J., & Day, E. (2019). A brief overview of NVR and glossary of terms. In E. Heismann, J. Jude, & E. Day (Eds.), *Non-violent resistance innovations in practice*, 291. Hove: Pavilion.

Henden, J. (2017). *What it takes to thrive. Techniques for severe trauma and stress recovery*. London: World Scientific.

Herman, J. (2015). *Trauma and recovery: The aftermath of violence – From domestic abuse to political terror* (2nd edition). New York: Basic Books.

Hermans, T. (2010). *Exhibition of the artist's work in Het Domein museum*. Sittard: Netherlands.

Hicks, S., Jakob, P., & Kustner, C. (2020). Engaging a family's support network in non-violent resistance: The experiences of supporters. *Journal of Family Therapy, 42*, 252–270.

Holt, A. (2013). *Adolescent to parent abuse. Current understandings in research, policy and practice*. Bristol: The Policy Press.

Holt, A., & Shon, P. C. (2018). Exploring fatal and non-fatal violence against parents: Challenging the orthodoxy of abused adolescent perpetrators. *International Journal of Offender Therapy and Comparative Criminology, 62*(4), 915–934.

Holzman, L. (2009). *Vygotsky at work and play*. New York: Routledge.

Honeycutt, J. M. (2021). Imagined interaction theory: Mental representations of interpersonal communication. In D. O. Braithwaite & P. Schrody (Eds.), *Engaging theories in interpersonal communication: Multiple perspectives* (3rd edition), 77–88. Newbury Park: Sage.

Honeycutt, J. M., Vickery, A. J., & Hatcher, L. C. (2015). The daily use of imagined interaction features. *Communication Monographs, 82*(2), 201–223.

Hughes, D. A., & Baylin, J. (2012). *Brain-based parenting. The neuroscience of caregiving for healthy attachment*. New York: Norton.

Imber-Black, E., Roberts, J. and Whiting, R.A. (Eds.) (2003). Rituals ion Families and Family Therapy, 2e. New York: W.W. Norton and Company.

Ingamells, K., & Epston, D. (2014). Love is not all you need: A revolutionary approach to parental abuse. *Australian and New Zealand Journal of Family Therapy, 35*(3), 364–382.

Jakob, P. (2018). Multi-stressed families, child violence and the larger system: An adaptation of the nonviolent model. *Journal of Family Therapy, 40*, 25–44.

Jakob, P. (2019). Child-focussed family therapy using nonviolent resistance: Hearing the voice of need in the traumatised child. In E. Heismann, J. Jude, & E. Day (Eds.), *Nonviolent resistance innovations in practice*, 51–65. Brighton: Pavilion.

Jakob, P. (2021). Die Neuerzählung des Selbst. Eine Wanderung durch Geschichten sozial engagierter Therapie. *Familiendynamik, 46*, 6–17.

Jakob, P. (2023). *Beyond "New Authority": The many dimensions of Non Violent Resistance*. Keynote presentation at 7th International Conference on Nonviolent Resistance, Osnabrück, Germany.

Jakob, P., & Sarah (anonymous co-author). (2021). Beyond parenting: Therapeutic integration of nonviolent resistance and narrative therapy. *Context, 175*, 18–25.

Jakob, P., Wilson, J., & Newman, M. (2014). Non-violence and a focus on the child: A UK perspective. *Context, 132*, 37–41.

Jay, M. A., McGrath-Lone, L., De Stavola, B., & Gilbert, R. (2023). Risk of school exclusion among adolescents receiving social care or special educational needs services: A whole-population administrative data cohort study. *Child Abuse & Neglect, 144*, 106325.

Jensen, T., & Tyler, I. (2018). Weaponising parent-blame in post-welfare Britain. In T. Jensen (Ed.), *Parenting the crisis*, 143–164. Bristol: Policy Press.

Kahn, D. T., Carthy, T. A. L., Colson, B., Tenne, T. A. L., & Omer, H. (2019). Measuring parental anchoring: The development and validation of the parental anchoring scale. *TPM: Testing, Psychometrics, Methodology in Applied Psychology, 26*(2), 271–286.

Käser, R. (1998). Die Schule als komplexes System. *Familiendynamik, 23*, 40–59.

Katz, E. (2022). *Coercive control in children's and mothers' lives*. Oxford, England: Oxford University Press.

Kelleher, K. (2021). Those secrets, they're literally eroding my bones. *The Psychologist, 34*, 24–27.

King, M. L. (1968). *I've been to the mountaintop*. Retrieved March 5, 2024, from https://www.americanrhetoric.com/speeches/mlkivebeentothemountaintop.htm

Kool, V. K. (2007). *The psychology of nonviolence and aggression*. London: Macmillan International Higher Education.

Køster, A. (2017). Mentalization, embodiment, and narrative: Critical comments on the social ontology of mentalization theory. *Theory and Psychology, 27*(4), 458–476.

Lankton, S. (1985). A state of consciousness model of Ericksonian hypnosis. In S. R. Lankton (Ed.), *Ericksonian monographs Vol. 1. Elements and dimensions of an Ericksonian approach*, 26–41. Abingdon on Thames: Taylor and Francis.

Lannamann, J. F., & McNamee, S. (2020). Unsettling trauma: From individual pathology to social pathology. *Journal of Family Therapy, 42*, 328–346.

Leary, M. R. (2015). Emotional responses to interpersonal rejection. *Dialogues in Clinical Neuroscience, 17*(4), 435–441.

Lebowitz, E., Dolberger, D., Nortov, E., & Omer, H. (2012). Parent training in nonviolent resistance for adult entitled dependence. *Family Process, 51*(1), 90–106.

Lebowitz, E., & Omer, H. (2013). *Childhood and adolescent anxiety*. Hoboken, NJ: John Wiley & Sons.

Little, M. (2011). Edward Lear's "The dong with a luminous nose". *The Explicater, 69*(1), 8–9.

Mackinnon, J., Jakob, P., & Kustner, C. (2023). Staff experiences of using nonviolent resistance in a residential care home for young people with high-risk behaviours. *Journal of Family Therapy, 45*(4), 444–458.

Macpherson, C. B. (1962). *The political theory of possessive individualism*. Oxford: Oxford University Press.

Madsen, W. C. (2013). *Collaborative therapy with multi-stressed families*. New York: Guilford Press.

Mallett, C. A. (2016). The school-to-prison pipeline: From school punishment to rehabilitative inclusion. Preventing school failure. *Alternative Education for Children and Youth, 60*(4), 296–304.

Maniadaki, K., Sonuga-Burke, E., & Kakouros, E. (2005). Parents' causal attributions about attention deficit/hyperactivity disorder: The effects of child and parent sex. *Child: Care, Health, & Development, 31*, 331–340.

Marchand, J. F., Hock, E., & Widaman, K. (2002). Mutual relations between mothers' depressive symptoms and hostile-controlling behavior and young children's externalizing and internalizing behavior problems. *Parenting: Science and Practice, 2*(4), 335–353.

Marshall, S. K., & Lambert, J. D. (2006). Parental mattering. A qualitative inquiry into the tendency to evaluate the self as significant to one's children. *Journal of Family Issues, 27*(11), 1561–1582.

Mason, B. (2015). Towards positions of safe uncertainty. *Interaction, 7*(1), 28–43.

McGlynn, F. D. (2002). Systematic desensitization. In M. Hersen & W. Sledge (Eds.), In chief: *Encyclopedia of psychotherapy*. Amsterdam: Elsevier Science, 755–764.

Meindl, P. (2021). From the thou to the we: Rediscovering Martin Buber's account of communal experiences. *Human Studies, 44*(3), 413–431.

Metzler, M., Merrick, M. T., Klevens, J., Ports, K. A., & Ford, D. C. (2017). Adverse childhood experiences and life opportunities: Shifting the narrative. *Children and Youth Services Review, 72*, 141–149.

Micucci, J. A. (1996). Adolescents who assault their parents: A family systems approach to treatment. *Psychotherapy, 32*(1), 154–161.

Mögel, M. (2019). Wie erleben platzierte Vorschulkinder die Zugehörigkeit zu ihren komplexen Beziehungswelten? Forschen mit dem Geschichtenstammverfahren der MacArthur Story Stem Battery. Perspektiven auf Vielfalt in der frühen Kindheit. In I. Hedderich, J. Reppin, & C. Butschi (Eds.), *Perspektiven auf Vielfalt in der frühen Kindheit. Mit Kindern Diversität erforschen*. 299–313. Bad Heilbrunn: Verlag Julius Klinkhardt.

Monson, C. M., & Shnaider, P. (2014). *Treating PTSD with cognitive-behavioral therapies: Interventions that work*. Washington, DC: American Psychological Association.

Murphy, F., & Gash, H. (2020). I can't yet and growth mindset. *Constructivist Foundations, 15*(2), 83–94.

Nelson, T. S. (2018). *Solution-focused brief therapy with families*. New York: Routledge.

Ngozi-Adichie, C. (2009). The danger of the single story. Retrieved January 30, 2024, from https://www.ted.com/talks/chimamanda_ngozi_adichie_the_danger_of_a_single_story?language=en

O'Hanlon, B. (2005). *The handout book*. Retrieved April 8, 2022, from https://www.possibill.com/download/bonus/files/HandoutBook.pdf

O'Hanlon, B. (2013). Solution-oriented therapy: A megatrend in psychotherapy. In J. K. Zeig & S. R. Lankton (Eds.), *Developing Ericksonian therapy*, 93–111. New York: Routledge.

O'Hanlon, W. H., O'Hanlon, B., & Beadle, S. (1999). *Guide to possibility land. Fifty-one methods for doing brief, respectful therapy*. New York: WW Norton & Company.

Ogden, P., & Fisher, J. (2015). *Sensorimotor psychotherapy: Interventions for trauma and attachment* (Norton series on interpersonal neurobiology). New York: Norton.

Ogden, P., Minton, K., & Pain, C. (2006). *Trauma and the body. A sensorimotor approach to psychotherapy*. New York: Norton.

Ohashi, K., Anderson, C. M., Bolger, E. A., Khan, A., McGreenery, C. E., & Teicher, M. H. (2019). Susceptibility or resilience to maltreatment can be explained by specific differences in brain network architecture. *Biological Psychiatry, 85*(8), 690–702.

Olthof, J. (2017). *Handbook of narrative psychotherapy for children, adults, and families. Theory and practice*. London: Karnac.

Omer, H. (2001). Helping parents deal with children's acute disciplinary problems without escalation: The principle of nonviolent resistance. *Family Process, 40*(1), 53–66.

Omer, H. (2011). *The new authority: Family, school, and community.* Cambridge University Press.

Omer, H. (2017). *Parental vigilant care: A guide for clinicians and caretakers.* London: Taylor & Francis.

Omer, H. (2021a). *Courageous parents: Becoming a good anchor for your children.* Self-published.

Omer, H. (2021b). *Courageous teachers: Developing a new authority to cope with violence and chaos.* Self-published.

Omer, H. (2021c). *Non-violent resistance: A new approach to violent and self-destructive children* (2nd edition). Cambridge: Cambridge University Press.

Omer, H. Personal communication.

Omer, H., & Alon, N. (1994). The continuity principle: A unified approach to disaster and trauma. *American Journal of Community Psychology, 22,* 273–287.

Omer, H., & Dolberger, D. I. (2015). Helping parents cope with suicide threats. An approach based on nonviolent resistance. *Family Process, 54*(3), 559–575.

Omer, H., Satran, S., & Driter, O. (2016). Vigilant care: An integrative reformulation regarding parental monitoring. *Psychological Review, 123*(3), 291–304.

Omer, H., & Schlippe, A. v. (2016). *Stärke statt Macht. Neue Autorität in Familie, Schule und Gemeinde.* Göttingen: Vandenhoeck & Ruprecht.

Omer, H., Steinmetz, S. G., Carthy, T., & Schlippe, A. (2013). The anchoring function: Parental authority and the parent-child bond. *Family Process, 52*(2), 193–206.

Otten, M., Seth, A. K., & Pinto, Y. (2017). A social Bayesian brain. How social knowledge can shape visual perception. *Brain and Cognition, 112,* 69–77.

Pandey, N., & Naidu, R. K. (1992). Anasakti and health. A study of non-attachment. *Psychology and Developing Societies, 4,* 89–104.

Patterson, G. R., DeBaryshe, B. D., & Ramsey, E. (1989). A developmental perspective on antisocial behavior. *American Psychological Association, 44*(2), 329–335.

Pérez-Hernando, S., & Fuentes-Peláez, N. (2020). The potential of networks for families in the child protection system: A systematic review. *Social Sciences, 9*(5), 70.

Peters, E. (2012). I blame the mother: Educating parents and the gendered nature of parenting orders. *Gender and Education, 24*(1), 119–130.

Phoenix, A. (2013). Social constructions of lone motherhood: A case of competing discourses. In E. B. Sylva (Ed.), *Good enough mothering?,* 183–198. London: Routledge.

Porges, S. W. (2011). *The polyvagal theory: Neurophysiological foundations of emotions, attachment, communication, and self-regulation* (Norton Series on Interpersonal Neurobiology). New York: WW Norton.

Porges, S. W. (2015). Making the world safe for our children: Down-regulating defence and up-regulating social engagement to 'optimise' the human experience. *Children Australia, 40*(2), 114–123.

Potter-Efron, R. (2007). *Rage: A step-by-step guide to overcoming explosive anger.* Oakland, CA: New Harbinger Publications.

Reed, G. J., & Parks, R. (1995). *Quiet strength. The faith, the hope, and the heart of a woman who changed a nation.* Grand Rapids, MI: Zondervan.

Reis, H. T. (2014). Responsiveness. Affective interdependence in close relationships. In M. Mikulincer & P. R. Shaver (Eds.), *Mechanisms of social connection. From brain to group,* 255–271. Washington, DC: American Psychological Association.

Reis, H.T., & Gable, S. L. (2015). Responsiveness. *Current Opinion in Psychology, 1,* 67–71.

Reynolds, V. (2019). *Justice-doing at the intersections of power: Community work, therapy and supervision.* Adelaide: Dulwich Centre Publications.

Rober, P. (2017). *In therapy together: Family therapy as a dialogue.* London: Bloomsbury Publishing.

Rodriguez, A. J., & Margolin, G. (2013). Wives' and husbands' cortisol reactivity to proximal and distal dimensions of couple conflict. *Family Process, 52*(3), 555–569.

Routt, G., & Anderson, L. (2011). Adolescent violence towards parents. *Journal of Aggression, Maltreatment & Trauma, 20*(1), 1–19.

Schechter, D. S., Zygmunt, A., Coates, S. W., Davies, M., Trabka, K. A., McCaw, J., & Robinson, J. L. (2007). Caregiver traumatization adversely impacts young children's mental representations on the MacArthur Story Stem Battery. *Attachment and Human Development, 9*(3), 187–205.

Schwarz, R. (2013). *Tools for transforming trauma.* Abingdon: Routledge.

Selwyn, J., Wijedasa, D., & Meakings, S. (2014). *Beyond the adoption order: Challenges, interventions and adoption disruption.* Department for Education research brief. Bristol: University of Bristol.

Sharp, G. (2012). *From dictatorship to democracy: A conceptual framework for liberation.* New York: The New Press.

Shelley, M (2014). *Frankenstein* (new edition). Wimbledon: Alma Classics.

Shoesmith, K., & Castle, E. (2019). *Creative protests as an act of reconciliation.* Workshop at the 3rd National NVR UK Conference.

Shotter, J. (2008). Dialogism and polyphony in organizing theorizing in organization studies: Action guiding anticipations and the continuous creation of novelty. *Organization Studies, 29*(4), 501–524.

Siegel, D. J. (2012). *Pocket guide to interpersonal neurobiology. An integrative handbook of the mind.* New York: Norton.

St George, S., & Wulff, D. (2014). Braiding socio-cultural interpersonal patterns into therapy. In K. Tomm, S. St. George, D. Wulff, & T. Strong (Eds.), *Patterns in Interpersonal Interactions,* 124–142. New York: Routledge.

Teicher, M. H., & Samson, J. A. (2016). Annual research review: Enduring neurobiological effects of childhood abuse and neglect. *Journal of Child Psychology and Psychiatry, 57*(3), 241–266.

Tomm, K. (2014a). Continuing the journey. In K. Tomm, S. St. George, E. Wulff & T. Strong (Eds.), *Patterns in interpersonal interactions. Inviting relational understandings for therapeutic change,* 13–35. New York: Routledge.

Tomm, K. (2014b). Introducing the ipscope. A systemic assessment tool for distinguishing interpersonal patterns. In K. Tomm, S. St. George, E. Wulff, & T. Strong (Eds.), *Patterns in interpersonal interactions. Inviting relational understandings for therapeutic change,* 13–35. New York: Routledge.

Van der Kolk, B. (2014). *The body keeps the score: Mind, brain and body in the transformation of trauma.* London: Penguin.

Van der Kolk, B. A. (2003). The neurobiology of childhood trauma and abuse. *Child and Adolescent Psychiatric Clinics, 12*(2), 293–317.

Van Holen, F. Personal communication.

Van Holen, F., Vanderfaeillie, J., & Omer, H. (2016). Adaptation and evaluation of a nonviolent resistance intervention for foster parents: A progress report. *Journal of Marital and Family Therapy, 42*(2), 256–271.

Wade, A. (1997). Small acts of living: Everyday resistance to violence and other forms of oppression. *Contemporary Family Therapy, 19*(1), 23–39.

Walker, C. (2020). *Frederick Douglass and the transformational power of courage in a fearsome world. Blog of the American Psychological Association.* Retrieved July 27, 2022, from https://blog.apaonline.org/2020/02/18/frederick-douglass-and-the-transformational-power-of-courage-in-a-fearsome-world/

Walters, M., Carter, B., Papp, P., & Silverstein, O. (1991). *The invisible web. Gender patterns in family relationships.* New York: Guilford Press.

Ward, K., Sanchez-Vaznaugh, E., Ryan-Ibarra, S., & Smith, M. (2021). *Adverse childhood experiences and cognitive disability in United States college-age adults.* In APHA 2021 Annual Meeting and Expo. APHA.

Watzlawick, P., Beavin, J., & Jackson, D. (2017). Some tentative axioms of communication. In *Communication theory*, 74–80. New York: Routledge.

Weber, T. (2001). Gandhian philosophy, conflict resolution theory and practical approaches to negotiation. *Journal of Peace Research, 38*(4), 493–513.

Weinblatt, U. (2018). *Shame regulation therapy for families.* Cham: Springer.

Weinblatt, U. (2022). *Contactivity: Advanced NVR interventions for overcoming avoidance.* Independently published.

Weingarten, K. (2003). *Common shock. Witnessing violence every day; how we are harmed, how we can heal.* Boston, MA: Dutton.

Weingarten, K., Galván-Durán, A. R., D'Urso, S., & Garcia, D. (2020). The witness to witness program: Helping the helpers in the context of the Covid-19 pandemic. *Family Process, 59*(3), 883–897.

Wheatley, T., & Sievers, B. (2016). Toward a neuroscience of social resonance. In D. Greene, I. Morrison, & M. E. P. Seligman (Eds.), *Positive neuroscience*, 37–54. Oxford: Oxford Scholarship online.

White, M. (1997). Re-membering and professional lives. In M. White (Ed.), *Narratives of therapists' lives,* 53–92. Adelaide: Dulwich Centre Publications.

White, M. (2007). *Maps of narrative practice.* New York: Norton.

White, M., & Epston, D. (1990). *Narrative means to therapeutic ends.* Adelaide: Dulwich Centre Publications.

Wiebenga, E., & Bom, H. (2023). Verbindende Autorität als Beziehungsangebot – konstruktive Allianzen zwischen Elternberatern und Eltern. *Familiendynamik, 48*(4), 306–317.

Wilson, J. (1996). Physical abuse of parents by adolescent children. In D. M. Busby (Ed.), *The impact of violence on the family: Treatment approaches for therapists and other professionals,* 101–123. Needham Heights, MA: Allyn and Bacon.

Wilson, J. (2017). *Creativity in times of constraint. A practitioner's companion in mental health and social care.* London: Routledge.

Wilson, J. (2018). *Child-focused practice. A collaborative systemic approach* (2nd edition). London: Routledge.

Wolcott, M. D., McLaughlin, J. E., Hann, A., Miklavec, A., Beck Dallaghan, G. L., Rhoney, D. H., & Zomorodi, M. (2021). A review to characterise and map the growth mindset theory in health professions education. *Medical Education, 55*(4), 430–440.

Wynne, L. C. (1984). The epigenesis of relational systems: A model for understanding family development. *Family Process, 23*(3), 297–318.

Young, A. (2002). The self-traumatized perpetrator as a »transient mental illness«. *L'evolution psychiatrique, 67*(4), 630–650.

Young, I. M. (2010). *Responsibility for justice.* New York: Oxford University Press.

Zaki, J., & Mitchell, J. P. (2016). Prosociality as a form of reward seeking. In J. D. Greene, I. Morrison & M. E. Seligman (Eds.), *Positive neuroscience.* New York: Oxford University Press, 57–72.

Index

For Product Safety Concerns and Information please contact our EU
representative GPSR@taylorandfrancis.com
Taylor & Francis Verlag GmbH, Kaufingerstraße 24, 80331 München, Germany